Tackling Domestic Violence

Tackling Domestic Violence

Theories, policies and practice

Lynne Harne and Jill Radford

Open University Press

Open University Press
McGraw-Hill Education
McGraw-Hill House
Shoppenhangers Road
Maidenhead
Berkshire
England
SL6 2QL

email: enquiries@openup.co.uk
world wide web: www.openup.co.uk

and Two Penn Plaza, New York, NY 10121-2289, USA

First published 2008
Reprinted 2010

A catalogue record of this book is available from the British Library

ISBN-13 978 0335 21248 4 (pb)   978 0335 21249 1 (hb)
ISBN-10 0335 21248 4 (pb)   0335 21249 2 (hb)

Library of Congress Cataloging-in-Publication Data
CIP data applied for

Typeset by RefineCatch Limited, Bungay, Suffolk
Printed in the UK by Ashford Colour Press Ltd, Gosport, Hampshire

The *McGraw·Hill* Companies

Contents

Preface

This book is inspired by the work undertaken by the authors across the last ten years during which we developed and delivered a 'University Certificate in Professional Development (Domestic Violence)'. Initially this was embarked upon as a response to a request from Cleveland Police in the late 1990s. Subsequently, it has been delivered several times a year at The University of Teesside and around England, Wales and Northern Ireland at the request of police forces, domestic violence forums and Women's Aid groups. Culturally sensitive versions of the course have also been delivered in Kazakhstan and Turkey, to police, lawyers, women's organisations and domestic violence groups with the support of the British Council. This book shares the course aims of bridging the gaps between 'academic' and professional/practitioner understandings of domestic violence in an academically rigorous but accessible way and thereby enriching both perspectives.

Acknowledgements

We would like to thank all those professionals and practitioners, from the voluntary and state sectors, who have contributed their knowledge and experience to this book. Their frontline experiences of dealing with domestic violence have highlighted best practice and shown some of the difficulties in implementing policy. This is reflected in some of the case studies contained in this book, and in the content generally.

Introduction

The recognition of domestic violence by the United Nations as a human rights abuse in the 1990s (CEDAW, 1992; Beijing Declaration and Platform of Action, 1995) has meant that domestic violence has achieved a much greater profile in terms of law and policy development in many countries. In the UK, recent changes at local and national levels have been far-reaching and domestic violence is now high on the agendas of many professionals, practitioners and policy-makers.

Centred on the UK, but located in a context of global change, this book aims to provide an informed background for those professionals and practitioners whose remit is to respond to domestic violence. Taking a multi-disciplinary approach and drawing on contemporary research findings, policy developments, innovative practice and case studies contributed by professionals on the front line, it is also highly relevant to those academics and students whose specialisations or studies include 'domestic violence'.

Key themes

Women's and children's safety

A major theme throughout this book is to consider how far changes in policy and practice have increased the safety of women and children experiencing domestic violence and enabled them to rebuild their lives free from violence. Although such aims are central to current policy, they do not always translate into practice, either because of resistance or misunderstandings in implementation or because other agendas take over. One example of this is in the implementation of criminal justice policy, where a focus on achieving managerial targets, such as improved conviction rates or 'sanctioned detections', can displace this primary goal. At the same time, we highlight examples of best practice where women's and children's safety has improved as a result of these initiatives.

Complexity and social inclusion

Another important aspect is highlighting the broader and more complex understandings of domestic violence, which have been developing in recent years. There is now a wider recognition that domestic violence is about perpetrators' power and control over women and involves not only physical and sexual violence, but can include a number of behaviours such as intimidation and threats, isolation and humiliation, behaviour often named as psychological coercion or 'violence'. Recent understandings are also more inclusive of a range of different women's experiences. For example, some of the differences for women living in 'honour' communities are reflected in recent government policies to address forced marriage and 'honour' killings and there is now a recognition that domestic violence can be perpetrated by other family members, not only partners, in official definitions of domestic violence. There is also more knowledge about the problems faced by women living in rural and travelling communities, and of the interconnections between domestic violence and women exploited and abused through prostitution.

Nevertheless, some social exclusions and problems remain. The experiences of disabled women are only beginning to be addressed, despite recent legislation against disability discrimination in the delivery of services. Furthermore, immigration laws continue to work against women with insecure immigration status, who seek and gain protection from different services. Young women below the age of 18 experiencing violence from boyfriends or partners are also often excluded from official definitions of domestic violence.

In addition, there remain problems about knowing the extent of domestic violence and its impacts, given some of the continuing social exclusions mentioned above. Further, despite overwhelming evidence that women in heterosexual relationships form the vast majority of victims of domestic violence, there remain ongoing debates about the extent of male victimisation and violence in lesbian and gay relationships. These are issues which are discussed in depth in Chapters 1 and 2 in looking at the nature and extent of domestic violence, its impacts on women and how perpetrators' power and control strategies, as well as limitations in some policy areas, can considerably affect the possibilities of obtaining safety. Such understandings are crucial for professionals in health, social care and criminal justice agencies if they are to be enabled to alleviate some of these impacts and take appropriate action to increase protection. Recent initiatives and case studies to address these impacts are discussed in Chapter 2.

A focus on perpetrators and the criminalisation of domestic violence

Another welcome development in recent years has been the increasing criminalisation of perpetrators of domestic violence. All too often in the past, blame has been placed on victims and the perpetrators' responsibility for the violence is ignored, as is the fact that they have committed serious crimes. Gradual changes in police policy and practice as well as recent legal changes and initiatives to improve prosecution and conviction rates have indicated a significant shift in government policy and are the result of extensive campaigning by women to achieve the recognition of domestic violence as a crime in criminal justice policy. Nevertheless, there remains unevenness in criminal justice practice and resistance to such changes, most obviously in the derisory sentences frequently handed out to chronic domestic violence offenders and in the differential treatment of men and women by the legal system when partners are killed in the context of domestic violence. Further resistance to change is highlighted in the civil law, which can be used to obtain injunctions against a perpetrator, since the conduct of survivors is still taken into account, in the granting or otherwise of certain orders, by the courts. In addition, the family courts remain a bastion of patriarchal reaction in their failure to recognise some fathers as violent perpetrators, who pose considerable risks to children and their mothers, when making decisions about child contact and residence post-separation. These themes are outlined and developed in Chapters 1 to 4.

Chapters 3 and 4 take a critical historical look at legal developments and policing practice, including recent initiatives to target prolific offenders and high-risk victims. Changes to support survivors through the prosecution process with multi-agency interventions represented in the specialist domestic violence courts initiative are examined as we question what more needs to be done to improve 'victim safety' and place survivors' needs at the heart of the criminal justice system.

The impacts of domestic violence on children

There has been a growing recognition of children as 'hidden victims' of perpetrators' domestic violence and of the interconnections between their violence towards mothers and their subsequent abusive parenting of children in families. This knowledge and understanding has been considerably enhanced by research that asks children themselves about the impacts of domestic violence, the many ways it has affected their lives, their feelings towards violent fathers and their ways of coping with the violence. However, children's views, particularly if they are under the age of eight, have continued to be ignored by professionals in some policy areas, most often by legal and welfare professionals in private family law proceedings and sometimes in criminal proceedings, when children want to act as witnesses to the violence against their mothers. In addition, discourses of child welfare and child protection, in contrast to those of criminalisation, can continue to blame non-abusing parents (usually mothers) and make them responsible for children's safety and protection, when it is impossible for them to do so because they live in fear of the perpetrators' violence. Since mothers and children constitute the majority of those affected by domestic violence, children's experiences and the implications for practice are discussed in detail in the second half of Chapter 2 and all subsequent chapters.

Preventing domestic violence

An understanding of domestic violence as a social problem implies that it is not inevitable and consequently that such violence can be prevented before it happens. Strategies and initiatives aimed at achieving this (known as 'primary prevention'), both public awareness campaigns and school education, have vastly increased in recent years. Nevertheless, considerable cultural toleration of men's violence towards women and children continues to exist in all its forms and this toleration and the way it can counter-act primary prevention interventions is discussed in the penultimate chapter in this book.

This chapter also discusses 'tertiary prevention' (secondary prevention being support to survivors), most significantly in efforts to change and rehabilitate perpetrators in the form of perpetrator programmes. These have vastly increased under New Labour, as a solution to dealing with offenders convicted by the criminal justice system, and are viewed by the family courts as a means of making violent fathers safe to have contact with their children, post-separation. This chapter takes a critical look at the difficulties involved in changing perpetrators, by examining how such offenders conceptualise their own violence and abuse and the effectiveness of different explanations and subsequent approaches to achieve such change. It also discusses whether these programmes are working to improve women's and children's safety and the evidence base for these developments.

Multi-agency working

Multi-agency and partnership approaches and co-operation in local areas have been viewed by government since the early 1990s as an 'inevitably good idea', since survivors require services from many different agencies if they are to achieve safety. Nevertheless, the research indicates that such approaches can produce mixed results and vary considerably within and between different local areas, with competition for funding between different services, conflicts over approaches and different understandings of domestic violence and the marginalisation of voluntary sector women's services occurring in some localities. More recently, research evaluations have shown the significance of women's independent advice and support services in enabling multi-agency approaches to work in improving the safety of women and children. The use of multi-agency approaches in specific recent initiatives is discussed and critically assessed in the final chapter, which addresses improving practice.

1 The nature and extent of domestic violence

Domestic violence exists in many but not all cultures throughout the world (Heise, 1995). Until the late 20th century, it was socially accepted in male dominant cultures, justified in customs and traditions and condoned by law. Women have also been expected to suffer in silence. Hostile criticism has been directed at feminists and women's liberation movements worldwide for challenging this violence and its condoning by governments at different points in history, most recently and powerfully in the last quarter of the 20th century.

Since the 1970s, albeit in the face of criticism, feminists successfully transformed domestic violence from a private trouble into a public issue, now high on the agendas of local, national and international governments. In the UK, feminist work in this period also included the establishment of a nationwide chain of refuges and other support services, which subsequently contributed to the vibrant women's voluntary sector of the 21st century. Other achievements included instigating research into the nature, extent and impact of domestic violence and successful campaigns for its recognition as criminal violence by the government, police and the criminal justice system.

The questions of 'exactly what is domestic violence' and 'how common it is' have been subject of much discussion within feminism, amongst policymakers, practitioners and in research since its (re)discovery as a social problem in the 1970s. This chapter explores these questions, beginning with an examination of the nature of domestic violence before moving on to explore its prevalence.

The nature of domestic violence

One starting point for an exploration of the nature of domestic violence is the 'Imagine' poster produced by Women's Aid Federation of England in 2002.

As illustrated in this powerful poster, domestic violence is a broad concept incorporating many forms of physical violence, sexual violence and a range of

---

So what is domestic violence?

We all know what a bully is . . .

- Imagine . . . living with a bully all the time, but being too scared to leave.
- Imagine . . . being afraid to go to sleep at night, being afraid to wake up in the morning.
- Imagine . . . being denied food, warmth or sleep.
- Imagine . . . being punched, slapped, hit, bitten, pinched and kicked.
- Imagine . . . being pushed, shoved, burnt, strangled, raped, beaten.
- Imagine . . . having to watch everything you do or say in case it upsets the person you live with – or else you'll be punished.
- Imagine . . . having to seek permission to go out, to see your friends or your family, or to give your children a treat.
- Imagine . . . being a prisoner in your own home – imagine being timed when you go out to the shops.
- Imagine . . . that you believe what he tells you – that it's your fault. That if only you were a better mother, lover, housekeeper, kept your mouth shut, could only keep the children quiet, dressed how he liked you to, kept in shape, gave up your job – somehow things would get better.
- Imagine . . . that you don't know where to get help, what to do, or how to leave.
- Imagine . . . that you can't face the shame of admitting what's really going on to family or friends.
- Imagine . . . his threats if you dare to say you will leave. How could you ever find the strength to leave? Will you ever be safe again?
- Imagine . . . threats to find and kill you and your children, wherever you go.
- Imagine . . . permanent injuries and sometimes death.

Domestic violence is physical, sexual and psychological abuse.

Women's Aid Federation of England (2002)

---

coercive, intimidating and controlling behaviours. It is damaging physically, psychologically and socially. Domestic violence can occur in any intimate or familial relationship, irrespective of whether the parties are living together or not, whether they are married or cohabiting or living in three-generational extended families. It is this relational element, rather than location that defines the violence as 'domestic', because while it commonly occurs in the home, it can spill out into the streets, bus stops, bars or even result in road traffic 'accidents'. It is the fact that the perpetrator and victim are not only well known to each other, but are (or were) in intimate or familial relationships, that makes it particularly hard to deal with by the survivor or victim, support and criminal justice agencies and the law.

Experiencing domestic violence

For those without personal experience, appreciating its nature requires the recognition that domestic violence is real and serious violence that can result in permanent injuries and sometimes death (Home Office, 2005). The 'Imagine' poster identifies and illustrates key elements of domestic violence including those summarised in the 'physical, sexual, psychological and financial violence' strap line of many formal definitions, and which form the basis of criminal offences in many legal systems, including those of England and Wales, Scotland and Northern Ireland.

Physical violence

Physical violence is represented in the 'Imagine' poster in its references to 'being punched, slapped, hit, bitten, pinched, kicked, pushed, shoved, burnt, strangled and beaten', as an illustrative but not exhaustive list. Although not specified there, it can involve the use of weapons and objects, which may be household items like knives, belts, scissors, furniture, hot irons, cigarettes or indeed anything that comes to hand.

Association of Chief Police Officers (ACPO) definition of domestic violence

Any incident of threatening behaviour, violence or abuse (psychological, physical, sexual, financial or emotional) between adults who are or have been intimate partners regardless of gender. It will also include family members who are defined as mother, father, son, daughter, brother, sister, grandparents, in-laws and step family.

ACPO Centrex (2004)

In societies where gun ownership is widespread, guns can be and are used in the perpetration of domestic violence. As McWilliams (1998) notes, in societies characterised by civilian or sectarian violence, like Northern Ireland, the availability of fire-arms is reflected in the forms of domestic violence and in the higher prevalence of domestic homicide.[1] Although less well documented in research, in rural areas too, the higher prevalence of shotgun ownership, as well as the availability of a range of farm implements that in the hands of perpetrators can become nasty weapons, shape the nature of domestic violence.[2] These examples illustrate the ways the forms of domestic violence can reflect their social and political context.

Similarly the cultural context can influence the forms taken by domestic violence. For example, The Human Rights Commission of Pakistan noted an increase in deaths by kitchen fires, reporting that at least four women a day are burned to death by husbands and family members as a result of domestic disputes (UNICEF, 2000). In India, although the institution of dowry has been abolished, dowry related violence is increasing and over 5,000 women a year are killed, burned in kitchen fires by husbands and in-laws (UNIFEM, 2003). In the UK, in 2002, Southall Black Sisters sought a judicial review of a coroner's decision not to hold an inquest after the collapse of a criminal trial against the husband of a woman who was burned to death with her child (Gupta, 2003). This illustrates the pervasiveness of cultural traditions in shaping forms of violence and the failure of authorities in the UK to recognise this.

Women's Aid definition of domestic violence

What is domestic violence?

In Women's Aid's view domestic violence is physical, sexual, psychological or financial violence that takes place within an intimate or family-type relationship and that forms a pattern of coercive and controlling behaviour. This can include forced marriage and so-called 'honour crimes'. Domestic violence may include a range of abusive behaviours, not all of which are in themselves inherently 'violent'. Crime statistics and research both show that domestic violence is gender specific (i.e. most commonly experienced by women and perpetrated by men) and that any woman can experience domestic violence regardless of race, ethnic or religious group, class, disability or lifestyle. Domestic violence is repetitive, life-threatening, and can destroy the lives of women and children.

Women's Aid (2005)

Sexual violence

The 'Imagine' poster identifies rape as a form of domestic violence, making the connection between sexual and domestic violence, which unfortunately is lost in UK law and much service provision (Kelly and Lovett, 2005). Sexual violence is a wide term used to describe rape and the humiliating range of unwanted, pressured and coerced sex that may be experienced in domestic violence contexts (Kelly, 1988). Sexual violence is often linked to physical violence, often perpetrated immediately after a physical assault and commonly accompanied by verbal violence (Johnson, 1995). It is normalised in malestream representations of heterosexuality, where sex was, and in some cultures still is, represented as a 'duty' for women. The continuing strength and prevalence of this myth is such that many women, including women in some minority communities in the UK, don't name rape in marriage as 'rape' (NISAA, 2004). Further, as Walby and Allen (2004) report, the media stereotypes of rape and the continuing stigma associated with it, is such that many women who suffer this crime do not identify it as 'rape'. The British Crime Survey 2001 asked women, who had experienced rape from a current or former intimate partner, how they would describe this experience. Only 28 per cent selected the option 'rape' with other women selecting 'sexual assault' (20%), forced sex (23%), sexual abuse (18%) and 12 per cent rejecting all these options, opting for 'something else' (Walby and Allen, 2004).

This difficulty with the language of rape, together with the fact that it is an intimate and intrusive violation of the self, makes sexual violence one of the hardest aspects of domestic violence for its victims to talk about. But it is nevertheless a common aspect of domestic violence (Painter, 1991; Dominy and Radford, 1996). The British Crime Survey 2001, found that 54 per cent of the 237,000 estimated incidents of rape or serious sexual assault perpetrated against women were perpetrated by intimate partners or former partners, and that 40 per cent of the women had told no-one prior to that survey (Walby and Allen, 2004).

Coercion and control

The 'Imagine' poster also identifies a range of coercive and controlling strategies commonly used by perpetrators; for example, 'having to seek permission to go out, to see your friends or your family'. In some cases women are prevented through violence or threats from seeing any family or friends or having social contacts with the outside world, unless accompanied by the perpetrator. They may also have their mail opened and their phone calls monitored, or literally be locked in the house when the perpetrator goes out. While this latter example constitutes the crime of false imprisonment, less extreme strategies of isolation and control that limit women's autonomy, freedom of movement and association with others, although not necessarily defined as criminal in themselves, are profoundly undermining and can constitute psychological abuse and maltreatment.

'Mind games' represent another form of emotional or psychological violence: 'Imagine . . . that you believe what he tells you – that it's your fault'. These are illustrations of psychological or emotional violence, which survivors commonly report as being the hardest form of domestic violence to bear (Kirkwood, 1993). As Kirkwood notes, because physical and sexual violence are also psychologically distressing, and reflected in anxiety, depression, eating and sleeping disorders, the psychological toll of domestic violence is a heavy one. Kirkwood (1993) offers a typology of six inter-related coercive and controlling strategies which serve to trap a victim in a violent relationship: threats, degradation, objectification, deprivation, an overburden of responsibility and a distortion of subject reality so that some women may begin to lose confidence and belief in themselves. As Mullender (1996) argues, perpetrators use these tactics in combination with physical and sexual violence to gain and reinforce their control:

> Once the fear of further attacks is established, threats, gestures and glares will be enough to maintain a constant atmosphere of fear. . . . Any behaviour that engenders fear can be used such as shouting, hitting walls, driving recklessly, displaying weapons, stalking, prolonged silence, destruction of objects, injuries to children or pets (inflicting the double torture of making her watch, with the clear implication that she will be next). Women live in constant terror and fear for their very lives.
>
> (Mullender, 1996:23–4)

Mullender (1996:25) further highlights the devastating nature of psychological violence pointing to its similarity both with the torture of hostages and the 'brainwashing of political prisoners', who similarly are 'stripped of all freedoms and deprived of sleep, never knowing when the next beating will be'. Due to its pervasiveness and continuing presence, as Kelly (1988) notes, psychological violence/emotional cruelty is hard to pinpoint and name, which adds to the difficulty of help-seeking or reporting to the police.

Pence and Paymar (1993) have emphasised that although domestic violence takes many forms, it is the physical and sexual violence or threats of these forms of violence, that serve to keep the other forms in place, because despite its pernicious nature, psychological violence and emotional cruelty take their power from the threats and realities of physical and sexual violence which contextualise it. Whether outside the context of this violence, such coercive and controlling behaviours constitute 'violence' in their own right is a matter of continuing definitional debate.

Economic control and material deprivation

Additionally the 'Imagine' poster makes reference to 'being denied food, warmth and sleep'. These can be part of the psychological violence discussed above and sleep deprivation is now recognised as a form of torture by Amnesty International (2004). However, other deliberate forms of material deprivation have been defined as economic deprivation or financial abuse in some definitions of domestic violence. Financial abuse refers to the distribution and control of income between the parties, and is not to be confused with poverty per se, as women with wealthy partners, as well as those from average or low income backgrounds, can be subjected to deliberate economic deprivation. Where women work or have their own income, one aspect of financial control by violent perpetrators is to take women's wages or social security benefits away from them through physical violence or threats of physical violence. Perpetrators may also deliberately harass women at work so that they lose their jobs and the degree of economic independence that employment provides (Pence and Paymar, 1993).

The power and control wheel

Engagement with the 'Imagine poster' has facilitated a discussion of the dynamics and nature of domestic violence. It illustrates its serious nature, which can result in death, serious injury or disability and mental distress, paralleling the violence of war and torture. The poster highlights its range of forms, physical and sexual violence and associated coercive and controlling behaviours, which are deeply embedded in the dominant and minority cultures of a society. It also illustrates a 'clustering' of its different forms, which can be combined in incidents, which may last for minutes, hours or days (Mullender, 1996). For example, the serious physical and sexual violence described above – 'being pushed, shoved, burnt, strangled, raped, beaten' – is frequently accompanied by threats, threats of more severe violence and threats of more dire consequences. These can include, as the poster illustrates, threats to kill women and/or their children if they dare to attempt to leave the relationship, speak out or seek help to escape the violence. The Duluth Domestic Violence Intervention Project has represented the different elements of domestic violence in a wheel of power and control.

The power and control wheel is an analytic model developed by the Domestic Abuse Intervention Project, Duluth, Minnesota, USA, to illustrate the power dynamics of domestic violence and how it constitutes an overall pattern of power and control. The hub of the wheel illustrates its gendered nature, highlighting how traditional power relations of male dominant societies not only make the choice to use violence more available to men than women, but also facilitate their ability to use a range of controlling strategies rarely available to women. For example, in a society like the UK, where the average weekly income of all men is twice that of all women (Women's Equality Unit, 2003) and gender inequality in wealth continues to accumulate over the life course (Warren et al., 2000) despite women's increased participation in the workforce, men have greater access to strategies of economic control.

The examples in the wheel are illustrative, not definitive or exhaustive, but highlight some of the most common strategies of domestic violence identified in Western cultures. The gendered power at the hub of the wheel is also mediated by other power structures. For example, historically in the UK

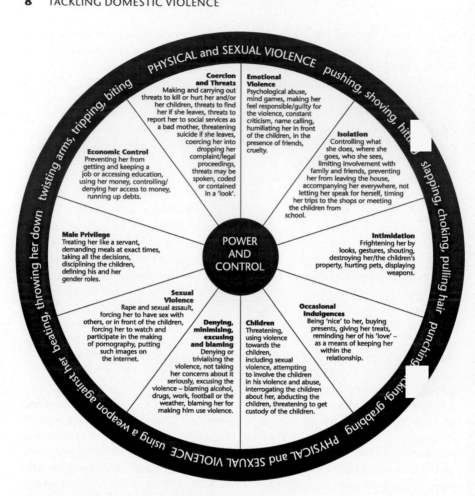

The power and control wheel (Adapted from Pence, 1987)

domestic violence has been legitimised in law, religion, and in cultural ideologies of male dominance and women's inferiority. Further, although there have been some legal changes, cultural discourses of masculinity continue to inform men's justications for violence (Hearn, 1998).

In some other male-dominant cultures, the notion that women are responsible for upholding family honour[3] remains a major force influencing law, religion and cultural values and shaping the nature of and responses to domestic violence. In such cultures it may be difficult for women to leave or seek help to escape domestic violence because to do so would bring shame on the whole family and could result in community ostracisation, further violence or even murder in the name of family honour (Gill, 2004).

Further, the re-emergence of fundamentalist religious practices and structures in all major religions including Christianity, Judaism, Islam, Hinduism and Sikhism also play a major part in justifying and legitimising domestic violence against women (Saghal and Davies, 1992).

Domestic violence as hate crime

The operation of the strategies of power and violent control described above has parallels with the ways in which those with power have the ability to commit other hate crimes against less powerful groups; for example, racist and homophobic violence. In hate crimes, those with power exploit cultural stereotypes to deny, minimise, excuse or justify their use of violence against vulnerable members of minority groups. In relation to domestic violence, perpetrators draw on the sexist attitudes, gender stereotypes and misogyny still endemic in the cultures of modern society. It is important to realise that personal relationships are not immune or isolated from dominant sexist cultural beliefs, power structures and discrimination of the wider society which contextualise them. This is why domestic violence is also considered by the police to be a hate crime.

Diversity in women's experiences of domestic violence

Black and minority ethnic women's experiences

Power structures constructed around 'race' and ethnicity, economics and class, age, disability and sexuality interact with those of patriarchy in constructing the prejudice and discrimination in the wider culture. While, as argued above, the occurrence of domestic violence does not respect social divisions, its nature reflects the wider power relations and cultural norms of specific societies. In consequence, while there are many common forms of domestic violence, some forms are culturally specific and others impact in particular ways on minority ethnic groups of women. The use of fire, for example, in the perpetration of domestic violence against some South Asian groups has already been illustrated (see page 4).

As part of the 1970s to 1980s feminist campaigns to transform domestic violence into an issue of public concern, UK feminists encouraged women to speak out about it. Many women, including some from black and minority ethnic communities, felt able to do this. For example, groups such as Southall Black Sisters and Brent Asian Women's group in London began their own campaigns highlighting the specific experiences of domestic violence in Asian communities (Patel, 2000).

Other black and minority ethnic women, however, concerned about the high levels of racism and racist violence in Britain in the 1970s and 1980s, took the view that, the time was not right.[4] Speaking out against domestic violence in their own communities could be seen as publicly criticising already stigmatised communities, and/or lead to racist suggestions that it was a specifically 'black' issue, thereby appearing to endorse negative racist stereotypes of black men. It was not until the publication of Mama's research in 1989, tellingly entitled 'The Hidden Struggle', that the specific impact of domestic violence on black women was recognised more broadly. Mama pointed to the complex gender and power relations embodied in black families, which can be both a source of strength and affirmation in struggles against racism, and a source of gender oppression. Consequently, struggling simultaneously against domestic violence and racism has posed contradictions for black women. Ten years later, Bernard (2000) identified similar complexities facing black mothers whose children disclosed sexual abuse:

> Black mothers struggle with inherent contradictions in conflict of loyalties to their male partners, their families and communities. These important factors will significantly influence how they make choices for themselves and their children. Social belonging in their families and communities is of the utmost importance to many black women in a society where race is a significant marker for experience . . . Black mothers may thus find it more difficult to resist the pressure not to involve outside agencies, as the consequences for women involving social services or the police could be exclusion or marginalisation from their wider families and communities.
>
> (Bernard, 2000:110)

South Asian Women's groups such as Southall Black Sisters and Brent Asian Women's Refuge in London have been in the foreground of feminist activism against domestic violence, highlighting South Asian women's experiences and campaigning to achieve legal and social change. During the early 1980s, they organised a number of public protests over the killings of Asian women by their husbands. It was also at this time that their famous slogan 'Black women's tradition, struggle not submission' was used in the UK and alliances with other feminist campaigns against domestic violence were formed (Gupta, 2003).

In 1986 Southall Black Sisters helped produce a film – 'A Fearful Silence' – on domestic violence in Asian communities and in 1990 they published 'Against the Grain', which celebrated ten years of 'struggle and survival' in supporting Asian women fleeing domestic violence. 'Against the Grain' revealed SBS to be feminist advocates in the fullest meaning of the word. Their work included personal support and advocacy in respect of a complex legal system, perceived as sexist and racist, and detailed casework to evidence their legal advocacy. Using the strategies of street campaigning and protests outside the Appeal Courts and the Home Office, while simultaneously acting as advocates in court, including taking cases to the High Court and House of Lords, SBS helped secure beneficial law changes. Through their campaigning, research and writing they have been influential in facilitating understanding, amongst government, politicians, policy-makers, researchers and practitioners of the specific forms and impact of domestic violence on South Asian women, as well as challenging dominant discourses that domestic violence in Asian communities should be tolerated as 'a traditional cultural practice'. Other examples relate to their engagement with and interventions in the struggle to seek wider recognition of and policy responses to women with insecure immigration status and forced marriage as a form of domestic violence.

Forced marriage

Forced marriage came to wider public attention in the UK in 1999 following the murder of a 19-year-old-woman, Rukshana Naz, in Derby, considered by her family to have shamed them, by refusing to remain in a forced marriage (Siddiqui, 2003).

> Forced marriage is a gross violation of women's human rights. It is a form of domestic violence and/or child abuse ... Although men can be forced into a marriage, research indicates overwhelmingly this affects women and young women adversely. In forced marriage situations, there can be a number of influencing factors for example, emotional blackmail, social pressure, threatening behaviour abduction, imprisonment, physical violence, rape, sexual abuse and even murder. . . .
>
> Forced marriage cannot be regarded as a cultural practice that is respected or tolerated because it is a violation of human rights.
>
> Asian Women's Resource Centre (2005)

Forced marriage is a violation of Article 16 of the Universal Declaration of Human Rights and contrary to the laws of all major religions, including Christianity, Judaism, Islam, Sikhism and Hinduism. As a human rights abuse, forced marriage is now acknowledged in domestic violence discourse, but as in so many aspects of both discourses, problems exist in understanding and defining the problem. Most commentators have followed the government in drawing on consent to make a clear distinction between forced and arranged marriages in order to avoid accusations of racism or being seen to criticise 'the tradition of arranged marriage (which) has operated successfully within many communities and many countries for a long time' (Home Office, 2005).

> In arranged marriages, the families of both parties take a leading role in arranging the marriage but the choice of whether to accept the marriage remains with the young people. In forced marriage, one or

both spouses do not consent to the marriage and some element of duress is involved.

(Foreign and Commonwealth Office, 2004)

However, others argue that reality is more complex. An-Na'im and Candler (2000) state that without stigmatising arranged marriages, it needs to be recognised that such a sharp dichotomy can be misleading because while some cases involve abduction, imprisonment and physical violence, in others the pressure is more subtle. Hannanah Siddiqui of SBS similarly argues that:

the line between an arranged marriage and a forced marriage is a fine one . . . Many women feel that in practice, there is little difference between the two. The desire to please parents who exert emotional pressure is itself experienced as coercion.

(Siddiqui, 2003:70)

Women with insecure immigration status

The situation of women with insecure immigration status experiencing domestic violence has been brought to public attention by the campaigning of Southall Black Sisters and other women's groups such as Imkaan. Yet while there has been some policy concessions,[5] these women's experiences continue to remain marginalised in public policy and are often hidden because of discriminatory immigration rules, which operate to entrap them in increasingly violent and often life-threatening relationships (Southall Black Sisters, 2006).[6] Although this kind of discrimination particularly affects South Asian women, as a consequence of capitalist globalisation and the demise of communist states, it also impacts on the increasing number of 'male order' brides from Eastern Europe and women who may marry UK 'sex tourists' in countries such as Thailand and the Phillipines. The experiences of domestic violence suffered by many 'female marriage migrants' to EU countries including the UK have recently been highlighted by cross-European feminist research (Daphne 11 Project, 2005), where researchers found that they can be compounded by immigration rules set up under the concept of Fortress Europe to deter immigration through denying access to social welfare provision. Such rules mean that women experiencing domestic violence cannot have access to public funds and they may therefore be unable to access refuge or other housing provision and can be left destitute if they contemplate leaving the relationship. Thus, perpetrators can use women's insecure immigration status as a strategy of power and control.

Travelling communities

Despite their diversity, which problematises their definitional status in terms of race, ethnicity and culture, women in travelling communities represent a group whose experiences of domestic violence have generally been hidden. For the women in these communities such experiences can be exacerbated by the negative attitudes of the dominant settled communities and ideologies of preserving family honour, which exist in some of the travelling communities. These present a conflict of loyalties for travelling women, making speaking out against perpetrators or help seeking difficult.

Young women

It is perhaps not surprising that young women's experiences of domestic violence are often hidden, since some official definitions are limited to adults, as in the ACPO definition, above. Yet there is increasing evidence that young women under 18 years, that is below the legal age of adulthood, may experience domestic violence from boyfriends or partners. This has been highlighted in self-selected surveys in teen magazines (NSPCC, 2006) as well as in research on teenage pregnancy and young women's involvement in prostitution. Because some definitions may exclude their experiences,[7] young women may have problems in naming their experiences as domestic violence – viewing it only as something that happens to older women, making help-seeking even more difficult. The extent of domestic violence experienced by young women in their teens is not yet known. But the British Crime Survey (2001), which looked at incidents of domestic violence, stalking and sexual assault from the age of 16, found that the younger women were, the more likely they were to experience any form of 'interpersonal violence,' and that young men were most likely to be the perpetrators of such violence (Walby and Myhill, 2004:84).

Women abused through prostitution

Also marginalised in the early feminist campaigns against domestic and sexual violence were women exploited and abused through prostitution. For some young women being forced into prostitution has been part of their experience of domestic violence from boyfriends/pimps where it has been used to groom and coerce them into selling sex (Barnardos, 1998). As well as being at risk of violence from punters, women involved in prostitution can experience domestic violence from partners/pimps in order to keep them in prostitution (Hester and Westmarland, 2005). In addition, the prevalence of drug use, including its use by pimps/partners as a form of control, together with the stigma associated with the sex industry and its links with crime, make speaking out, help-seeking and escaping domestic violence even more difficult for the women involved.

Case study: Domestic Violence and Prostitution: the need for specialist support

Karen left home at the age of 15, after witnessing domestic violence by her father towards her mother and being physically abused herself. She was homeless and sleeping on friends' floors when she met Jimmy who offered her a place to stay for the night. Shortly after, they started a relationship and Jimmy began to isolate Karen from her friends and became physically violent towards her. As a drug user, he also introduced her to heroin and Karen used it to help her to cope with the violence. As a result of money problems and debt due to heroin use, Jimmy forced Karen into prostitution making her have sex with his friends and taking her to places where men were looking to purchase sex. At aged 16, Karen became pregnant and the physical violence became more severe. At this point Karen decided to end the relationship and sought the help of a local service that supports young people involved in prostitution. She was referred to Women's Aid, because of her experiences of domestic violence. She was able to go into the local refuge, after going on a methadone programme to help her withdraw from heroin. When she entered the refuge, she had very low self-esteem and believed that she had deserved the violence. She was supported in the refuge and soon realised that it was not her fault. Unfortunately, before she was due to move into a new home with her baby, it was discovered that she had been using heroin and had to leave. Although she continued to be supported by Women's Aid, she continued to use heroin and her baby was removed by social services.

(Based on information provided by Janet King, Eva Women's Aid)

Disabled women's experiences

Disabled women's experiences of domestic violence have been significantly marginalised both in public policy and feminist research until fairly recently in the UK.[8] This is despite the fact that it has long been recognised in the refuge movement that domestic violence itself can cause permanent injuries and impairment (Radford *et al.*, 2005). International research has suggested that disabled women may experience domestic violence for much longer than non-disabled women (Young *et al.*, 1997; Cockram, 2003) and this can partially be explained by disabling and discriminatory social barriers and attitudes which make it much more difficult for them to gain access to the same services and protection of the law, that are available to non-disabled women.

In disabling societies social barriers such as inaccessible buildings, communication systems and transport as well as social stigma and prejudice continue to marginalise disabled women's experiences and has led to a focus on impairments by some agencies as an excuse for inaction, rather than focusing on disabled women's equal rights to safety and justice (Radford *et al.*, 2005). Thus, agencies may assume that physically disabled women are dependent on non-disabled violent partners and are therefore better off staying in the relationship, despite the violence. Such approaches can also be characterised by patronising attitudes where choices are made for disabled women, rather than consulting with the women themselves about what actions they want agencies to take (LIAP, 2005).

Disabled women are not a homogenous group and as with groups of non-disabled women, their experiences of domestic violence can vary and take different forms (LIAP, 2005). For example, as well as inflicting or threatening physical and sexual violence, non- or less disabled perpetrators may remove aids, means of communication and transport from physically disabled women, as a form of power and control to deny women their means of independence and prevent help-seeking. Non-disabled partners may also use prejudices about disabled people combined with patriarchal ideologies to humiliate their partners, undermine their sense of self-worth and tell them they will not believed if they report the violence (Cockram, 2003). Where domestically violent perpetrators are also women's carers they may withhold medication, food or essential assistance which themselves should be viewed as serious forms of violence, because such actions can be life-threatening (Erwin, 2000).

Perpetrators can also use prejudices about mental illness to reinforce commonly held prejudices and successfully deny the violence if women with mental health problems seek help from agencies. In some communities mental illness may carry a particular stigma, and these women may find themselves ostracised or forced into marriages to the 'lowest bidder' (Siddiqui and Patel, 2003).

Women with learning difficulties face particular prejudicial attitudes and because of this often have to endure repeated physical and sexual violence – most frequently from boyfriends or partners who also have learning difficulties (McCarthy and Thompson, 1997). The reluctance of certain services to act against such violence means that women with learning difficulties experience higher rates of rape and sexual assault from boyfriends/partners than any other group, to the point where sexual violence has become a normalised part of their experience (McCarthy, 1999). This situation is a continuing scandal that still needs to be addressed adequately in policy approaches today. For example, by 2006, Powerhouse (established by women with learning difficulties) was the only specialist refuge in the UK for this group of women, despite key recommendations made by McCarthy in 1999.

Violence in lesbian relationships

Although domestic violence can occur in some relationships between women, there exists a profound lack of knowledge about its extent and a lack of understanding about differences between violence in intimate lesbian relationships and violence in heterosexual relationships. One problem, which has arisen in relation to the research and analysis undertaken in this area, is that much broader definitions of what constitutes domestic violence have been used in lesbian populations, leading to exaggerated claims that lesbian violence is highly prevalent. Such claims themselves can lead to heterosexism, and prejudicial attitudes and responses towards lesbians. These definitions, used in both US and UK research, often define domestic violence as 'disrespectful treatment' or 'manipulative behaviour' without the occurrence of other strategies of power and control, such as physical violence or intimidation or threats of violence, used in heterosexual definitions. This expansion of the definition of domestic violence renders it virtually meaningless, since disrespectful or manipulative behaviour can occur in almost any intimate relationship (Kelly, 1996). A further problem is that there have been no random prevalence studies asking questions about lesbian violence and current knowledge is therefore limited to small self-selected surveys where participants usually respond to advertisements asking them about their experiences of domestic violence. This makes it difficult to make any claims about the extent of domestic violence amongst lesbians.

Existing knowledge suggests that the continuing marginalisation of lesbians, and their lack of social power compared to that of heterosexual men provides a different context for conflicts, which can sometimes lead to violence. As Kelly has highlighted

> Lesbians frequently have to manage contradictory public and private identities and meanings and struggle to develop positive identities for themselves in a context of invisibility, being defined as 'abnormal' and frequent subjection to hostility and abuse.
>
> (Kelly, 1996:39)

Although there is now more formal recognition of discrimination against lesbians, this different context is illustrated through the findings from one recent self-selected study, which suggests that the fear of being 'outed' to relatives or work colleagues may lead to violence against a partner who does not have the same fears (Donovan et al., 2006). Such studies also suggest that lesbians who experience violence from a partner are less likely to seek assistance from mainstream agencies for fear of prejudice and some may prefer to deal with it within their own networks and communities.

Violence in gay men's relationships

Although gay men's relationships are more visible and less marginalised in mainstream society, knowledge about violence is again limited to self-selected studies and because of this claims of extensive violence in men's gay relationships, as in lesbian relationships, are likely to be exaggerated. Self-selected studies suggest that sexual violence is more frequent than in lesbian relationships and gay men are slightly more prepared to report sexual violence such as rape to the police. However, under-reporting and actual agency responses indicate that in some cases homophobia continues to be a block to obtaining appropriate services in some geographical areas (Donovan *et al.*, 2006). Existing evidence therefore suggests that some agencies do need to develop appropriate responses to same-sex domestic violence and there may be a need for some specialist services. But, simultaneously, it also needs to be recognised that while it has become fashionable in current 'equality discourses' to simply represent violence in lesbian and gay relationships as similar to and occurring at the same rate as violence in heterosexual relationships, there is no credible evidence that this is the case. As with claims that women are equally as violent as men in heterosexual relationships, such representations often serve to disguise the main occurrence of domestic violence as a gendered problem.

Domestic violence as gender violence

Despite the cultural variability in the forms of domestic violence, there is one clear pattern in its occurrence. The gendered nature of domestic violence, the fact that its perpetrators are overwhelmingly men and its victims mostly women and children, has led to its recognition as a form of 'gender violence' by the United Nations and in international discourse, where it is recognised as a worldwide 'major public health and human rights problem' (World Health Organisation, 2005). Gender violence can be defined as: Violence involving men and women, in which the female is usually the victim and which arises from unequal power relations between men and women (UNIFEM, undated).

As illustrated, the concept 'gender violence' identifies it as a problem with roots in women's subordinate gender status in all cultures, and is reflected in the beliefs, norms, morals, laws and social institutions that legitimise and normalise it, and, in so doing, perpetuate this violence. Gender violence is a broad human rights concept which:

> . . . encompasses a wide range of human rights violations, including sexual abuse of children, rape, domestic violence, sexual assault and harassment, trafficking of women and girls and several harmful

traditional practices. . . . Violence against women has been called 'the most pervasive yet least recognized human rights abuse in the world'.
(United Nations Population Fund, undated)

Identifying the embeddness of gender violence in male dominated or patriarchal cultures importantly brings a critical focus to the wider culture as well as to the need for specific strategies of prevention, protection and justice and support for survivors of domestic violence. Reasons why carefully developed domestic violence crime reduction strategies can fail to realise their potential may be located in the wider culture, if this is not also addressed. Consequently, in male dominant or patriarchal cultures, effective action to end domestic violence must include changes to that culture, as well as specific preventative strategies.

Myths of domestic violence

Tangible evidence of the power of cultural attitudes towards domestic violence lies in the myths generated in many cultures, which convey popular 'woman-blaming' and excusatory attitudes to domestic violence. Some of these cultural myths are illustrated in this poster from Northern Ireland, Women's Aid.

As this summary illustrates, these myths can impact on domestic violence survivors, deterring help-seeking. They can also impact on the wider public, including professionals in the law and order industry, care or welfare services and the media and inevitably influence representations of domestic violence in popular discourse and influence the attitudes of and responses to survivors on the part of judges, lawyers, police and the caring professionals.

Women's Aid Federation, Northern Ireland

There are many popular myths and prejudices about domestic violence. Not only do these myths lead to many women feeling unable to seek help, but they can cause unnecessary suffering. They may come to believe these myths in an attempt to justify, minimise or deny the violence they are experiencing. Acknowledging these cultural barriers can be an important part of coming to terms with what is really happening.

'It's just the odd domestic tiff, all couples have them.'

Fact: Violence by a man against the woman he lives with commonly includes rape, punching or hitting her, pulling her hair out, threatening her with a gun or a knife or even attempting to kill her. Often women who have been abused will say that the violence is not the worst of their experiences – it's the emotional abuse that goes with it that feels more damaging.

'It can't be that bad or she'd leave.'

Fact: Women stay in violent relationships for many reasons ranging from love to terror. There are also practical reasons why women stay; they may be afraid of the repercussions if they attempt to leave, they may be afraid of becoming homeless, they may worry about losing their children. Some women who have experienced domestic violence just don't have the confidence to leave.

They may be frightened of being alone, particularly if their partner has isolated them from friends and family. If they leave, they may decide to go back because of . . . fear and insecurity or because of a lack of support. Some women believe that their partners will change and that everything will be fine when they go home. (Sometimes the separation does provide a catalyst for real change.)

'Domestic violence only happens in working-class families.'

Fact: Anyone can be abused. The wives of doctors, lawyers, businessmen, policemen and teachers have all sought help as a result of domestic violence. Domestic violence crosses all boundaries including: age, sexuality, social and economic class, profession, religion and culture.

Unemployment and poverty are circumstances which can of course be very distressing, especially to those trying to bring up children. However, unemployed and financially challenged people do not have a monopoly on domestic violence. Many people survive the misfortune of unemployment and poverty retaining dignity, good humour and a caring response to their families.

'They must come from violent backgrounds.'

Fact: Many men who are violent towards their families or their partner come from families with no history of violence. Many families in which violence occurs do not produce violent men. The family is not the only formative influence on behaviour. Blaming violence on men's own experience can offer men an excuse for their own behaviour, but it denies the experiences of the majority of individual survivors of abuse who do not go on to abuse others.

A violent man is responsible for his own actions and has a choice in how he behaves.

'It's only drunks who beat their partners.'

Fact: Domestic violence cannot be blamed on alcohol. Some men may have been drinking when they are violent but drink can provide an easy excuse. Many men who are violent do not drink alcohol.

'*She must ask for it.*'

Fact: No one 'deserves' being beaten or emotionally tortured, least of all by someone who says they love them. Often prolonged exposure to violence has the effect of distorting perspectives so that the woman believes that she deserves to be hurt. It also distorts her confidence and some women may start to rationalise their partner's behaviour. Often, the only provocation has been that she has simply asked for money for food, or not had a meal ready on time, or been on the telephone too long.

Domestic violence as crime

The pervasiveness of the myths in the cultural context against which new laws and policies are introduced can generate resistance to, misunderstandings of and confusion about changed policy, often leading to its delayed and partial implementation. For example in the UK, 1990 marked government recognition of the criminal nature of domestic violence, in a guidance circular which advised the police that force policies were needed to deal with this serious violent crime. But subsequent evaluations found the development and implementation of police policies to be patchy and partial (Grace, 1995; Plotnikoff and Woolfson, 1998). In highlighting the need for professional (re)education in terms of recognising and responding to domestic violence as criminal violence and a human rights violation, these studies revealed the continuing currency of such myths. This directs attention to contradictions involved in attempting to eradicate gender and domestic violence, without a wider cultural transformation of gender power relations.

Nevertheless, government recognition of domestic violence as a serious violent crime marked a significant historical moment in domestic violence discourse. Historically, and still to a considerable extent today, the privacy accorded to the family shielded perpetrators from the public gaze, police intervention and criminal prosecution. In the UK, this was reflected in another patriarchal myth that 'a man's home is his castle'. This myth is a legacy of the tradition that the man is the head of the family or household with the legitimate authority to protect and control its members. However, during the past two hundred years, (some) women have secured citizenship rights and have been accorded formal legal equality and are no longer legally subject to the rule of the husband and father. In consequence, the status and form of the family has undergone significant changes. In the UK, although marriage is still common, the increased popularity of cohabiting relationships and legal recognition of lesbian and gay partnerships means that marriage is no longer a defining characteristic of family. As legal persons in their own right, it is now recognised that women, including married women, have civil rights and are entitled to protective remedies and criminal sanctions against domestic violence. Nevertheless, a continuing reluctance to recognise women's citizenship status is reflected in the belief that home and family are private spheres, beyond the reach of law. This partially explains why domestic violence continues to be a hidden crime.

The long-standing failure of governments around the world to recognise the criminal nature of domestic violence was highlighted at the United Nations 4th World Conference on Women, Beijing 1995. The Declaration and Platform of Action adopted by 189 nation states, including the UK, recognised violence against women as a 'critical issue'.

> Violence against women is an obstacle to the achievement of the objectives of equality, development and peace. Violence against women both violates and impairs or nullifies the enjoyment by women of their human rights and fundamental freedoms.
>
> (Para 112 Violence Against Women, Diagnosis, UN, 1995)

The Platform of Action (UN, 1995) among other things called for governments to:

> Enact and/or reinforce penal, civil, labour and administrative sanctions in domestic legislation to punish and redress the wrongs done to women and girls who are subjected to any form of violence, whether in the home, the workplace, the community or society;

and

> Adopt and/or implement and periodically review and analyse legislation to ensure its effectiveness in eliminating violence against women, emphasizing the prevention of violence and the prosecution of offenders; take measures to ensure the protection of women subjected to violence, access to just and effective remedies, including compensation and indemnification and healing of victims, and rehabilitation of perpetrators.
>
> (United Nations 1995 Strategic objective D.1. para c and d)

These strategic objectives, agreed at the Beijing 1995 conference by the governments of 189 nation states, formed the basis of new approaches to law and policy in relation to a range of forms of gender violence, including domestic violence in many countries of the world.[9]

Square pegs and round holes

Central to this new approach was the recognition of domestic violence as criminal violence and as a human rights abuse. Many countries, including the

UK, had begun to move in this direction in the years leading up to the Bejing conference, but while some European countries, like Cyprus and Sweden, introduced specific domestic violence legislation that attempted to address its complexity, the UK has relied on a less radical, more piecemeal strategy of applying existing criminal law provisions to domestic violence incidents. The difficulty in this approach is that much of this legislation, primarily that relating to 'violence against the person' was introduced over a hundred and fifty years ago, to deal with the problem of stranger violence and public order. Its efficacy in relation to domestic violence, in the contemporary era, is limited because it fails to address the additional complexities presented by violence perpetrated by familial men, most commonly in the privacy of the home. Domestic violence differs significantly from stranger violence, which occurs in public and community locations. Exploring the differences between stranger and domestic violence explains the limited efficacy of this legal strategy as well as providing further insight into the nature of domestic violence.

Similarities and differences between stranger violence and domestic violence

While the forms and seriousness of the physical violence, as measured by physical injury, can be similar in stranger and domestic violence situations, there are significance differences, between the two. Firstly, although domestic violence is now recognised as criminal violence, existing legal provisions relate to physical violence, sexual violence and threats, but generally do not cover the range of coercive strategies also associated with domestic violence,[10] and consequently labelled 'sub-criminal' in Home Office guidance documents. So, the first problem is that not all aspects of domestic violence are criminalised.

Further, assaults perpetrated by intimate partners are aggravated by several factors, which do not generally arise in stranger violence contexts. Domestic violence is aggravated by a betrayal of trust entailed in assaults perpetrated by intimate partners. Being assaulted by an intimate partner generates massive emotional distress and sense of loss, leading to insecurity and a questioning of life decisions. It forces an uncomfortable recognition on the part of the survivor that the home, the heart of personal life often considered a haven of security, is no longer safe. This recognition entails real fears about the future, future violence and future life. In contrast, while stranger attacks most commonly occur in public places, and may make its victims nervous about that space, there is the possibility of escaping to the safety of the home, an option not available to victims of domestic violence.

This fear of future violence points to another significant difference between stranger assault and domestic violence. The former usually constitutes a one-off incident, however unpleasant, whereas domestic violence is continuing violence. Studies indicate that without effective intervention, domestic violence increases in frequency and severity and so is very rarely a 'one-off' episode with resolution and ending (Kelly, 1988; Hanmer, Griffiths and Jerwood, 1999; Kelly *et al.*, 1999). Thus, the continuing nature of domestic violence produces a cumulative impact. A survivor/victim is not simply affected in an incident-by-incident way, as presumed by the criminal justice system. On the contrary, the impact of an incident is shaped by previous incidents and the fear of future ones. Agencies sometimes express surprise that it is not always the most serious incident that leads a woman to begin help-seeking or to make an official report.

For a survivor, acknowledging that domestic violence is occurring heralds a new, unsought, frightening chapter in life. It is likely to involve re-thinking or ending the relationship and starting over, raising worries about how and where to live safely. Deciding to leave a violent perpetrator may constitute a further more dangerous episode in a woman's life, as he seeks revenge against her for daring to leave (Kelly, 1999). She may also have to decide how to support herself and the children and tell relatives and friends, as well as deal with incident related matters like calling the police, seeing solicitors, giving evidence in court and dealing with injuries and psychological harms.

Another significant difference is the stigma attached to gender violence, a powerful legacy from the recent history of social acceptance, reflected in the series of cultural myths, proverbs, folk or fairy tales found in many cultures, which aim to blame women for the violence used against them. In male dominant societies, this victim blame is attached to all forms of gender violence and has been most visible in relation to sexual violence, which tends to receive more media coverage because rape trials are, for example, usually heard in the Crown Court.

Although domestic violence has been recognised as a crime since the 1990s in the UK, the failure to introduce specific domestic violence legislation, which could reflect its complexity, has resulted in a series of difficulties which have limited the effectiveness of legal responses and in part explains why it continues to be largely a hidden crime.

Prevalence of domestic violence

Returning briefly to the Women's Aid 'Imagine' poster, there is one further point to be made. Although the hidden nature of this problem means that exact prevalence figures are hard to find, all sources indicate that many women, including readers of this text, will have no need to 'imagine' domestic violence, as its reality may be all too well known to them. While the methodological difficulties involved in estimating its extent are explored later, the Home Office headline figure indicates that as many as one in four women in the UK have experienced domestic violence at some point in their life-times

(Home Office, 19/2000). This high prevalence figure means that in whatever context domestic violence is discussed, if women are present, regardless of their social status, there is a possibility that as many as a quarter of them may have been subjected to domestic violence, whether or not they choose to identify as either survivors or victims.[11] Logically too, to the extent that men are present, there is a possibility that perpetrators are amongst them.[12] This highlights the need for care, caution and sensitivity in all discussions of and work around domestic violence because personal dynamics are intrinsic to all domestic violence contexts.

Domestic violence as a gendered crime

Understanding domestic violence in the conceptual framework of gender violence reflects the reality that in the UK, as internationally, the overwhelming majority of its survivors who seek help from the police and support agencies and who require medical attention are women and the vast majority of its perpetrators are men (Home Office, 19/2000). When seen in the context of crime more broadly, this becomes less surprising, as men commit the vast majority of violent crime and sexual offences, indeed the majority of all crime:

> Men outnumber women in all major crime categories. Between 85 and 95 per cent of offenders found guilty of burglary, robbery, drug offences, criminal damage or violence against the person are male. Although the number of offenders is relatively small, 98 per cent of people found guilty of, or cautioned for, sexual offences are male.
>
> (Home Office, 2002/2003)

Given the gendered nature of crime and particularly violent crime and sexual offences, the gendered nature of domestic violence should not be surprising. This gendered patterning, the operational reality for police, health authorities and support agencies, does not mean that men are never its victims, yet as will become clear, there is no evidential support for claims from the UK's men's movement that there is an increasing number of men amongst its silent victims. Rather than being an equal opportunities crime, all sources (official crime statistics, national crime surveys, local and international studies) indicate that the gender patterning of domestic violence is stronger than that found for general crime categories.

Problems occasioned by the lack of accurate statistics

While this patterning is clear, considerable methodological difficulties have plagued the many different approaches to ascertaining precise statistics, which makes assessing the scale of this problem, and whether it is increasing or decreasing, difficult. It also means that it is hard to know with certainty whether domestic violence impacts on all groups of women to the same extent and this enables stereotypes and misperceptions to flourish.

These methodological difficulties create problems for policy-makers and practitioners in ascertaining the scale of resources needed to address the problem, both on the part of statutory agencies like the police or voluntary sector agencies like Women's Aid. Further, it makes for problems in assessing 'what works' in terms of domestic violence reduction policies and strategies because the lack of reliable 'base-line' figures means the effectiveness of interventions cannot be assessed with any accuracy. By the same token, the lack of reliable statistics undermines risk assessment tools used by practitioners in attempting to assess risks posed by perpetrators to individual clients.

As this section reveals, there are many reasons why it is hard to assess the prevalence of domestic violence. One problem is the recording of domestic violence as a crime in official statistics. For example, although criminological wisdom holds that the official statistics for murder are the most accurate because it is a hard crime to conceal, recent events like the Harold Shipman murders have cast doubt on this wisdom. In relation to domestic violence, Southall Black Sisters have expressed concern that the murders of some South Asian women have been concealed as accidents or suicides (Gupta, 2003). The recognition that murders can be concealed suggests that official statistics can be undercounted. The possibility that the figures for domestic murder of women (on average two a week (Home Office, 2005)) are an underestimate is a real issue and not merely an academic quibble, because a reduction in the level of domestic homicide is now used as the primary 'proxy' performance indicator against which the government intends to measure 'the medium- to long-term success' of their domestic violence strategy.

Problems with reporting domestic violence

For a series of reasons, women may be reluctant to report the violence and some women are unable to speak out. Disabled women experiencing domestic violence may be particularly isolated, for example, and have no independent access to telephones or other means of communication (Radford et al., 2005). Women from some minority ethnic communities may be isolated by language and have no independent access to help-seeking outside of their own communities, where cultural values may mitigate against reporting to or seeking help from an outsider (NISAA, 2004).

Naming domestic violence

Some women may be unaware that what is happening to them counts as domestic violence (Walby and Allen, 2004). Radford and Kelly (1991) have argued that recognising that domestic violence is occurring is itself a process involving several steps. The first involves recognising that what is happening is unacceptable. Whether this is recognised will be influenced by many things, including what actually happened, how family life was experienced in childhood or how it is represented in influential cultural portrayals of 'family life', whether by the media or in different cultures and religions.

The second step involves naming the behaviour as violent. This may seem straightforward, and sometimes it can be but, on the other hand, a 'push', 'shove', or even a slap may be dismissed as accidental or playful. Radford and Kelly (1991) found that what triggered a recognition of the behaviour as violent was different for different women. For some it was being seriously injured and needing medical treatment, for others the presence of a third party enabled them to view the incident through the eyes of another and see it as violence, and for some it was its impact on their children. The complexities involved in naming perpetrators' actions as 'violent' is an important, but neglected, reason why many women are reluctant to name or report domestic violence. Yet this study found that listening to women's accounts of 'violent' incidents also revealed a range of subtle violations that can have long-term repercussions. Even where there had been serious physical injuries, women tended to minimise the violence, perhaps accepting it was serious, but not frequent. The study identified a range of reasons for this including: not wanting to deal with the consequences of naming incidents as violent; not seeing any alternatives, but putting up with it; focusing on day-to-day survival.

Research on perpetrators (Hearn, 1998) shows they hold very narrow definitions of violence, largely restricted to punching with fists or use of weapons. Further, Hearn found that denying or minimising the violence is a common strategy adopted even by convicted perpetrators and it seems likely that they would attempt to persuade their partners to their point of view. Walby and Allen (2004) report that it was women who had experienced repeated victimisation who were more likely to name their experiences as domestic violence. Consequently, in familial or intimate contexts, recognising behaviour as 'violent' can be complex for those experiencing it. Discussing or speaking out about it, even to family or friends can also be embarrassing because of the continuing stigma associated with domestic violence. Further reluctance may stem from the fact that naming the violence, even to friends and family, carries with it an imperative to do something. The British Crime Survey (BCS) 2001 found that 31 per cent of women victimised by domestic violence had told no-one.

Reporting to the police

Beyond this, making the decision to seek outside help requires courage. Calling the police or making an official report requires the further recognition that the behaviour in question is criminal violence. Again the 2001 BCS found that 64 per cent of women who had been subject to domestic violence in the previous year did not name their experiences as 'crime' and only 23 per cent of women reported it to the police.

The police themselves were only advised that domestic violence should be considered and treated as a crime in 1990. Despite publicity campaigns, and given the longevity of folk myths, it is not surprising that some victims might not think of domestic violence as a police matter, or that it has to be very serious violence to warrant police involvement. Others may be deterred from reporting by remorseful apologies and promises that 'it won't happened again', or be persuaded that is was somehow their fault, again pointing to the power of the myths. Others again may be discouraged by fear or threats of 'consequences' if they do report. The BCS (2001) found that 43 per cent of women did not report domestic violence because they thought it would be considered 'too trivial', 38 per cent considered it a private family matter, 7 per cent wanted to avoid further humiliation and 13 per cent thought involving the police would trigger further violence.

For many women reporting domestic violence can feel like a betrayal, although the actual betrayal was the perpetrators' decision to use violence. Some women may simply want the violence to be stopped, rather than their former/partner or family member to be labelled and dealt with as a criminal. Earlier in the chapter the acute conflict of loyalties experienced by some black and minority ethnic women in respect of help-seeking in a society where racism is a continuing problem was discussed. This becomes even more pertinent to decisions on reporting to the police, an institution labelled as 'institutional racist' as recently as 1999.[13] The fear of exposing themselves, or even the perpetrator, to racism can be a further deterrent to reporting to what may be perceived as 'white authorities'. Other women, particularly those involved in prostitution and women from travelling communities, may for these reasons fear police intervention, given again very mixed histories of previous encounters with the police. Asylum seekers and refugees may also be reluctant to involve the police, perhaps as a consequence of negative encounters with the police in their home countries or through fear that police involvement could impact negatively on their claims for asylum. Other migrant women may be deterred through fears in relation to nationality and immigration law. Barron (1990) found that, on average, a woman experiences 35 incidents before making a report.

While this reluctance to report raises many issues, in relation to assessing the extent of domestic violence, it means that all official figures relating to domestic violence generated by the police and criminal justice system are likely to be undercounted and consequently unreliable as a basis for policy-making, planning, risk assessment or research. Statistics generated by Women's Aid or other support services count the number of women accessing their services, so while demonstrating a real need for these services such figures are not comprehensive as estimates of domestic violence, given women's reluctance to help-seek.

Community studies of violence against women

Prior to 1990, the official crime figures were even less help as domestic violence was not considered as a crime, so was rarely reported and rarely recorded by the police. As a response, feminist academics began undertaking research, as part of the wider feminist campaign, to secure effective public and political responses to the problem and to provide statistical support for Women's Aid campaigns to secure public funding for refuges. An early study was undertaken by Hammer and Saunders (1984) in West Yorkshire, who found that 59 per cent of women interviewed had experienced at least one incident of domestic violence in the previous year. Radford (1987) found 70 per cent of women interviewed in the London Borough of Wandsworth had experienced at least one incident of domestic violence, again in the year prior to interview. These were both community studies, and were based on the concept of 'violence against women', rather than 'crime'. They both used random sampling techniques and adopted women-centred interviewing methods, employing women as interviewers. They rejected the 'hit-and-run' methodology of formal research, and ensured that women received details of the limited sources of help and support available at the time. These studies together with Edwards' (1989) study of the police responses to domestic violence in north London led to changes in police policies in London and West Yorkshire, changes which foreshadowed those introduced nationwide from 1990. These 1980s studies were followed by Painter's (1991) study of relationship rape which found, contrary to public perceptions, that 'rape' by husbands or male partners was seven times more common than stranger rape. 1994 saw the publication of Mooney's Islington randomised study of 500 women which found that between one in three and one in four women had experienced domestic violence in the previous year, a finding very similar to that of Dominy and Radford (1996) in Surrey.

Although local, these studies have played an important role both in highlighting domestic violence as a serious and prevalent problem and in developing knowledge regarding its nature. The 1980s studies also highlighted the failure of statutory agencies in terms of their lack of response to this serious and prevalent problem. Importantly too, they drew attention to the limitations of the official crime statistics as a measure of domestic violence.

Problems with British Crime Surveys (BCS)

Recognising that there is a large number of crimes not reported to the police, or not recorded by them as crimes, the Home Office introduced the BCS in

1982.[14] It is primarily a 'victimisation' survey in which respondents are asked about particular incidents of crime they have experienced in the previous year. The rationale is that these figures are more accurate than official crime statistics because they are not affected by the problem of under-reporting, or police policies in recording crime. However, it was soon realised that women's reluctance to talk about domestic violence, particularly to a stranger on the doorstep who was not in a position to access help, resulted in domestic violence being seriously undercounted in the early sweeps of the BCS.

In the 1996 BCS the Home Office introduced a new methodology, which recognised that the disclosure of sensitive and potentially distressing incidents, like domestic violence, could be affected by the way interviews were conducted, the presence of other household residents and the gender of the interviewer (Mirrlees-Black, 1999). This innovation was further developed in the 2001 BCS and included a detailed 'interpersonal violence' computerised self-completion schedule designed to produce an 'accurate estimate of the extent of domestic violence, sexual assault and stalking' (Walby and Allen, 2004:v). It was considered that this approach would be less embarrassing for respondents who would be more likely to disclose incidents.

However, several problems remained, a major one being that only residents in private households were interviewed, so women and children who had fled to refuges or were living in temporary accommodation continued to be excluded. Although the authors of the report considered these numbers too small to be significant, they also noted that they received more reports pertaining to the earlier part of the research year. This could suggest that the lower numbers in the second half of the year were explained by the fact that some women were still in refuges and/or other temporary accommodation. Thus in concentrating on private households, the BCS is still likely to exclude considerable numbers of women experiencing domestic violence.

Another problem in crime surveys relates to definitions. The 2001 BCS counted separately the numbers of women and men reporting domestic violence, sexual assault and stalking, yet these crimes can all occur in a domestic violence context. Although it found that 54 per cent of rapes, 47 per cent of serious sexual assaults and 37 per cent of aggravated stalking were perpetrated by current or former partners, it was not possible to know whether all these assaults were carried out by the same perpetrator who was also domestically violent.

A further problem with crime surveys asking about domestic violence is that they do not reflect the context in which the violence takes place. Thus, in asking about particular incidents of physical assault of women and men, it is not clear whether physical assaults carried out by women partners are mainly 'self-defence' in response to male partners' violence (see Dobash and Dobash, 1992). One key qualitative study which looked at the incidents of violence between 100 UK heterosexual couples found that when they were just asked about these incidents, rates between women and men appeared to be similar. However, when each partner of the couple were asked about the context and impacts of the violence, it was found that women's use of violence (except in three cases) consisted of one-off acts such as a slap or throwing an object and usually occurred in self-defence. In contrast, all of the 100 men interviewed used 'threatening violence' which was based on a combination of repeated physical attacks, intimidation and humiliation of their partners and was intended to inflict both physical and psychological harm (Nazroo, 1995). Further, the vast majority of men in this study stated that women's (self-defence) violence was 'laughable' and had had no impact on them in relation to causing them fear or concern.

More recent crime surveys have attempted to reflect some of the differences in impacts between heterosexual men and women, particularly with regard to repeated assaults and impacts in relation to ill-health and injuries and employment (Mirrlees-Black, 1999; Walby and Myhill, 2004) and these are discussed in the next chapter.

The British Crime Survey (2001) continued to highlight the overall gendered patterning of domestic violence. It concluded:

> While some experience of inter-personal violence (defined as domestic violence, sexual violence and stalking) is quite widespread, a minority is subject to extreme violence, consistent with exceptional degrees of coercive control. . . . Women are the overwhelming majority of the most heavily victimized group. Among the people subject to four or more incidents of domestic violence . . . 89% were women.
>
> (Walby and Allen, 2004:vii)

Despite this gendered patterning, the numbers relating to male victimisation were surprisingly high and appeared to suggest that large numbers of men were experiencing domestic violence. This clearly raised questions about male victimisation and was addressed in a follow-up study to the Scottish Crime Survey (2000), which used similar methods to the BCS.

The Scottish Crime Survey (SCS) found that 6 per cent of women and 3 per cent of men reported being victimised by domestic violence (McPherson, 2002). These figures were far higher than the numbers of men reporting to the police or help-seeking from local agencies. Concerned that the needs of these men were not being met, the Scottish Executive commissioned a follow-up study. But far from revealing a hitherto unrecognised group in need of domestic violence services, this study, which involved retracing and re-interviewing the men who had participated in the SCS, found that some had misinterpreted the questions and believed they were being asked about non-domestic assaults, vandalism and property crimes occurring near their homes when they ticked the domestic abuse box in the survey. Others, on re-interview, admitted to being the main perpetrators of domestic violence. The authors of this second study found that only 9 of the men interviewed from the original survey claimed to be victims of domestic violence, where women's violence caused fear or concern. They reported:

> Only a minority of the men referred to as 'victims' within published reports about the Scottish Crime Survey 2000 actually perceived themselves as victims. This remained the case even when the responses of those men who misinterpreted the remit of the self-complete questionnaire were omitted from the calculation.
>
> (Gadd, Farrall, Dallimore and Lombard, 2002:2)

These authors also cautioned that future researchers 'should pay particular attention to ensuring respondents fully understand the nature of the experiences they are being asked to disclose' (Gadd *et al.*, 2002:2) to prevent inappropriate comparisons being made. There is a clear message for future British Crime Surveys here, given the similarities of their methodologies.

These findings are significant given the periodic revival of debates in the UK around men's victimisation as new researchers (re)discover the limitations of official statistics and crime surveys in terms of estimating the prevalence of domestic violence and attempt to present it as an 'equalities' issue, with a view to securing funding for new projects or meeting local authority equalities targets.

Conclusion

This introductory chapter has examined the nature of domestic violence and its global recognition as a form of both gender violence and hate crime. It has discussed recent research into its prevalence in the UK. The final question addressed here relates to its naming. Several criticisms have been aimed at the term domestic violence, but it is the one used in this text because it reflects the historical struggle by women for such violence to be recognised as criminal, despite its problematic gender-neutral connotations. This is in contrast to the increasing use of the term 'domestic abuse' by various agencies and statutory bodies. The term 'domestic abuse' has been adopted by some agencies because it is regarded as reflecting a broader range of harmful experiences than is contained in the word 'violence'. But, problematically, 'abuse' is also a minimising term and has, for example, commonly been used to accord lesser status to children's experiences of physical and sexual assault and rape. The term 'domestic' can also be limiting because not all domestic violence takes place in the home and violence from partners, ex-partners or family members can occur in other settings. Nevertheless, it continues to convey a common aspect of many women's experiences of violence.

Another area of debate has been in relation to the terms 'victims' and 'survivors' when referring to women's experiences of violence. In the criminal justice context 'victim' is a useful term to denote who has been on the receiving end of a crime and consequently is used here when discussing policing and the law. But apart from this context, many women prefer the term 'survivor' where they have struggled against domestic violence and rebuilt their lives. But not all survive, and some are still struggling to cope with continuing violence and its impacts and feel the latter term is inappropriate (Radford and Hester, 2006). The next chapter discusses these impacts for women and children in more depth and highlights some of the real barriers to escaping domestic violence.

Notes

1   During 'the troubles' the level of domestic homicide in Northern Ireland was higher than that in both the Irish Republic and England and Wales, McWilliams (1998).
2   From work undertaken by the authors with North Wales Domestic Violence Forum.
3   Cultures of honour include many in Eastern and Southern Europe and South America and not only those in South East Asia, the Middle East and Africa.
4   Benjamin Bowling (1998) describes the late 1970s as the period in which the extent and ferocity of violent racism in Britain was unprecedented.
5   The domestic violence concession allows women to apply for indefinite leave to remain if they can 'prove' they have experienced domestic violence.
6   Such rules apply to women who enter the UK as the wives, unmarried partners or fiancées of UK citizens who have not gained indefinite leave to remain in this country, because they have not been in the relationship for two years. They also apply to women who enter as the partners of EEA citizens who come here to work.
7   Some official definitions include these experiences under child abuse and child protection and in this regard it could be argued that this diminishes young women's experiences, since they may not be entitled to the same protection under the law as adults.
8   National research is currently being undertaken in conjunction with Women's Aid at the time of writing on the experiences of physically disabled women. In 2000 disabled women were recognised as a 'hard to reach group' in equal opportunities statements by domestic violence agencies in the statutory sector.
9   Leading to the present authors, along with other UK domestic violence experts, being invited to work with law makers, members of the judiciary and police officers in developing and implementing new domestic violence legislation in countries as diverse as Japan, Turkey and Kazakhstan.

10 The exception to this is the Protection from Harassment Act (1997) which recognises psychological violence, but only in circumstances where partners are not living together.

11 Language issues are important in discussions of domestic violence – the debate around the identities 'victim' or 'survivor' is explored later in this chapter.

12 The Home Office figure that one in four women have been subjected to domestic violence in their life-times cannot be directly transposed to suggest that one in four men are domestic violence perpetrators, because it is recognised that perpetrators may commit violence in more than one relationship, i.e. victimise more that one woman. Nevertheless, these figures do suggest a significant prevalence of 'hidden perpetrators'.

13 The Stephen Lawrence Inquiry Report (1999).

14 Initially the scope of the BCS was UK wide but in more recent years Scotland and Northern Ireland have conducted their own. Eight crime surveys were conducted prior to 2001, subsequently they have been conducted annually.

References

Amnesty International, UK (2004) *USA: Patterns of Brutality and Cruelty: War Crimes at Abu Ghraib.*

An-Na'im, A. and Candler, C.H. (2000) *Forced Marriage.* www.soas.ac.uk/honour crimes/FM

Asian Women's Resource Centre (2005) *Forced Marriage: Training Development Seminar Report.* Asian Women's Resource Centre, London.

Association of Chief Police Officers (2004) *Guidance on Investigating Domestic Violence.* ACPO Centrex.

Barnardos (1998) *Whose daughter next? Children abused through prostitution.* London: Barnardos.

Barron, J. (1990) *Not worth the paper.* Bristol: Women's Aid Federation, England.

Bernard, C. (2000) Shifting the margins: black feminist perspectives on discourses of mothers in child sexual abuse, in Radford *et al.* (eds) *Women, Violence and Strategies for Action.* Buckingham: Open University Press.

Cockram, J. (2003) *Silent voices: women with disabilities and family and domestic violence.* Perth: WA Edith Cowan University.

Daphne II Dissemination Project (2005) *Female Marriage Migrations – Awareness raising and violence prevention.* Brussels: European Commission.

Dominy, N. and Radford, L. (1996) *Domestic Violence in Surrey: developing an effective inter-agency response.* London: Surrey County Council and Roehampton Institute.

Donovan, C., Hester, M., Holmes, J. and McCarry, M. (2006) *Comparing domestic abuse in same sex and heterosexual relationships.* Universities of Sunderland and Bristol.

Edwards, S. (1989) *Policing Domestic Violence, Women, the law and the state*. London: Sage.

Erwin, P. (2000) *Intimate and caregiver violence against women with disabilities*. www.bwip.org/documents/Erwin

Foreign and Commonwealth Office (2002) *Guidelines for Police: Dealing with cases of forced marriage*. London.

Foreign and Commonwealth Office (2004) *Practice Guidance for Social Workers: Young people and vulnerable adults facing forced marriage*. London.

Gadd, D., Farrall, S., Dallimore, D. and Lombard, N. (2002) *Domestic Abuse against Men in Scotland*. Criminal Justice Research Findings no.61. Edinburgh: Scottish Executive.

Gill, A. (2004) 'Voicing the silent fear: South Asian Women's Experiences of Domestic Violence', *The Howard Journal*, 43 (5): 465–483.

Grace, S. (1995) *Policing Domestic Violence in the 1990s. Home Office Research Study 139*. London: Home Office Research and Planning Unit.

Gupta, R. (2003) Some recurring themes: 'Southall Black Sisters, 1979–2003 and still going strong', in Gupta (ed.) *From homebreakers to jailbreakers: Southall Black Sisters*. London: Zed Books.

Hanmer, J. and Saunders, S. (1984) *Well-founded Fear: A Community Study of Violence to Women*. London: Hutchinson.

Hanmer, J., Griffiths, S. and Jerwood, D. (1999) *Arresting evidence: domestic violence and repeat victimisation*. London: Home Office.

Hanmer, J., Radford, J. and Stanko, B. (1989) 'Women and Policing, Contradictions Old and New', in Hammer *et al.* (eds) *Women, Policing, and Male Violence*. London: Routledge.

Hearn, J. (1998) *The Violences of Men*. London: Sage.

Heise, L. (1995) 'Overcoming violence: A background paper on violence against women as an obstacle to development'. Unpublished.

Home Office (2001–2003) *Criminal Statistics, England and Wales 2001, Crime in England and Wales, 2002/2003*. National Statistics on-line www.statistics.gov.uk

Home Office 19/2000 *Domestic Violence: revised circular to the police*. London: Home Office.

Home Office, Crime Reduction Unit (2005) *Domestic Violence: A National Report*. www.crimereduction.gov.uk/domesticviolence51.htm

Johnson, N. (1995) 'Domestic Violence: An overview,' in P. Kingston and B. Penhale (eds) *Family Violence and the Caring Professions*. Basingstoke: Macmillan.

Kelly, L. (1988) *Surviving Sexual Violence*. Oxford: Polity Press.

Kelly, L. (1996) 'When does the speaking profit us? Reflections on the challenges of developing feminist perspectives on abuse and violence by women', in M. Hester *et al.* (eds) *Women, violence and male power*. Buckingham: Open University Press.

Kelly, L. (1999) *Domestic Violence Matters: an evaluation of a development project*. London: Home Office.

Kelly, L. and Lovett, J. (2005) *What a Waste: The Case for an Integrated Violence Against Women Strategy*. Women's National Commission.

Kirkwood, C. (1993) *Leaving Abusive Partners*. London: Sage.

Leeds Inter-Agency Project (LIAP) (2005) *Disabled women experiencing violence from men they know*. Leeds.

Mama, A. (1989) *The Hidden Struggle: Statutory and Voluntary Sector Responses to Violence against Black Women in the Home*. London: Race and Housing Research Unit, Runnymead Trust.

McCarthy, M. (1999) *Sexuality and women with learning disabilities*. London: Jessica Kingsley.

McCarthy, M. and Thompson, D. (1997) 'A prevalence study of sexual abuse of adults with intellectual disabilities referred for sex education', *Journal of Applied Research in Intellectual Disability*, 10 (2).

McPherson, S. (2002) *Domestic violence: findings from the 2000 Scottish Crime Survey*. Edinburgh: Scottish Executive.

McWilliams, M. (1998) 'Violence Against Women in Societies Under Stress', in R.E. Dobash and R.P. Dobash (eds) *Rethinking Violence Against Women*. London: Sage.

McWilliams, M. and McKiernan, J. (1993) *Bringing it out into the open: Domestic violence in Northern Ireland*. Belfast: HMSO.

Mirrlees-Black, C. (1999) *Domestic Violence: Findings from the BCS Self-Completion Questionnaire. Home Office Research Study 191*. London: Home Office.

Mullender, A. (1996) *Rethinking Domestic Violence*. London: Routledge.

Nazroo, J. (1995) 'Uncovering gender differences in the use of marital violence: the effect of methodology', *Sociology*, 29:49–95.

NISAA project in Partnership with My Sisters Place (2004) *Identifying Gaps in Services for Black and Minority Ethnic Women experiencing Domestic Violence in Middlesbrough, A Case Study*. University of Teesside.

Painter, K. (1991) *Wife rape, marriage and law: survey report, key findings and recommendations*. Manchester: University Department of Social Policy and Social Work.

Patel, P. (2000) 'Southall Black Sisters: domestic violence campaigns and alliances across sex, race and class', in Hanmer, J. and Itzen, C. (eds) *Home Truths about Domestic Violence*. London: Routledge.

Pence, E. (1987) *In Our Best Interest: A Process for Personal and Social Change*. Deluth: Minnesota Program Development Inc.

Pence, E. and Paymar, M. (1993) *Education Groups for Men who Batter*. New York: Springer.

Plotnikoff, J. and Woolfson, R. (1998) *Policing Domestic Violence: Effective Organisational Structures*. London: Home Office, Policing and Reducing Crime Unit.

Radford, J. (1987) 'Policing Male Violence: Policing Women', in J. Hanmer and M. Maynard (eds) *Violence and Social Control*. London: Macmillan.

Radford, J. and Kelly, L. (1990–1) 'Nothing Really Happened: The Invalidation of Women's Experiences of Sexual Violence', *Critical Social Policy 30*; reprinted in

M. Hester, L. Kelly, and J. Radford, (eds) (1996) *Women, Violence and Male Power: Feminist activism, research and practice.* Buckingham: Open University Press.

Radford, J., Harne, L. and Trotter, J. (2005) *Good Intentions and Disabling Realities.* Middlesbrough Domestic Violence Forum and Teesside University.

Radford, L. and Hester, M. (2006) *Mothering through Domestic Violence.* London: Jessica Kingsley.

Saghal, G. and Yuval Davies, N. (1992) *Refusing Holy Orders.* London: Virago.

Siddiqui, H. (2003) 'It was written in her kismet: forced marriage', in R. Gupta (ed.) *From homebreakers to jailbreakers: Southall Black Sisters.* London: Zed Books.

Siddiqui, H. and Patel, M. (2003) 'Sad, mad or angry? Mental illness and domestic violence', in R. Gupta (ed.) *op cit.*

Southall Black Sisters (2006) *Domestic Violence, Immigration and No Recourse to Public Funds.* Paper: Gender, Marriage Migration and Justice in Multi-cultural Britain Conference. London: Roehampton University.

The Charity Commission (2000) *Operational Guidance, Human Rights Act 1998, Article 8 – Right To Respect For Private And Family Life.* http://www.charity-commission.gov.uk/supportingcharities/ogs/g071c002.asp#a

UNICEF (2000) *Domestic Violence against Women and Girls.* Innocenti Digest, No.6. June, Innocenti Research Centre, Florence, Italy.

UNIFEM (2003) *Not a minute more: Ending violence against women.* New York: UNIFEM.

UNIFEM (undated) *Masculinity and Gender Violence.* UNIFEM Gender Fact Sheet 1.

United Nations (1995) *Fourth World Conference on Women: Beijing Declaration.* www.un.org/womanwatch/daw/beijing/platform/declar.htm

United Nations Population Fund (undated) *Ending Widespread Violence Against Women.* www.unfpa.org/gender/violence.htm

Walby, S. and Allen, J. (2004) *Domestic violence, sexual assault and stalking: Findings from the British Crime Survey,* Home Office Research Study 276. London: Home Office. www.homeoffice.gov.uk/rds/pdfs04/hors276.pdf

Warren, T., Rowlingson, K. and Whyley, C. (2000) 'Gender and Wealth Inequality,' *Radstats Journal,* Spring Issue, 75:49–54.

Women's Aid (2005) womensaid.org.uk/home/domestic violence A–Z/domestic violence (general).

Women's Aid (2000) 'So what is domestic violence?' Women's Aid Campaign: a future without fear. www.womensaid.org.uk/campaigns

Women's Aid Federation England (1992) *Written Evidence to the House of Commons Home Affairs Select Committee Inquiry into Domestic Violence.* Bristol: Women's Aid Federation.

Women's Equality Unit (2003) *Individual Incomes of men and women 1996/97 to 2001/02.* Department of Trade and Industry (June 2003).

Young, M., Nosek, M., Howland, C., Chanpong, G. and Rintala, D. (1997) 'Prevalence of abuse of women with disabilities,' *Archives of Physical Medicine and Rehabilitation, Special Issue 78.*

2   Impacts, coping and surviving domestic violence

This chapter looks in more detail at the impacts of domestic violence on women and children. Understanding these impacts can help dispel some of the myths and reduce woman blame, as well as identify how policy-makers and agencies can improve policies and practice to enable women to rebuild their lives in safety and gain protection and justice. Although women and children's experiences of domestic violence are interconnected, not all women who are subjected to domestic violence have children and there are differences in experiences based on age and power. Children's perspectives are therefore specifically addressed in the second part of this chapter.

The impacts on women

The focus in the first part is on women's experiences because all the research indicates that they are far more likely to experience negative impacts in comparison to male victims, in relation to anxiety and fear, injury and ill health and depression and, in extreme cases, death (Mirrlees-Black, 1999; Walby and Myhill, 2004). Examining these issues continues to underline domestic violence as a gendered crime which is used by men to dominate and control women, and which in male-dominating societies often leave women with few options to escape the violence. The question 'Why don't they just leave?', although complex and variable depending on women's different circumstances, can still be partially explained by women's lower access to financial and other resources than men in the UK (Home Office, 2000). It also needs to be recognised that even where women and children do leave, violence from perpetrators can continue and escalate and the possibilities for post-separation violence can be facilitated by government policies and by inaction by agencies. These issues, which are discussed later, demonstrate why some women experience ongoing violence for very long periods of time.

This does not mean, however, that women should be viewed as passive victims, nor that women 'learn helplessness' as is suggested in some psychological discourses on domestic violence, such as 'battered women's syndrome' (see, for example, Walker, 1979). In contrast, the research evidence indicates that women cope and adapt according to the circumstances in which they find themselves and the options that are open to them, to protect themselves and their children (Kelly, 1988; Mama, 2000; Siddiqui and Patel, 2003). Women also resist through challenging perpetrators and some may fight back but this can result in them experiencing more serious violence (Dobash and Dobash, 1992; Nazroo, 1995). In a few cases women may be driven to kill their partners in self-defence and as the only way to survive to protect themselves and/or their children, often after years of living with the violence (Griffiths, 2000; Siddiqui and Patel, 2003). Further, where they can women seek help but although there have been considerable improvements in some services, inappropriate responses, which can continue to put women at risk from further violence, remain. This is highlighted in this chapter in looking at how the medicalisation of some women's experiences and the policies and practices of other agencies can compound the impacts of violence and prevent women from rebuilding their lives in safety.

Injuries and ill health

One of the most obvious impacts in relation to women's experiences of domestic violence is the physical harm caused through injuries. This can range from bruising to more serious injuries some of which can result in permanent impairment such as loss of hearing or sight (WHO, 1997). Less obvious but equally serious are the mental impacts, particularly when these drive women to self-harm and suicide, and these are discussed in further detail below.

Canadian health statistics indicate that women are three times more likely to be injured and five times more likely to require medical attention or hospitalisation than men as a consequence of domestic violence (Statistics Canada, 2003). In the UK, there are currently no national health statistics in relation to domestic violence,[1] but there is some indication of the impacts and extent of physical injury from survivors' reports to the British Crime Survey studies and from local surveys and research. For example, the 2001 BCS indicated that 75 per cent of women sustained some kind of physical or mental injury, with 21 per cent sustaining severe bruising, black eyes or cuts. Further, 8 per cent of women reported serious physical harm in the form of broken bones, teeth or internal injury compared to 2 per cent of men. The Scottish Crime Survey (2000) found that 47 per cent of female victims required hospitalisation, compared with no male victims. Women who had sustained severe injuries as defined in the BCS were those who were more likely to have experienced frequent severe assaults. The BCS does not, however, give much information on the kind of injuries sustained. A local survey in Hackney found that as well as broken bones and bruising these also included burns, miscarriage and attempted strangulation, and 10 per cent of women in this study had been knocked unconscious (Stanko *et al.*, 1998).

General ill health

Only recently has recognition been given to how domestic violence affects women's general health. World Health Organisation (WHO) studies, which have gathered data from industrialised and developing countries, give some indication of the extent of ill health caused by domestic violence. For example, the 2002 WHO survey found that women who had experienced domestic violence were more likely to experience chronic pain, gastro-intestinal disorders, irritable bowel syndrome, ocular damage, disability and reduced physical functioning than other women (WHO, 2002). The 2005 survey found that in the majority of settings, women who had experienced sexual and/or physical partner violence were more likely to report poor or very poor health compared to women who had never experienced domestic violence. Common problems reported by women included difficulties 'with walking and carrying out daily activities, pain, memory loss and vaginal discharge' (WHO, 2005:16). As these were life-time experiences it is suggested that these findings indicate the cumulative impacts of chronic domestic violence. Other studies have suggested that women experiencing domestic violence are more vulnerable to illness and infections due to lower immunity, caused by the stress related to the violence (Koss *et al.*, 1991).

Sexual and reproductive health

Women who experience sexual violence in partner relationships are more likely to have sexually transmitted diseases, urinary tract infections and have more gynaecological complaints than other women (WHO, 1997; WHO, 2002). A study from the US (Plichta and Abraham, 1996) indicated that they were three times more likely to suffer menstrual problems, STDs or a urinary tract infection. Rape by partners and boyfriends can produce unplanned and unwanted pregnancies and international research indicates this is particularly high for teenage women, who also delay seeking antenatal care (Quinlivan and Evans, 2001; Taft, 2002). Further, research in the UK indicates that pregnancy and the time after birth can involve increased risks of violence for some women. Pregnancy can, for example, be the point at which the physical violence starts. For others it may escalate and include sexual violence (Mezey and Bewley, 1997; McGee, 2000). Some research with women suggests that an escalation of the violence relates to perpetrators' jealousy of women's pregnant state itself or of the unborn child, often because women who are pregnant are viewed as taking on a different role, which the perpetrator cannot control and where they are no longer the centre of attention (McGee, 2000). On the other hand, forced pregnancies through rape can be used by perpetrators to keep control of women and prevent them from escaping violent relationships.

Women who experience physical and sexual violence in pregnancy are at increased risk of inadequate weight gain, anaemia, miscarriages, infections, premature birth, haemorrhage, and having low birth weight babies (Parker *et al.*, 1994; BSA, 1997; WHO, 2005). Some perpetrators may also prevent women from attending post-natal care (McGee, 2000). Women who are subjected to severe domestic violence are most likely to experience negative impacts in pregnancy as has been indicated by a survey of 127 women in refuges in Northern Ireland (McWilliams and McKiernan, 1993). This study found that 60 per cent reported violence in pregnancy with 13 per cent losing their babies and a further 22 per cent being threatened with the loss of their baby as a consequence of this violence.

Deaths

It also needs to be recognised that while many women are able to survive domestic violence some women do not. UK homicide statistics indicate that women are five times more likely to be killed by a male partner than men by a woman partner and as was seen in Chapter 1, the numbers of women killed by partners have averaged over one hundred a year.

The number of women who are recorded as being killed do not, however, reflect the numbers of women who die as a result of domestic violence. The Confidential Enquiry into Maternal Deaths in the UK between 1997–1999 (DoH, 2002) stated that violence against women causes more deaths and disability among women aged 15–44 than cancer or traffic accidents. Deaths may therefore result from injuries or ill health, which can be a direct consequence of women's experiences of domestic violence.

Suicide – 'a hidden crime'[2]

Deaths resulting from suicide among women are a hidden aspect of the most serious impacts of perpetrators' violence on women. Suicide and suicide attempts are usually carried out when women are so entrapped in relationships as a result of the coercive control carried out by perpetrators that they feel the only control left to them is to take their own lives (Stark and Flitcraft, 1995; Siddiqui and Patel, 2003; Humphreys and Thiara, 2003). As one survivor who had attempted suicide from the latter study said

> I had no life. I had nothing. I had me kids . . . then I thought me kids would be better off without me because . . . it were like I had no

control over anything, to what I wore, to when I went to sleep, to
when I woke up; everything I did was what he let me do really. (Gail)
(Humpreys and Thiara, 2003:215)

Stark and Flitcraft (1995), in their ground-breaking research demonstrating the causal links between domestic violence and suicide attempts amongst
abused women, noted that the medical profession's failure to identify these
links and the resultant pathologising of these women could increase their
sense of isolation and further entrap them in the relationship. A US review of
13 research studies (Golding, 1999) has indicated that women experiencing
domestic violence are three and a half times more likely to be driven to attempts
at suicide than other women.

Stark and Flitcraft (1995) noted that suicide attempts were higher amongst
black women experiencing domestic violence and suggested that strategies of
isolation which cut black women off from informal support networks and fear
of homelessness and racism from agencies such as the police, can contribute to
black women's sense of entrapment. Mama (2000) has suggested that similar
pressures exist in the UK for black women.

In the UK, suicide and suicide attempts have been identified as up to three
times higher for Asian women under 30 than for white women (Merril *et al.*,
1990; Raleigh, 1996; Bhugra *et al.*, 1999). For example, Bhugra *et al.*, looking at
rates of self-harm at a West London hospital, found that for Asian women it
was two and half times higher than white women and seven times higher than
for Asian men, with qualitative research indicating that domestic violence,
including forced marriage, is a factor for many (Yazdani, 1998).

Southall Black Sisters (SBS) highlight that some suicides of Asian women
are 'encouraged' by partners and other family members and in this context
should more properly be regarded as murder. They have therefore struggled to
get coroners courts to acknowledge the direct connections between suicide
and domestic violence and to regard such suicides as an abuse of women's
human rights (Siddiqui and Patel, 2003; Patel, 2003). However, they also
emphasise that the fact that more Asian women commit suicide than white
women does not mean that Asian society is more oppressive than white
society. Rather they stress that 'Asian and other women from minority
communities have greater obstacles to overcome both inside and outside the
community when escaping abuse' and that such suicides are a consequence of
the 'double discrimination of racism and sexism against black and minority
women' (Siddiqui and Patel, 2003:114–15). In this regard, internal pressures
include the notion that women in Asian cultures are held responsible for
upholding family honour, and this can mean 'pressures to make the marriage
work at all costs' (Siddiqui and Patel, 2003:127).

Gill (2004) has stressed that 'the ideal of feminine sacrifice and family
loyalty tends to be strongest in cultures of honour'[3] and the fear of bringing

shame on the family can prevent women from speaking out about the violence in order to uphold the family's reputation. In her research women who expressed suicidal thoughts or had attempted suicide 'felt trapped by the shame' and the 'overwhelming fear from living with the violence' (Gill, 2004:468).

However, SBS also emphasise that suicide attempts and other means of self-harm can be forms of coping and survival strategies which are used by South Asian women as a form of protest or to alleviate tension to regain some control over their lives. In this sense they are 'a cry for help and a desire for a better life rather than death' (Siddiqui and Patel, 2003:115).

Anxiety, fear and depression

Women are far more likely to experience increased fear and anxiety than men as a result of their experiences of domestic violence. The 1996 BCS found that 60 per cent of women interviewed were frightened and anxious as a result of their experiences compared with 5 per cent of male victims (Mirrlees-Black, 1999). In Humphrey and Thiara's study of 180 women who had used Women's Aid outreach services, 60 per cent had left as a result of being threatened with being killed (Humphreys and Thiara, 2003).

On separation the women in this study who had experienced life-threatening violence or threats of being killed continued to experience extreme fear, which could involve flashbacks, panic attacks and sleeplessness (sometimes defined in medical discourse as post-traumatic stress disorder) as is indicated by one survivor's account from this study,

> I've put a phone in and I take my mobile to bed every night. I keep doors wide open so I can hear all through the house and I sometimes just don't sleep anyway. It comes in fits and starts. I have panic attacks . . . It can be absolutely anytime anywhere. Its just certain things trigger a flashback. And if I have a flashback then they always follow with a panic attack. (Elaine whose husband was charged with attempted murder)
>
> (Humphreys and Thiara, 2003:215)

Internationally, the fear of being killed by intimate or familial violent perpetrators is high for women; for example, in Canada women fear being killed five times more than men (Statistics Canada, 2003).

Depression is also a common response amongst women who feel that perpetrators' control strategies have rendered them powerless and trapped in relationships. For example, Mooney's (1994) study in Islington, North London found that 46 per cent of the sample of women interviewed, who had experienced domestic violence, were or had been depressed, and Golding's US review of 17 research studies found similar rates of depression with its occurrence being three times higher than for non-abused women. These studies further indicated that the severity of women's depression was directly connected to the severity of the violence and the length of time that women lived with the violent perpetrator. Depression amongst women experiencing domestic violence also appears to be connected to perpetrators' use of humiliation as a power and control tactic as well as repeated sexual violence, both of which can destroy women's self-confidence and sense of self (Humphreys and Thiara, 2003; Walby and Myhill, 2004). This is illustrated from a survivor's account in Humphreys and Thiara's research

> I suppose he was mentally abusing me in a way. I was just becoming some subservient doormat of a wife for him. . . . My confidence was at rock bottom when I was at home. I got to the point where I was no good at cooking, no good at basic things. He didn't let me have any opinions of my own. His opinion counted for everything and everybody else's was totally worthless . . . he had total control over me. He had total control over me sexually, like control over my body, so he'd thrust himself on me and take me anyway he liked just to like . . . you're my wife . . . it's pathetic . . . I'd just cry afterwards. Its sick really . . . I suppose I did get depressed. (Sally)
>
> (Humphreys and Thiara, 2003:214)

Substance dependence

Substance use and dependence has also been identified as a means of women coping with domestic violence (Golding, 1999; Humphreys et al., 2005). Golding's review (1999) found that women experiencing domestic violence were six times more likely than non-abused women to use alcohol to help them cope and were five times more likely to use illicit and licit drugs. Such dependence can impact long term on women's physical health and ultimately result in death (see case study). Women who are prostituted by partners/pimps as part of an overall pattern of domestic violence can be particularly at risk of substance dependence, either through being forcibly given hard drugs such as crack cocaine or heroin, or they may take these drugs as a means of coping with the violence from the partner/pimp and from the 'punters'.

Medicalisation and revictimisation

While depression, self-harm, stress and substance dependence can be defined as the 'health' and 'mental health' consequences of domestic violence, responding to these signs of emotional distress by medicalising women's experiences can result in their revictimisation and prolong the violence.

For example, women experiencing domestic violence who seek help from GPs or other health workers may have been diverted into mental health services or given anti-depressants or other drugs when what they need is confirmation that their experiences are a result of the violence and so require appropriate support to be able to escape the violent man (Humphreys and Thiara, 2003). Some women may fear that drugs will lower their responses and reduce their capacity to protect themselves and their children. As one survivor said

> I don't want to be put on medication. I find it better being able to talk about the problem rather than talk to the bottle of pills they want to give me . . . I've got two children. I can't afford to be drugged up. I've been on anti-depressants before and ended up worse than before I started. (Mary)
>
> (Humphreys and Thiara, 2003:218)

There are also real problems in diagnosing women's normal emotional distress as a consequence of domestic violence as 'mental illness'. The label carries a social stigma, which can provide perpetrators with further weapons to allege that because women are 'mad' they should not be believed when they report violence to agencies such as the police, as research with disabled women defined as mentally ill has demonstrated (Cockram, 2003). It can also enable perpetrators to allege that mothers are not capable of caring for their children in custody battles post-separation, or where there are child protection concerns (Radford *et al.*, 1999). Further, it can reinforce the 'distorted perceptions' of perpetrators and deepen women's 'sense of disempowerment and loss of self-esteem' (Humphreys and Thiara, 2003:219).

The label of mental illness can be particularly harmful for Asian women, and families can allege that women are 'mad' when they resist forced marriage or attempt to escape domestic violence. In this regard, SBS has highlighted the collusion by some GPs with such families to put women on drugs or have them sectioned (Siddiqui and Patel, 2003).

Recovering from the health impacts of domestic violence

The negative health impacts of domestic violence and how women cope and survive are diverse and vary according to women's different circumstances, their own resilience and the different forms of violence experienced. On the whole, they depend on the severity of the violence, its frequency and the extent of the perpetrators' control, as well as how long women have to cope before they are able to obtain appropriate help and support. The research evidence suggests that women who experience chronic physical and sexual violence and are trapped in relationships by perpetrators for long periods are more likely to experience severe impacts than others in relation to anxiety, depression and physical harm (Golding, 1999). Nevertheless, international research has shown that women can 'recover' from the mental impacts of domestic violence, such as panic attacks and depression, if health agencies respond appropriately (Golding, 1999; Coker *et al.*, 2002).

Coker *et al.*, in their large-scale study of women reporting to health agencies, found that disclosure of domestic violence made no difference to women in lessening these impacts unless they received repeated positive affirmation that the women who had experienced domestic violence *were not to blame*. Alongside such affirmation, these studies have emphasised that women need strong social support in safety planning to escape the violence (Coker *et al.*, 2002). In this regard, Golding's review (1999) looking at the mental health impacts of domestic violence found that the longer women were away from the violence, the more likely they were to recover from depression or the impacts of extreme fear such as panic attacks. Further, the research indicates that although some women may value counselling or other types of therapeutic interventions, the impacts of the violence are unlikely to lessen without measures to address women's safety.

Thus, as Southall Black Sisters have emphasised 'many women can recover or cope with depression and mental illness' if they are provided with the appropriate help and support (Siddiqui and Patel, 2003). This involves addressing a range of needs that women may have in order to obtain safety and be able to move on in their lives, from emotional and social support to safety planning, legal protection and having somewhere to live. While health, mental health and social care services cannot meet most of these needs themselves, they need to have strong links with other agencies including women's support services, such as Women's Aid (Department of Health, 2005).

Case study: Alcohol use in the context of domestic violence

Irene, in her 50s, had been in a relationship for 12 years with Paul and suffered years of domestic violence from him. She had been hospitalised and had suffered a stroke, all as a result of his violence. He had used various strategies of power and control over her including: isolating her from her family and friends; taking control of her money through getting himself recognised as her carer; threatening and repeatedly physically assaulting her. He had also put her down so much that she was convinced she could not look after herself and he even controlled when she should eat. As a consequence, Irene had very low self-esteem and believed that no one cared what happened to her.

Over the years, she had called the police on several occasions but on many of these she had been identified as smelling of drink and having slurred speech. She was therefore viewed as being as bad as the perpetrator and no police action was ever taken since her evidence was considered unreliable. There was also no recognition that her speech could have been affected by the stroke. When the police did take statements she usually retracted them, and so she was considered even more unreliable. Irene was an alcoholic but had become so because of the violence.

Eventually she received the recognition and support for the causes of her alcoholism by a domestic violence police officer, who had the knowledge and understanding of the interconnections between domestic violence and substance misuse. Her partner was remanded in custody for the various reported assaults over the years and Irene was able receive visits from family and friends and receive home visits from social services. Unfortunately, three months after her partner had been remanded in custody and before the final court case, Irene died from causes attributed to poor diet and alcohol abuse. However, if the interconnections between her substance misuse and domestic violence had been identified years earlier, Irene might still be alive.

(Based on information provided by Tracey Bellamy, Detective Sergeant, Domestic Violence Officer, Nottinghamshire Police Force, 2004).

Why don't women just leave?

Professionals may get frustrated when women stay with a violent perpetrator (BMA, 1997) and one of the main myths about domestic violence is that it is easy for women to leave, but this is not the case. As seen earlier in looking at the health impacts, common power and control strategies used by perpetrators that make it difficult for women to leave include: threats to kill women and/or children; intimidatory tactics such as destruction of women and children's possessions; threats and harm to pets; increased use of sexual violence; isolation, humiliation, constant surveillance, and virtual imprisonment.

Economic and social consequences

If women leave they may also lose their jobs, or fear losing their only means of financial support, their home and possessions. They may also fear having to move away from family, friends and their own communities and social networks in order to find safety. The assumption that it is women and children who should leave the family home, and experience deprivation as a result of this, rather than the perpetrator is itself problematic. Nevertheless, it is women and children who are often driven to move because agencies, including criminal justice agencies, are frequently unable to provide sufficient protection.

The impacts on mothers

Perpetrators may also threaten mothers with the loss of custody of their children or with allegations of 'bad motherhood' to social services, if they attempt to leave. Alternatively, they may keep the children with them, knowing that many mothers will not leave without them. Ironically, some mothers will also stay because of familial ideology, which tells them that children need fathers, despite their violence and abuse (McGee, 2000; Mullender *et al.*, 2002). A common strategy of perpetrators is to attempt to destroy mothers' relationships with their children, through verbally undermining their parenting in front of the children and destroying children's respect. While many mothers and children resist these strategies of control, some violent fathers succeed in permanently destroying these relationships (Radford and Hester, 2006). Most mothers struggle to protect their children from their fathers' violence and abuse, and some decide to leave, despite the dangers, when they become aware how far their children are affected. However, a significant number lose their children in this context. Some are forced to send their children to live with previous partners in order to keep the children safe. Others may have to leave without their children because they are in fear of their lives, and some have their children taken into care as a consequence of the impacts of a perpetrator's violence, which leaves the mothers unable to cope through illness, disability, substance use or mental health problems (Humphreys and Thiara, 2002).

Compounding the impacts for mothers – child protection policies

Mothers experiencing domestic violence often fear seeking help from child protection agencies, believing that they will be blamed and have their children removed. Such views are not without foundation since traditionally child protection work has focused on mothers and held them responsible for protecting their children. Further, although there have been changes in social work practice, and more recognition has been given to the need to support mothers experiencing domestic violence in the last few years, mothers can still be blamed if they do not act to end the relationship with the violent perpetrator and either leave or get an injunction to get him out of the family home. In this context, there can be lack of understanding of the fear created by the perpetrator and of the extent of his power and control. There can also be assumptions that the family will be safe once the relationship is over, when this is not necessarily the case (see below). In other circumstances, child protection professionals may not be aware of how far a perpetrator's violence and power and control strategies have undermined a mother's parenting capacities, and her need to obtain safety before this can be addressed (Radford and Hester, 2006).

Traditionally, there has been a lack of focus on domestic violence perpetrators and their responsibility for the direct abuse and neglect of children in child protection procedures (Farmer, 2006). Although practice in this area is changing, there remain considerable problems in holding perpetrators accountable. For example, as seen above, violent fathers can make counter-allegations of child abuse against mothers and child protection agencies may take these at face value and collude with perpetrators' allegations of mothers as inadequate parents (Hester and Scott, 2000). Perpetrators can also allege that their partners are equally violent and this can lead professionals to viewing the problem as one of 'mutual violence', where there is no identification of a primary perpetrator, or who does what to whom. In these circumstances there can be a lack of understanding of women's violence used in self-defence or their fear of their violent partners (Radford *et al.*, 2006).

A further problem is that some childcare workers (and particularly women) experience intimidation and threats from violent fathers and this can lead them to avoid visiting families or holding perpetrators' accountable. This is one *hidden* reason why the attention may turn on mothers to protect their children and the perpetrator's responsibility for the violence and abuse disappears (Littlechild and Bourke, 2006; Humphreys, 2000). In extreme circumstances a lack of focus on domestically violent perpetrators and their responsibility for the violence and abuse has led to their killings of children (see below). A failure to address the impacts of violence on mothers and their need for safety can also ultimately lead to the permanent removal of children, since, as seen above, mothers are no longer able to protect. In recent years there have been changes in child protection law and policy (see Chapter 3) and local initiatives in some areas to assist mothers in early disclosure of domestic violence and help to gain safety for themselves and their children. These can assist in avoiding some of the problems in child protection practice highlighted above and are discussed below.

Isolation and racial discrimination

Isolation has already been mentioned as a frequent strategy developed by perpetrators to cut women off from informal support from families or friends, and to prevent them from seeking help from agencies. Such strategies can have acute impacts for certain groups of women, and be compounded by institutional discrimination. For example, in some South Asian communities leaving home can be viewed as 'a betrayal of the family and community', and families may put considerable effort into finding and bringing women and children back (Gill, 2004: 468). But minority women can also fear being isolated from their own communities because of institutional racism from the wider society, which can make their own survival that much harder (Siddiqui and Patel, 2003).

Racism and immigration laws

As seen in Chapter 1, the difficulties of leaving are particularly acute for minority women whose immigration status is insecure. This includes women who come to the UK to marry or who accompany partners on work visas or as asylum seekers. Women who marry must now remain in the relationship for two years before they can obtain settled status and be able to have recourse to public funds, such as housing benefits and social security (Gill and Sharma, 2005). Perpetrators may also tell them they will be deported if they leave and take possession of their passports and they may deliberately fail to apply for settled status for their wives at the end of the two-year period. In effect this can make women 'overstayers' who are eligible for deportation under the immigration rules. Although the government now allows women who are subject to the two-year rule to stay in this country on the grounds of domestic violence, this rule excludes women who are viewed as 'overstayers' (Gill and Sharma, 2005). Thus immigration rules can constitute a form of institutional discrimination, which prevents women in this position from leaving their violent partners.

Case study: problems with immigration law

Tatanya came to England from Eastern Europe after she had married her husband who had settled status in the UK. Tatanya's immigration status to stay in this country was dependent on her husband's and was governed by the then one year rule (now 2 years) which stated that she must remain living with her husband for at least one year, before she could apply for leave to remain and have access to public funds. Tatanya had been told by her husband that she would be deported if she left him and as a consequence suffered regular physical and sexual violence as well as mental abuse and was treated like a slave. Tatanya eventually reported a violent assault at a police station, after her husband had systematically kicked and beaten her. He was subsequently arrested and charged with Actual Bodily Harm, but he was allowed bail, albeit with conditions not to contact her or to go near to the mobile home where she lived. However, because he was allowed bail, Tatanya continued to be at risk and although the domestic violence officer contacted several refuges, none were able to offer her a place, since her lack of access to public funds meant she could not claim housing benefit. She had been financially dependent on her husband and had no money to buy food or clothing, but was denied access to income support under the same immigration rules. The police were able to provide Tatanya with a panic alarm and mobile phone, but she was too afraid to use them for fear of being deported and her only contact with the outside world was with an English language college, once a week.

Eventually, the domestic violence officer was able to obtain support for Tatanya through the local refuge outreach service. This service was able to organise an interpretator and access to an immigration lawyer, who made an application for leave to remain under the domestic violence concession rule. She finally obtained limited leave to remain and gained access to social security benefits and social housing. However, for several months she had to live in a precarious and unsafe situation, because she was denied access to public funds.

(Based on information provided by PC Lisa Skeggs Hertfordshire Constabulary)

Disabled women and institutional discrimination

Disabled women are another social group particularly affected by perpetrators' strategies of isolation. But this isolation can be made far worse by agency responses. As seen in Chapter 1, perpetrators can isolate physically disabled women by removing all aids and equipment, which enable independence and contact with the world outside the home. This is illustrated in survivor accounts from Australian research with disabled women.

> He got a car I couldn't drive, so he had complete control over me . . . he insisted on doing everything, he took away my independence . . . he took away my wheelchair so I couldn't get up off the floor . . . He abused me for years. He really believed I owed him everything because he cared for me, but he took away my independence and nearly my life. (Anne)
>
> (Cockram, 2003:21)

Where the perpetrator is also the primary carer he may attempt to cut off and prevent contact with agencies, making it much harder for women to get assistance to deal with the impacts of the violence and get out of the relationship (BSA, 1997; Cockram, 2003). But when disabled women do report the violence, they can still face considerable prejudice and disbelief, particularly when they are reporting violence from an able-bodied partner, as one Australian survivor said:

> I believe the big difference for a woman with a disability experiencing domestic violence is that people don't believe you. They still have this underlying assumption that the able-bodied partner is wonderful for taking on a person with disabilities. (Rebecca)
>
> (Cockram, 2003:21)

Such disbelief was illustrated by another survivor with mental health problems from the same research

I was getting my medication from my doctor; I don't know if he knew I was involved in domestic violence, he never asked me so I never talked about it. Once I had had enough and I called the police. They came after about an hour, but when my husband saw them he said she's crazy look at the medication she takes and they left. I never called them again. (Amanda)

(Cockram, 2003:25)

Further, research indicates that women with learning disabilities experience extreme disbelief and discrimination from agencies when they report physical or sexual violence, even though the levels of partner sexual violence are extremely high for this group of women (McCarthy and Thompson, 1997; McCarthy, 1999). For example, studies on attrition in rape cases have found that this group is more likely to face prejudice, disbelief and inaction when reporting rape to the police (Keilty and Connolly, 2001; Kelly *et al.*, 2005) and that some disability agencies have tolerated partner rape and sexual assault (Thompson, 2000).

The Leeds Inter-Agency project confirms that in the UK disabled women face similar experiences when reporting violence to different agencies and states in its report on five years' work with disabled women that many who 'had disclosed [domestic violence] felt they had not been taken seriously or had not been believed' (LIAP, 2005:16).

However, even where agencies acknowledge the violence experienced by disabled women, prejudical attitudes and assumptions of dependency on the perpetrator can mean that no action is taken (Cockram, 2003; Radford *et al.*, 2005). In this regard, it needs to be recognised that not all physically disabled women need care and 'dependency' can be created or made worse by the partner's violence. Moreover, where disabled women do require personal support, this can be provided by paid personal assistants[4] rather than the violent perpetrator.

Research and practice with disabled women in general suggests that both domestic violence agencies and disability support services are far more likely to focus on impairments and view these as a barrier, rather than acting to protect disabled women from the violence (Cockram, 2003; LIAP, 2005; Radford *et al.*, 2005). Paternalistic attitudes and the failure to consult and offer the same choices as are given to non-disabled women experiencing domestic violence contribute to this lack of protection (LIAP, 2005; Cockram, 2003). As the LIAP reported: 'Many disabled women spoke of patronising and negative attitudes from professionals. This often left them feeling as if choices and decisions were being made for them' (LIAP, 2005:16).

In addition, a failure to provide accessible information on domestic violence services means that disabled women are often unaware of the help and support that is available and they therefore feel that they are excluded from domestic services (LIAP, 2005). As a consequence of these discriminatory practices, disabled women have had unequal access to the protection afforded to non-disabled women and the international research indicates they are therefore more likely to have to remain in violent relationships much longer than other women (Young *et al.*, 1997; Cockram, 2003). Recent UK disability discrimination legislation (Disability Discrimination Act, 2005) has made it illegal to treat disabled people less favourably in the delivery of public and statutory services, including criminal justice agencies such as the police and the CPS. However, it remains to be seen whether legal change will improve agency practice, unless it is also supported by an appropriate level of funding to assist them in training and in developing the means to overcome many of the inaccessibility barriers that disabled women face.

Post-separation violence

One of the most problematic assumptions in asking the question 'Why don't women leave?' is that it is then presumed that they will be safe from the violence. But at least a third of women will continue to experience violence after they have ended the relationship. In this context, perpetrators' violence can become far more severe and potentially lethal in cases where they are intent on punishment and getting revenge on partners for daring to leave, resulting in attempts to kill or actual homicides of women (Kelly, 1999; Humphreys and Thiara, 2002; Walby and Myhill, 2004).

The level and severity of such violence is illustrated from this survivor's account from Humphreys and Thiara's research with women in contact with Women's Aid outreach services.

> My ex-partner asked a friend of his to come to my home and beat me up because I left him. I did not know this man. I opened the door to a knock one night, a man asked my name. I told him and basically he kicked and punched the hell out of me. He got hold of my three-year-old son and literally threw him into the glass door which smashed. My son needed his head injuries glued at hospital. I had a fractured skull and extensive bruising to my body and a couple of broken ribs . . . All this because I wouldn't go back to my husband.
>
> (Humphreys and Thiara, 2002:13)

White Western men who kill women in this situation often regard such killings as justified because they view women as their personal possessions who they have the right to dominate and control. Women who dare to leave the relationship are therefore regarded as challenging their masculine status and their view of themselves as men (Campbell, 1992). Within a different patriarchal discourse, those living in traditional honour communities may justify such killings on the grounds that women who dare to leave a marriage or forced marriage have brought shame and dishonour on the whole family and diminished their status in the eyes of the community. Women who are in these situations are often aware of these risks and some may decide to stay in the relationship rather than risk the possibility of lethal violence (Gill, 2004).

Compounding the impacts of post-separation violence – family law policy

For women with children, who are three times more likely to experience domestic violence than other women (Mirrlees-Black, 1999), family law policy which insists that all children must have contact with fathers increases the amount of severe post-separation violence. This is indicated from several research studies, which demonstrate that much of this violence is directly connected to child contact arrangements (Hester and Radford, 1996; Radford *et al.*, 1999; Humphreys and Thiara, 2002). Opportunities to perpetrate violence are created through child contact visits and handovers, whether organised at contact centres or elsewhere (Radford *et al.*, 1999; Aris *et al.*, 2002). Violent fathers often also find out where women live even if they escape to refuges, through making child contact applications to the family courts (Saunders, 2003a). Despite government policy, which aims to provide safe contact (Home Office, 2003), the research suggests that for some women and children contact can never be organised safely (Aris *et al.*, 2002; Mullender *et al.*, 2002). Many of the post-separation homicides of women and children can directly be related to these contact policies and practices (Saunders, 2003b, 2004). In addition, they can prolong women's experiences of violence, harassment and stalking which can continue for years after the relationship has ended (Humphreys and Thiara, 2002). Further, mothers who attempt to protect their children from violent fathers post-separation can face increased hostility from family court professionals and punitive measures, such as the threat of imprisonment if they fail to force reluctant children to have contact with violent fathers. This can place considerable strain and stress on whole families, including the children, as they may be subjected to years of what has been named as 'litigation abuse' through repeated court hearings.

The problem of woman blame and the need for perpetrator accountability

In focusing on the impacts of domestic violence on women, some contexts have been highlighted where agency interventions and policies have worsened the situation, rather than providing these women with appropriate support and protection.

State agencies may often blame women for failing to leave a violent relationship or for failing to seek help to deal with the violence. As seen above, mothers can be blamed for not protecting their children from the impacts of a perpetrator's violence and abuse by social care agencies and this can lead to them being fearful of seeking further help. In the post-separation family law context, however, when mothers do try to protect their children by preventing contact with a violent father, they are also blamed, indicating contradictions in policy and practice.

It has also been seen how medicalisation can displace the responsibility for the violence from perpetrators and result in a form of woman blame where women become defined as mentally ill, or substance dependent, without any recognition that these are the consequences of domestic violence and women's need for support and protection in these circumstances. In addition, medicalisation discourses affect how agencies respond to disabled women's experiences of violence, through focusing the blame on women's impairments rather than on the actions of perpetrators. These examples continue to underline the depth of patriarchal ideologies and culture in affecting policy and practice in shifting blame onto women and can have profound implications for survivors who may believe they are at fault. Another theme is the way institutional racism can combine with sexism to prevent women from gaining protection and contributes to a lack of understanding of the way racism operates to prevent women from leaving violent perpetrators.

Implications for practice

Although the treatment of disabled women has been specifically highlighted as an example of where some agencies can exclude women from services, it is important to recognise that all women have rights to protection. Many women remain unaware of the specific help they can obtain from Women's Aid and refuge services or the rights they have to legal protection and social housing. This includes women who live in rural areas, who may have less access to information and support than those who live in cities.

In addition, some examples highlighted above have emphasised how inappropriate or woman-blaming responses can deter women from seeking further help. Although practice has improved greatly in the last few years, differences still remain within and between services in the way women who experience domestic violence are treated. Listening to women, believing them and being non-judgemental are therefore prerequisites in empowering women to gain safety and protection (Mullender and Hague, 2000). Professionals also need to be aware of the close interconnections between mothers' safety and that of children and this issue is discussed further in looking at children's experiences.

Asking about domestic violence – routine enquiry

One specific initiative to assist women to disclose domestic violence and gain appropriate help and support in many areas has been the introduction of asking all women routinely about whether they have experienced domestic violence, when they come into contact with health or social care agencies (DoH, 2005).

Routine enquiry recognises that for several reasons some women may be reluctant to disclose domestic violence to professionals. Such reasons include fear of the perpetrator, feelings that they are to blame or will be blamed by agencies, fear that they will not be believed, and the perceived stigma of experiencing domestic violence. Asking all women about domestic violence (also known as screening) is one way to overcome these problems. However, routine enquiry only works where professionals receive sufficient training in understanding the dynamics of domestic violence and how to ask women about their experiences in confidential settings. Some local initiatives have undertaken routine enquiry through using tools such as the Duluth power and control and equality wheels (see Chapter 1) and have found that using these to assist women understand their experiences empowers survivors and gives them back some control over their own lives. Some also offer crisis safety planning until women can get further help from specialist agencies (Hester and Westmarland, 2005). It needs to be recognised, however, that opportunities need to be created which enable women to see professionals without their partners, and that agencies have sufficient information and contact with appropriate domestic violence services.

Why routine enquiry is needed

Case study

Sandra was living part-time with her parents, but spent most of her time at her partner, Allen's flat. She was first seen with Allen at the ante-natal clinic, when she was ten weeks pregnant. Allen insisted that all the examinations were organised around his work shifts so he could be present. He also wanted to stay with Sandra in hospital when she came in for the birth, and requested that she only be seen by women doctors, as he did not want any man to examine his partner in the intimate way necessary for childbirth. When questions were directed at Sandra, she would look at him and he would answer for her.

At the first parenthood class Allen's behaviour became more aggressive and he refused to participate in the class activities. Soon after this, he dragged Sandra down the stairs by her hair and the midwife was called out by Sandra's mother. Sandra had sustained severe bruising to her arms and both sides of her body and was admitted to hospital for monitoring. She was later visited by the midwife and she revealed that this was not the first violent attack she had experienced from Allen and that he had total control over her. She said she was not allowed to see any friends because he disliked them, he had stopped her working and going to college and had told her she was 'thick'. She said she could not take any more and was going to end the relationship. The midwife initiated an inter-agency meeting with professionals from the police, health and social services and it was decided that no further action would be taken if Sandra ended the relationship. But later Sandra changed her mind and said she wanted Allen to attend the birth. She minimised the violence and felt it was mostly her fault because she had wound him up. She also felt he would never hurt the baby, and regretted disclosing the incident. However, during a post-natal visit Allen pulled the curtains round the bed and punched her in the face because she would not agree with him about the baby's name. A case conference was held before she left hospital because of the risks to the baby and Sandra said she wanted nothing more to do with Allen. She also registered the birth as 'father unknown' so he could not claim parental responsibility.

As a result of this case, midwife practice changed in the local area. Women were routinely asked about domestic violence and supplied with opportunities to disclose it through at least one appointment being provided where the partner could not be present. Women were also provided with other opportunities through a regular drop-in session at the ante-natal clinic, as it was recognised that it may take some time to build up trust in health service professionals.

(Based on information provided by a midwife, midwifery services, North Wales, 2004. NB Some details have been changed in order to protect the anonymity and confidentiality of the survivor.)

The impacts on children

There is now considerable research evidence which demonstrates that children are also distressed by living with domestic violence, alongside their mothers. This research denotes three overlapping contexts in children's experiences – the witnessing either directly or indirectly of fathers' violence towards mothers; situations where children can be 'caught up' in the violence and/or used in the abuse of the mother; and situations where they themselves are being directly abused, by the violent father or father figure. In many cases, it can be hard to differentiate between violence towards mothers and that directed towards children, as perpetrators often keep whole families in a state of fear through their power and control strategies (Kelly, 1994). This section outlines the different ways that domestic violence impacts on children, emphasising their own voices and experiences.

Although some of the information on the impacts of domestic violence on children comes from adult observations, there are now a number of UK studies which have specifically sought children's views and regarded children as social actors, rather than merely as passive objects of concern (see, for example, Abrahams, 1994; McGee, 2000; Mullender *et al.*, 2002). This research indicates that nearly all children are aware of domestic violence and are affected by it, even where mothers think that they have kept it hidden from them. However, children in families may have different experiences because of their age or role within the family and because some domestically violent fathers target specific children for abuse. Children's experiences are also framed by their ethnicity and racism can vary because of different family structures or because they have a disability (Imam and Acktar, 2005; Mullender *et al.*, 2002).

The existing research shows that children are not necessarily passive witnesses of the violence and may take action to try to protect their mothers, themselves, or their siblings and have their own coping strategies and resilience, depending on their age and the resources and support available to them. These issues are discussed in more detail later in the chapter.

Witnessing violence

Children can witness domestic violence in a number of different ways. They may, for example, overhear it and this can be equally if not more traumatic than direct observation, because the sounds of the violence may lead them to imagine the worst possible events. 'Paul and Tracey were crying and I was . . . we were all just crying, because we could hear our mum crying and screaming and our dad shouting at her' (McGee, 2000:71).

Jaffe *et al.* (1990) emphasised that children 'witnessing' domestic violence involves a range of experiences including: observing fathers being directly violent or threatening to mothers; overhearing it; seeing physical injuries and/ or observing 'the emotional consequences of fear, hurt and intimidation which may be very apparent to them' (Jaffe *et al.*, 1990:17). They found that children could provide detailed accounts of events that their mothers had not been aware they had witnessed and noted that parents had considerably underestimated children's own knowledge of the violence. This and other studies have found that babies as young as six weeks old can be affected by witnessing domestic violence and learn to stay silent during such events in order not to further aggravate the violence (Suderman and Jaffe, 1999).

The impacts of witnessing violence – fear and anxiety

One of the main consequences for children in witnessing domestic violence is that they are more likely to be fearful and anxious than other children (Rossman, 2001). Abraham's study (1994) found that witnessing a father's violence created a climate of intimidation and fear which made children constantly anxious as they did not know what was going to happen next. As one child said, 'He just had like an aura around him, like it made you frightened all the time' (Abrahams, 1994:33). Children can be particularly frightened by witnessing the sexual abuse of their mothers. McGee (2000) found that 10 per cent of children witnessed the rape of their mothers and that violent fathers carried on regardless of children's protests. Some mothers report perpetrators deliberately raping them in front of children, so that they will acquiese to unwanted sex, in order to protect children from witnessing such violence. This is illustrated in the following account of a mother talking about being raped in front of her three-year-old son.

> I didn't want to have sex with him . . . I would pretend to be asleep and he would cause a scene and wake me up – and wake up John – because he was hitting me and getting on top of me – you are my wife – my property – and then he would just do it to me and John would go 'What are you doing? What are you doing to Mummy?' so I just let him do it in the end. (Pat)
>
> (Harne, 2004b)

Children can also be as frightened by overhearing threats and intimidation, as by witnessing physical or sexual violence and can be afraid to go to sleep, in case the threats are carried out, as is illustrated in the following children's accounts.

> He used to always say that he was going to kill my mum, he used to always say that he was going to kill all my family and if like, and he really sounded serious like he would do it . . . (Mona, aged 17)
>
> (McGee, 2000:62)

> He used to say he was going to put petrol in the house and burn it whilst we were asleep, we were always frightened he was going to do that. (8-year-old Asian girl)
>
> (Mullender *et al.*, 2002:183)

Mona (cited above) described how the impact of hearing such threats at the age of 11 made her feel 'constantly on edge, never free never safe . . . You don't sleep properly, you just sit there and wait for something to happen' (McGee, 2000:72).

Witnessing emotional and psychological abuse – undermining children's relationships with their mothers

Children report witnessing the emotional and psychological abuse of their mothers, which often takes the form of deliberately belittling their mother in front of them and criticising her ability to parent. They can be particularly disturbed by such power and control tactics, as is illustrated by this eight-year-old child in McGee's research.

> He just said to me last night, he said, 'Mum, my brain feels like a volcano, as though all the lava is going to erupt' and he said, 'I've only got a little brain, Mummy, why is he doing this to me? Why is he saying all these things?' (Kim)
>
> (McGee, 2000:70)

Other research has found that violent fathers may attempt to get their children to participate in the verbal and sometimes physical abuse of mothers. Radford *et al.*'s 1999 survey, for example, found that 43 per cent of mothers reported that fathers had attempted to use children in their abuse, which included making them spy on their mothers and participate in verbal abuse. A further 9 per cent were coerced or incited to participate in more physical forms of abuse, as is illustrated from the following example.

> (They were) encouraged to repeat 'Your mother is a stupid woman, we'll spit on her'. He had my daughter by the hand – she spat.
>
> (Radford *et al.*, 1999:15–16)

Such attempts by violent fathers to undermine young people's respect for their mothers and mothers' parenting abilities do have an impact and, whilst some children as they get older see through their violent fathers' tactics, others do not. Moreover, in the longer term, children's confidence in their mothers may be undermined and their relationships destroyed (McGee, 2000; Mullender *et al.*, 2002). Yet such behaviour may be accorded little significance by professionals, who may not acknowledge how violent fathers have attempted to undermine children's relationships with their mothers and how far they have used the children as a weapon against them (Jaffe *et al.*, 2003).

Violent fathers' parenting and their extreme control of children

Further, children can experience extreme control from a domestically violent parent, which can have a profound impact on their own physical and emotional development and socially restrict their lives. For example, they may have their movements restricted, be prevented from sleeping and be prevented from talking, as is illustrated in the following accounts:

It would be 11 o'clock at night . . . he wouldn't let my daughter go to bed. He made her just sit there all evening, and I kept on saying to her go to bed, and he'd say, 'She's not f . . . ing well going anywhere . . . she will go when I tell her.'

(Abrahams, 1994:32)

They were never allowed to talk, they were never allowed to play, they had to be quiet. My son did not talk until a year after we left the refuge, because that's what they did at home.

(Mullender *et al.*, 2002:159)

He never hit K, but every time he cried or anything he used to put him in his pushchair and make him sit there all day long. So he wasn't allowed to walk around. He was very quiet . . . he never used to bother playing he just used to sit.

(Hague *et al.*, 1996:44)

McGee's research indicates that children's movements could be controlled to such a degree that, in any other context, it would be regarded as imprisonment. For example, children described being locked in their rooms, or only being allowed out of their bedrooms to eat:

I wasn't very happy and we [my sister and I] wasn't allowed down in the front room at all, we had to stay in our bedrooms. We had to stay, the only time we could come out was when we eat. (Ralph, aged 9)

(McGee, 2000:54)

McGee's study highlighted several other forms of controlling and cruel behaviour. This included sleep deprivation; destroying children's toys; harming pets; destroying school work and reports; not allowing children to play outside the home; not allowing them to speak to their mother and not allowing friends to phone or come to the house. In addition, some children reported being emotionally abused in a similar way to their mothers. This included calling them names, deliberate humiliation and some fathers making fun of disabled children's impairments. In both McGee's and Mullender *et al.*'s studies, older girls described being called 'slags' and 'sluts' by their fathers.

The impacts of such controlling behaviour and emotional abuse can be serious and need to be recognised by professionals as being as harmful as physical and sexual abuse. For example, infants and toddlers who are prevented from moving or speaking can suffer significant developmental delays, although they may eventually catch up with other children if they are able to escape such forms of control and feel safe, as is illustrated in the following example from a refuge study.

Our worse case was a child who hadn't developed physically – a six-year-old in nappies and not talking, unable to communicate. But in the refuge the child developed well eventually.

(Hague *et al.*, 1996:32)

Older children who experience isolation from their peers and constant emotional abuse may also suffer problems of self-confidence and difficulties in making friends (Abrahams, 1994). Nevertheless, these forms of maltreatment are not necessarily acknowledged as causing significant harm to children by professionals and can be viewed merely as 'excessive discipline' (Farmer, 2006).

Physical abuse of children

Children who are living with chronic domestic violence are also at significantly increased risk of being directly physically assaulted by violent fathers. While recognising that mothers may also perpetrate physical abuse, extensive US research has found that violent fathers are three times more likely to physically assault children in the domestic violence context, with the overlap between repeated violence towards the mother and physical abuse of children ranging from 34 per cent to 100 per cent in some studies (Edleson, 1999; Ross, 1996).

UK research has also found a high overlap between violence towards mothers and violence towards children. McGee's study (2000) found that 52 per cent of children had experienced a range of physical violence from violent fathers, including 'extreme punishment' such as hitting children around the head with a fist or a weapon, to throwing things at them, hanging them out of windows and pushing their heads in a dishwasher. An analysis of a random selection of calls to ChildLine found that 38 per cent of children living with domestic violence had experienced physical abuse mainly from biological fathers, with reports of being hit with pokers, bottles and furniture and frequently being 'banged against walls and stairs'. In many of these cases children had called the helpline because the abuse was so severe they were too frightened to return home and did not know where to turn for help (Epstein and Keep, 1995:53). In other research, children have described their siblings being targeted.

> [He] didn't like my mother or my sister . . . He used to shout . . . He threw hot coffee on my sister, he used to bang her head on the floor and on the wall. (8-year-old Asian girl)

(Mullender *et al.*, 2002:187)

In addition, children can be physically harmed because such fathers have a reckless regard for their safety when they are attacking mothers, such as when mothers are holding babies in their arms, or when children may intervene to try and protect their mothers (Radford *et al.*, 1999; McGee, 2000).

The impacts of violent fathering

Research with fathers (Harne, 2004a) has found that they can engage in violence towards very young children, when looking after them, because they are generally annoyed by their behaviour and because the children have failed to meet their expectations of how they believe they should behave. Such authoritarian parenting, which can also involve extreme control, is not uncommon amongst violent fathers and is similar to the violence used against mothers when they do not immediately comply with the perpetrator's wishes. In its most extreme form this use of physical violence can result in children's deaths (O'Hara, 1994; Alder and Polk, 1996). For example, Alder and Polk found that some fathers had killed two- and three-year-olds, when they were looking after them, because they were annoyed with them for crying or because they had soiled themselves and because the children were seen as threatening their paternal authority.

Although there is now more recognition of the possibly lethal risks to children when they are living with a chronically violent father (Department of Health, 1999) there is less understanding that these risks are associated with their care and parenting of children. Such fathers may be encouraged to undertake more care of children, since it may be viewed as a means of lessening their violent tendencies (Pringle, 1998). But the consequences of following these approaches without holding perpetrators accountable for stopping their violence, and dealing with their desire for power and control, can be lethally harmful to children.

Domestic violence and sexual abuse of children

Studies of child protection records indicate that a significant minority of children are also at risk of being sexually abused by violent fathers (Farmer and Pollock, 1998; Hester and Pearson, 1998; Brown *et al.*, 2000). In McGee's study (2000) 11 per cent of children revealed they had been sexually abused even though they were not specifically asked about this. Radford *et al.*'s (1999) study of mothers reported that 14 per cent of children had been sexually abused by fathers when a broad definition was used, which included making children watch pornography or sexual acts, as well as direct sexual touching and penetration. However, one problem of identifying children at risk of sexual abuse in the domestic violence context, is the fact that some children may not feel it is not safe to disclose the abuse, until they are separated from the abuser. Threats from abusers including killing their mothers can prevent such disclosures and, in some cases, the violence towards mothers can be used to conceal the sexual abuse of children (McGee, 2000; Forman, 1995). In this context, professionals may have little understanding that children were too fearful to disclose abuse before separation and often regard their mothers as making false allegations, despite the vast majority of such allegations eventually being substantiated (Brown *et al.*, 2000).

A further problem in acknowledging that children can be sexually abused by domestically violent fathers, is that child sexual abusers may be constructed within medicalised discourses as 'abnormal men' and therefore as substantially different from more 'normal' men in families who perpetrate domestic violence (see, for example, Daniel and Taylor, 2001). Bancroft and Silverman (2002), however, indicate that domestic violence perpetrators often have a strong sense of 'entitlement' to having their own needs met by their children as well as by their partners and this can extend to having sexual access to their children.

The social consequences for children

In studies where children's views have been sought, older children and young people highlighted the social consequences and disruption caused by their fathers' violence. For example, many children talked about the social embarrassment and humiliation they felt from having a violent father, as is illustrated from the following accounts:

> I remember it was my tenth birthday. I just remember being in the kitchen, crying my eyes out that he embarrassed me so in front of my friends.
>
> (Abrahams, 1994:39)

> I am ashamed of him   I can't tell anyone because then they will know I haven't got a proper father.
>
> (Epstein and Keep, 1995:48)

Children also emphasised the disruption to their lives and schooling and social losses, such as friendships and the loss of pets, that had been caused as a consequence of having to leave home due to a father's violence. For some black and minority children the consequences of having to leave home could mean that they experienced racism, as they had to move into other areas. These impacts are illustrated through the following examples from children's accounts:

> When I went to school it affected me a lot because all day I was thinking about what would happen at home. So at school my work dropped for quite a bit. (Regina, aged 9)
>
> (McGee, 2000:79)

[I] failed all my exams, I put it down to him, what had happened at home . . . (Karina, aged 16)

(McGee, 2000:81)

He made me leave my home. He made me leave all my best friends. He made me leave all my things behind.

(Mullender *et al.*, 2002:108)

Sometimes people tease me and call me names, especially white people in the area . . . Mum is trying to get me a transfer to another school. I am just worried about being teased by white people – they do it because they don't like black people and can cause problems and be violent so you can feel really unsafe. (10-year-old Asian boy)

(Mullender *et al.*, 2002:139)

Children living with domestic violence

Once violence has a presence in the home, it does not need to be constantly repeated in order to engender fear and distress in children and their mothers. There is often a pervasive atmosphere of threats and intimidation that mean life is lived in constant dread.

(Mullender *et al.*, 2002)

As has been seen, children may have various experiences of domestic violence and of direct abuse, when living with a violent parent. It is important, however, to recognise that even where there has been no direct abuse, children living with episodes of violence and overall patterns of power and control still experience harm.

Age-related impacts

Although each child's experience is different, international research and UK studies suggest that some impacts are age related. Babies and very young children may fail to thrive and have problems of weight gain, eating and sleeping and relating to adults. Children over 18 months can experience developmental delays and develop stress-related health problems such as bedwetting and hair loss. They may experience sadness and crying, problems with sleeping and relating to other children and adults (Jaffe *et al.* 2003; Radford *et al.*, 1999). Children from the age of five may suffer depression, sleeplessness and nightmares and begin to develop self-harming behaviours (McGee, 2000).

In general, US reviews of psychological studies suggest that both genders may be more aggressive than those children not exposed to domestic violence, and/or be more withdrawn and depressed than other children (Edleson, 1999). There is no evidence, however, that children's cognitive abilities are affected, although children's academic progress, as has been seen above, may be reduced and disrupted as a consequence of the violence. However, other children may spend more time at school in order to escape the violence and achieve better as a consequence (Mathias *et al.*, 1995). Some young people may have lower self-esteem than others and find it difficult to relate to their peers, and depression and other kinds of emotional and psychological harm can also be a long-term consequence (Mullender *et al.*, 2002).

The cycle of violence

Some professionals may also be worried that children and particularly boys will also grow up to repeat the violence in their own adult relationships, although there is a lack of evidence of this for three-quarters of children (Stark and Flitcraft, 1996). In contrast, research with children themselves suggests that some older boys are protective of their mothers and other siblings and are very concerned *not* to end up like their fathers (Mullender *et al.*, 2002). However, a minority of adolescents (mainly boys), who have lived with chronic domestic violence and been physically abused themselves, do become violent and aggressive in their relationships towards others, including their peers and sometimes their mothers. A background of chronic domestic violence has also been found to be one key factor in young male offenders who sexually abuse (Farmer, 2006). Nevertheless, the association between living with domestic violence and the small minority who become perpetrators themselves is complex, since, as seen above, young people can make the choice to reject violence.

Children's coping strategies

Children's own accounts indicate that their experiences are mediated by their own individual coping strategies and resilience, as well as other factors such as how much support they get from significant others. This suggests that there are different impacts for individual children, which can change over time (McGee, 2000; Mullender *et al.*, 2002). Children's accounts indicate that some coped better where they were able to get support from other siblings, or from friends at school. Having a close relationship with their mothers and/or relatives in extended families has also been found to be a major protective factor in lessening the impacts of the violence (McGee, 2000; Mullender *et al.*, 2002; Jaffe *et al.*, 2003). However, while many older children may have a good understanding that their fathers are responsible for the violence, younger children may be confused about this responsibility because of what their fathers have told them, with some feeling guilty because they may blame themselves and this can lessen their capacity to cope. Other children may also blame their mothers for staying with the violent perpetrator. As McGee has noted, this is 'sadly ironic' where mothers have stayed in the relationship because they believed that it was in the best interests of the children to live with their fathers (McGee, 2000:97). In addition, children of various ages may use different strategies to avoid the violence and to try to keep themselves safe and some may call the police or try to intervene to protect their mothers. In general young children have fewer resources and less understanding to cope with the impacts of violence than older children. But some older children who have lived with repeated violence for most of their lives can still suffer significant mental harm (Mullender *et al.*, 2002).

Recovering from the impacts of domestic violence

Research with children indicates that they can eventually recover from some of the worst impacts of the violence, once they feel safe and are living in a stable environment away from the abusive father (Humphreys and Thiara, 2002; Wolfe *et al.*, 1986; Mertin, 1995). Children's own accounts illustrate how their feelings and anxiety change when they are in this situation, as is illustrated from the account below.

> I feel really different. I can sleep without any fear. I can really live like any other young person in the community . . . Now he is not around to terrorise me I can get on with my studies. (16-year-old Asian girl)
> (Mullender *et al.*, 2002:196)

Post-separation violence

Unfortunately, as has been seen earlier, family law policies underlined by ideological beliefs that children are more likely to benefit in the long term by maintaining contact with violent and abusive fathers do not allow many children who are fearful of their fathers to have this sense of safety. As seen in looking at the impacts of violence on mothers, child contact arrangements provide the 'greatest opportunity for the continuation of post-separation violence' and children are usually witnesses to this violence (Humphreys, 2006). Children also often experience a range of post-separation harassment alongside their mothers, from their homes being broken into, to threatening phone calls, to having the electricity and gas cut off and their possessions destroyed by revengeful fathers (Humphreys and Thiara, 2002).

Children's fears of post-separation violence can also continue long after separation, as is illlustrated in this mother's account:

> For some time after he had gone the kids were still very fearful, because they never knew when he would come back and try and break into the house. For a long time we had a panic alarm and when they took it away, they said 'What are we going to do mum? What are we going to do?' (Fiona)
>
> (Harne, 2004b)

Some children may experience direct post-separation harassment and stalking by their fathers, which can further disrupt their lives because the family has to keep moving so that they cannot be found. This is not helped by laws under human rights legislation which allow all parents to have information on their children at school, even if they constitute a danger to the family,

> I hate him. We've been in three refuges. When I was in the second one I liked it. One day, when I was coming home from school – he knew which school I was at – I turned round and saw him following me . . .
>
> (Mullender et al., 2002:108)

Abuse through contact with a violent father

For children who are fearful of violent fathers and are forced to have contact, their fearfulness and anxiety is unlikely to lessen (Church, 1984; Mertin, 1995; Humphreys and Thiara, 2002). They frequently witness life-threatening attacks on their mothers during contact handover and many experience further direct abuse themselves during contact visits ((Hester and Radford, 1996; Radford et al., 1999; Brown et al., 2000; Harne, 2004b). A minority of children will also experience abduction by violent fathers and experience increased emotional trauma and feelings of insecurity as a consequence (Aris et al., 2002).

Children's views on contact

A common misconception amongst some child protection, legal and court professionals is that most children want to see their fathers and must have affection for them, despite their violence. However, the research with children indicates that although some may have conflicted feelings, for many this is not the case. In one of the studies with children, only one out of fifty-four expressed the view that she missed her father after leaving the family home (Mullender et al., 2002:209). This study also illustrates how strongly some children felt about not having to see him, after separation.

> We don't see my dad now and don't want to see him. I am happy about not seeing him. (8-year-old Asian girl)

> I don't want to see him because he makes me upset. (9-year-old Asian boy)

> No. What he did to my mum – I don't really want to see him. I don't forgive him. (9-year-old white boy)
>
> (Mullender *et al.*, 2002:195–6)

In cases where violent fathers have made applications for contact through the family courts, children may not even be given the choice about whether they want to have contact, particularly if they are thought to be too young to be consulted (Harrison, 2006). But even if they are asked, their views can be ignored if they state they do not want contact (Bretherton, 2002). Alternatively, children may be put under considerable pressure to agree to contact, as is made clear in the following young person's account.

> To be honest, I used to not know what to say. I used to think I was saying the wrong thing . . . The worst thing I could think of was actually having to see him again . . . I don't think most of them believed me. I thought that after saying it once, that would be it. But it happened about six times. Each time the main question was if I wanted to see him again . . . Maybe it's just because I'm a child and they probably think my mum got me to say whatever . . . One of them asked if it was my own views or not.
>
> (Mullender *et al.*, 2003:33)

The above quote indicates another common attitude of legal and court welfare professionals towards children who express views about not wanting to see a violent father. These professionals often believe that children are incapable of expressing their own views and must have been manipulated by their mothers (Radford *et al.*, 1999; Aris *et al.*, 2002; Brown, 2006).

One survey found that initially a third of children wanted to have contact with violent fathers on separation, but this lessened as contact became violent and abusive (Radford *et al.*, 1999). Other research has found that children only wanted contact when it was clear that it was safe for themselves and their mothers and that their fathers have stopped the violence and changed. In this study some children wanted to stop contact with their fathers when they resumed being violent towards their mothers (Mullender *et al.*, 2002).

Children who have experienced domestic violence for most of their lives may never want contact and have no feelings of attachment to their fathers, as is indicated from this 14-year-old Asian/Carribean boy in a refuge study.

> My Dad cut my Mum with a knife; children left and went to Auntie – I was there – I used to hear arguments and shouting and drinking

('Alcoholic!') Unhappy I felt – I'd go to my room and play, I was ten years old. Domestic violence is horrible – not worth it, people getting hurt. I never see my dad – I saw him once a year ago, walking down the street; we just walked on. I don't feel anything for my dad.

(Higgins, 1994:20)

Further, young children who are very fearful and forced to have contact may have fantasies about killing their fathers.

My Dad really wants to kill us and shoot us. He will lock us in a room and we will never get out and have nothing to eat. I must look after my Mum, my Dad is really bad. When I am big, I could be Batman and go and kill my Dad and throw him in a dustbin . . . I am scared when I have to see my Dad sometimes, that he will hurt me and shoot me. He said lots of times he would do that to all of us. (6-year-old Asian boy)

(Higgins, 1994:20)

Other children may just express their view that they 'wished' contact 'never happened' as was indicated by an 11-year-old girl at a supervised contact centre (Harrison, 2006).

The direct abuse of children during contact visits

Very young children often experience the worst impacts of forced contact, as they are perceived by the family courts as being most likely to benefit from seeing their fathers and are least likely to be consulted as to whether they want contact. Radford *et al.*'s study, which looked at contact for children who were mainly under the age of five, found that 76 per cent of children who had court-ordered contact were abused once contact visits had been set up. This included a range of abusive experiences including neglect, emotional and physical abuse, and most children who had been sexually abused prior to separation continued to be sexually abused during contact. The neglect of young children was particularly apparent during contact visits, which comprised a failure to pay attention to children's basic health needs, such as not changing nappies, children being left alone for hours or locked in rooms and a quarter of fathers getting drunk while caring for the children. One mother whose child's father was a drug user described what happened during her child's contact.

He had our child overnight and locked [her] in a bedroom with a bucket to wee in. All this because he was using heroin downstairs with partner and friends.

(Radford *et al.*, 1999:22)

Further, some children can be psychologically harmed through fathers continuing to undermine their relationships with their mothers and being told their mothers lie to them or don't love them (Radford *et al.*, 1999; Harne, 2004b).

> He was telling him, mummy's a liar and don't believe anything she says – she is a thief and stole your Christmas stocking – daddy's house is better than mummy's and you're going to live at daddy's house soon anyway ... because when you lose a mummy it's not so bad – because sometimes mummies die. (Pat)
>
> (Harne, 2004b)

This five-year-old child was also being told by his father that he could 'misbehave' at his mothers' house and 'kick his friends' [at school], which he continued to do. Because of his behaviour at school, he was assessed by a child psychologist who diagnosed him as depressed and having a number of other stress related disorders, as a direct result of what he was being told by his father. Needless to say, despite this evidence of psychological harm, the family court refused to place restrictions on the father's contact.

Supervised and supported contact

Where professionals do recognise that children need some protection, contact may initially be organised at a supported or supervised contact centre. But even in this context children do not necessarily feel safe. One study (Aris *et al.*, 2002) found that most contact for children with a violent father took place in supported contact centres, where vigilance was low and where the aim was to facilitate a 'constructive role' for fathers. In these centres, mothers' concerns about the safety of themselves and their children were often dismissed by centre workers[5] and children continued to witness violence towards their mothers and some experienced direct emotional abuse from fathers in the form of threats or threatening behaviour and being told to carry abusive messages to mothers. Children's feelings of safety were enhanced by the knowledge that their mothers were nearby, but even so a third of children still did not feel safe in this setting (Aris *et al.*, 2002).

Supervised centres provide a higher level of vigilance for both mothers and children, but children can still be distressed by having to have such contact and their views being ignored when they want it to stop (Aris *et al.*, 2002). Some children also continue to be abused as is seen in the following mother's account. In this case the father was supervised and assessed over a period of a year, because he was known by social services to have sexually abused his children in a previous relationship, but as he had not been convicted the family court still considered allowing him contact.

> Throughout the supervised contact he was observed engaging in sexually abusive behaviour with his four-year-old daughter. (I was told) he was being very 'physical' with her and getting her to jump on top of him and lie on top of him. He would also hold her between her legs. One time when they were in the garden he had her head on his groin and her legs in his face and he was always trying to play with her where the other workers couldn't see what he was doing – the workers who were observing him recorded details.
>
> (Harne, 2004b)

Another problem is that the aim of both supported and supervised contact centres is to move the contact on as soon as possible to unsupervised visits, thus potentially putting the children at further risk. Violent and abusive perpetrators often perform well under observation and where supervised contact is being used to assess their 'fitness' for more open contact, their performance in these circumstances is not necessarily an indication that they pose no risk (Bancroft and Silverman, 2002). The idea that violent fathers can become 'rehabilitated' through short periods of supervised or supported contact is common among professionals involved in such provision, but there is no evidence that such arrangements reduce the risks to children or that children gain long-term benefits from contact with a violent father (Radford and Hester, 2006).

The impacts of abusive contact

Research with mothers indicates that being forced into abusive contact can have considerable impacts on the children, particularly when they are very young (Radford et al., 1999; Harne, 2004b). Mothers report a range of impacts when children returned from direct contact. These include: behavioural problems such as uncontrollable anger and aggression or withdrawal; stress-related problems such as anxiety and fear; sleeplessness and nightmares; bedwetting; self-harm; inappropriate sexual behaviour; delayed speech problems, nausea, skin disorders and hair loss. Further, fearful children who are threatened with increased contact can experience worse problems as their fears increase, as happened to these children (aged two, five and seven) when the court ordered overnight staying contact, in the following mother's account.

> Coming back from contact they are very quiet – they don't speak. It was after a few days they started saying he's told them that mummy will go to prison if they don't go. Since they've known they're going for staying contact Jane has asked me what they should do when they wake up – should we stay in the bedroom? I say she should ask him and she says – I'm too frightened, I'm too scared to ask him. He's not

> hitting them – he's a control freak – he doesn't even have to say anything – he only has to look and it's the tone of his voice – he knows they are terrified of him. Jane is now crying all the time and abusing herself ... I stay up till eleven or twelve o'clock at night reading to her because she won't sleep. (Tina)
>
> (Harne, 2004b)

Child homicides and the failure to protect children

Several children have been killed during contact visits or at contact handover since the early 1990s, when the legal changes on contact and residence were implemented and the family courts established a presumption of contact in nearly all circumstances. By 2004 Women's Aid had documented the killing of at least 29 children by violent fathers during contact visits or handover, which included fathers who already had criminal charges for violence pending against them (Saunders, 2004). In three of these cases the judges had ordered unsupervised contact, against professional advice. The research also indicates that there is considerable pressure put on mothers by solicitors to agree to unsafe and possibly lethal contact arrangements, without these concerns ever being raised in legal proceedings (Radford and Hester, 2006).

Apart from the possibly lethal risks to some children, children having long-term contact with a chronically violent father are more likely to experience emotional and psychological harm, as is indicated in the following account from a mother talking about her 18-year-old daughter who had continuous weekly contact with her father after separation until she was 16.

> She is seeing a psychiatric nurse and is on anti-depressants. This is because she was living on an emotional roller coaster, constantly being badgered and told by her father that she was useless ... He made the children feel the separation was their fault – he said if they had done such and such he wouldn't have had to leave – if they had gone to sleep when he told them to he wouldn't have had to lose his temper. So basically he blamed them for the violence and the ending of the relationship. (Margaret)
>
> (Harne, 2004b)

On the other hand, children who are not forced to have such contact are more likely to recover and experience fewer long-term impacts from living with the violence and abuse. In Australia, one study found that children who were fearful of their violent fathers had considerable reduction in anxiety and fear after ten months of no contact (Mertin, 1995). Other research has suggested that the time it takes for children to recover is variable depending on children's particular experiences (Humphreys and Thiara, 2002; Harne, 2004b). The following account from a mother who eventually managed to convince the family court that her children should not have direct contact with their father illustrates this:

> The children used to be really withdrawn and subdued – now two years on [aged 7 and 8] they are lively. Sarah [the youngest] was very withdrawn for a long time – at one point she was smearing faeces on the bathroom wall. She had this ongoing fear that she was the one who was going to be hit next ... She is only just about calm now. Kirsty would cope whatever – but it's all the shouting she remembers. After two years they are confident little devils – but not in all circumstances. Whenever someone gets angry, Sarah will get terrified because she knew I would get hit and 'dad' is a fearful word to her now.
>
> (Harne, 2004b)

Child protection agencies and child contact

Although there is increased awareness about the impacts of domestic violence on children in child protection policy when children are still living with a violent perpetrator, practice may vary considerably when child contact issues are raised post-separation. In some cases unsafe contact has been encouraged with a violent and abusive father (Humphreys, 2000). There are also examples where support has been withdrawn once the family has separated from the perpetrator (Humphreys and Thiara, 2002). In the latter study, mothers interviewed felt that child protection services were most unhelpful or disbelieved them when they raised problems of abusive contact, as seen from the following accounts:

> I told the social worker about concerns, but they found no case to answer.

> The child living with me has told me about the physical abuse of herself and her two sisters by their father. (Simone)
> Social services and court welfare made aware of it. They did an investigation and believed him rather than the children. (Miranda)
>
> (Humphreys and Thiara, 2002:95)

Understanding children's perspectives – implications for practice

Barriers to disclosing the violence

As with their mothers, some children may, for a variety of reasons, have difficulties disclosing domestic violence and or/direct abuse to professionals. One key reason is their fears about lack of confidentiality and fears that the perpetrator will find out and they will not be protected. For example, in private family proceedings, children know that their views will be contained in a report to the family court, which their fathers will see. On the other hand, some children also fear disbelief and as has been seen above, these fears are amply justified when professionals prefer to believe the perpetrator rather than the children.

Other reasons for not talking about the violence include feelings of shame and stigmatization and children may be specifically concerned to ensure that other children at school do not know. Some children will also not have the language skills to describe the violence or their feelings towards it, particularly in communication with adults. Where children are too young to have language skills, the impacts of violence can still be observed through their own demeanour and other communication forms such as drawings, but such work with children takes time, something that is often not permitted to children's workers in statutory services.

Mothers can be the most reliable resource on the impacts of violence on children and related child abuse and, in the family law context, professionals need to stop treating them as unreasonable and selfish parents who are deliberately waging a war on their ex-partners, but to act on their concerns for their children's safety. Although the prevailing discourse that all mothers make false allegations of harm to their children post-separation is beginning to be challenged in family law policy (see Chapter 3), professionals need to be aware that such false allegations are actually rare and were shown to be less than 2 per cent in one large-scale study of divorce proceedings (Thoennes and Tjaden, 1991).

Professionals also need to be aware that children who are having problems at school may be experiencing domestic violence and respond sensitively to these children and the non-abusing parent. They need to be aware of the stigma that children can feel and keep their circumstances confidential from other children (Mullender *et al.*, 2002). Children who have experienced domestic violence can be bullied at school or turn into bullies, and awareness of this needs to be addressed in school policies and practice (James-Hanman, 2004).

Children may also fear that speaking about the violence to children's services could mean that they are removed from their mothers and their home. On the other hand, children who do act to report the violence, for example to the police, often feel ignored when the police arrive and may be given no or little information about what is happening or what the police are going to do. Some older children may also want to act as witnesses of violence towards their mothers in criminal proceedings against their fathers but may not be allowed to do so because of over-protective discourses.

Key messages from the research with children are that, firstly, they want to be safe and, secondly, they want to have someone to talk to about the violence. As with their mothers, they want to be listened to, to be believed and told it is not their fault. Children who report domestic violence to professionals often expect that they will act to protect them and to punish the perpetrators and are dismayed when criminal justice proceedings are dropped or when professionals have failed to listen them in contact decisions and they are put at further risk (Mullender *et al.*, 2002).

Supporting children

Children also want information about domestic violence and where they can get help. Giving all children in schools information about domestic violence and sources of support, for example through lessons on domestic violence, reduces the stigma children can experience and can help them gain support from others including their peers.

Case study: Support for young people

At age 16 Anna was visited by a Specialist Domestic Violence Worker from the Young Carers Service, after a referral from the Education Welfare Officer, due to frequent school absenteeism. Anna was involved in caring for her mother who was a wheelchair user. During these visits it gradually emerged that both Anna and her mother were experiencing physical violence and verbal abuse from her father and her two older brothers and Anna was offered support to leave the family home. At this time she wanted to stay to continue to support her mother. Sometime later, however, Anna left and became homeless, as a result of further violence from her father and her mother turning on her and hitting her.

Through the young carers' service, Anna was able to obtain temporary housing and then her own flat. Eventually she was in the position to organise support for her mother to get her help to deal with the domestic violence, and she helped her to get a solicitor to stop her husband illegally taking her disability benefits. Anna was also able to gain strength from a young carers' domestic violence interest group, one of the few services provided for young people experiencing domestic violence in the statutory sector.

(Based on information provided by Julie Dempsey, Domestic Violence Specialist Worker, DISC Young Carers Group, Durham. NB some details have been changed to protect the anonymity and confidentiality of the survivors.)

Children and young people often benefit from gaining support from others who have had similar experiences. Mullender (2000) indicates that children's and young people's groups for those who have experienced domestic violence can assist them in understanding that domestic violence is wrong and not their fault; that they are not alone in their experiences; as well as supporting them to regain confidence and control over their lives in safety. Individual counselling can also help some children. However, apart from the significant support which is provided by Women's Aid for children who enter refuges, and in some areas through children's outreach services, this kind of service is not often available through statutory agencies.

The interconnections between domestic violence and child abuse – safeguarding children and supporting mothers

Earlier in this chapter, the interconnections between domestic violence and the direct abuse of children by violent fathers has been shown to be very high. Yet some mothers may be afraid to disclose to professionals, through shame, fear of the perpetrator and the impacts of the violence on them, and/or through fear that they will be blamed and their children will be removed. Asking all mothers about domestic violence (through routine enquiry), if it is undertaken in an appropriate way, can help in overcoming these problems.

At the same time, children need to be protected and agencies need to take seriously suspicions of harm and give children opportunities to disclose violence and abuse, without their parents. The following case study illustrates the need for domestic violence to be recognised as a major factor in the abuse and neglect of children (Hester, 2006) and highlights the importance of different agencies acting on suspicions of risk and following child protection procedures in reporting harm to children.

Case study: Domestic violence and child abuse

Steve and Adele had been married for ten years. Steve had been identified as having mental health issues, which were exacerbated by his misuse of alcohol. Adele had struggled to cope with his unpredictability and suffered depression herself as a consequence. There were four children in the family aged between eight months and nine years. Social services had been involved at various times as a result of neglect of the children's physical needs, but there appeared to be no awareness that these problems were related to domestic violence. The first identification of domestic violence came due to health visitor involvement when the eight-month-old baby was failing to thrive. Adele had bruising on her face when she attended the mother and baby clinic and was asked if she had been hit by her husband. Adele eventually acknowledged that this had happened but said the children had not been present and were not involved.

Two weeks later the health visitor received a call from the school nurse about a possible non-accidental injury to Gemma, the oldest child. Adele had claimed it was accidental and the headteacher was reluctant to report it to social services, but at the instigation of the school nurse, he eventually did so. Gemma had also been taken to the GP by her mother. The GP was so concerned about the injury that he called an ambulance to take Gemma to hospital. He did not, however, inform social services or the A and E staff about his suspicions that the injury was non-accidental. When the A and E nurse saw the injury she told Adele she would inform social services. Adele became very upset and left the department taking Gemma with her. The nurse did phone social services but no record of the call was kept. Social services only went to the family home four days later, when they received the written referral from the headteacher. However, since they met with hostility from Adele and accepted her explanation that the injury was accidental, they did not interview Gemma. Two weeks later, Gemma told the school nurse that her father had hit her when she had intervened to try and prevent him from hurting her mother. She said the violence was very frequent and she could stand it no longer and wanted it to stop. As a result of this Adele later disclosed that she had been experiencing the violence for nine years ever since she became pregnant with Gemma and eventually she and the children gained the help and support they needed. If, however, Gemma had not been brave enough to disclose the violence at school, the situation might have worsened, as the various agencies involved had been reluctant to follow child protection procedures and appeared unaware of the serious consequences that living with domestic violence can have for children.

(Based on information supplied by Catherine Masson, Senior Nurse – Safeguarding Children, Denbigh, North Wales.)

Supporting mothers in their parenting of children, which may have been negatively affected by the perpetrators' strategies of power and control, helping them and their children to communicate about the violence and most significantly helping them and their children to gain safety, rather than blaming them for failing to protect, is an ongoing message to those statutory services, who have responsibility for protecting children (Mullender *et al.*, 2002; Radford and Hester, 2006).

Holding violent fathers accountable

The overwhelming ideology that all children benefit from the presence of fathers in families, whatever these fathers are like and whatever crimes they have committed, means that all too often violent fathers are not held to account for their violence and abuse and its impacts on children. This is one major reason why many children continue to be harmed and cannot feel safe. As has been seen in private family law practice, this lack of accountability enables professionals either to dismiss mothers' concerns or to fail to listen to children's fears. Further, in criminal law practice, violent and abusive perpetrators as fathers may be given lower sentences (for example, a non-custodial sentence) in order that they can maintain contact with their children without any consideration of the risks to children that this may involve (Radford and Hester, 2006). It has also been seen that while child protection practice has improved in this area, there remain problems, particularly post-separation, when child contact issues can arise. A renewed emphasis on prioritising the safeguarding of children in law and policy in recent years and multi-agency working provide further opportunities to take the impacts of domestic violence on children seriously and address their needs and this is discussed further in the next and later chapters.

Notes

1   This is partly because the question has not been consistently asked, or domestic violence as a cause of injuries or ill health has not been recorded by health agencies. Practice is now changing to gather this information. Even so, any health statistics are likely to be underestimates because many women do not or are prevented by perpetrators from seeking medical help – only 30 per cent of women who received any injury according to the 2001 BCS (Walby and Myhill, 2004).

2   This term is taken from Southall Black Sisters (see Gupta, 2003).

3   These include a wide range of cultures from Southern and Eastern Europe, the Middle East and South East Asia.

4   Funding for personal assistance has been reduced in recent years. Nevertheless in the light of recent government legislation on disability discrimination in

the provision of services, it is important that funds are recommitted to assist in overcoming this type of barrier to equal treatment for disabled women.

5   Most supported centres are staffed by volunteers, rather than trained staff, although some may employ a part-time paid co-ordinator.

References

Abrahams, C. (1994) *The Hidden Victims: Children and Domestic Violence*. London: NCH Action for Children.

Alder, C. M. and Polk, K. (1996) 'Masculinity and child homicide', *British Journal of Criminology*, 36 (3): 396–411.

Aris, R., Harrison, C. and Humphreys, C. (2002) *Safety and Child Contact: an Analysis of the Role of Child Contact Centres in the Context of Domestic Violence and Child Welfare Concerns*. London: Lord Chancellor's Department.

Bancroft, L. and Silverman, J.G. (2002) *The Batterer as Parent: Addressing the Impact of Domestic Violence on Family Dynamics*. Thousand Oaks, CA: Sage.

Bhugra, D., Desai, M. and Baldwin, D. (1999) 'Attempted suicide in west London, rates across ethnic communities', *Psychological Medicine*, 29: 1125–30.

Bretherton, H. (2002) ' "Because it's me the decisions are about" Children's experiences of private family law proceedings', *Family Law*, 32: 450–5.

British Medical Association (1997) *Domestic Violence: A healthcare issue*. London: BMA.

Brown, T. (2006) 'Child abuse and domestic violence in the context of parental separation and divorce: New models of intervention', in C. Humphreys, and N. Stanley, (eds) *Domestic Violence and Child Protection: Directions for Good Practice*. Jessica Kingsley Publishers.

Brown, T., Frederico, M., Hewitt, L. and Sheehan, R. (2000) 'Revealing the existence of child abuse in the context of marital breakdown and custody and access disputes', *Child Abuse and Neglect*, 24 (6): 849–59.

Campbell, J. (1992) 'If I can't have you no one can – power and control in homicide of female partners', in J. Radford, and D. Russell, (eds) *Femicide*. New York: Twayne Publishers.

Church, J. (1984) *Violence against Wives: Its Causes and Effects*. Christ Church, NZ: John Church publisher.

Cockram, J. (2003) *Silent Voices: Women with Disabilities and Family and Domestic Violence*. Perth, WA: Edith Cowan University Centre for Social Research.

Coker, A., Smith, P., Thompson, M., McKeown, R., Bethea, L. and Davis, K. (2002) 'Social support protects against the negative effects of partner violence on mental health,' *Journal of Women's Health and Gender-Based Medicine*, 11 (5): 465–76.

Daniel, B. and Taylor, J. (2001) *Engaging with Fathers: Practice Issues for Health and Social Care*. London: Jessica Kingsley.

Department of Health (1999) *Working Together to Safeguard Children*. London: The Stationery Office.

Department of Health (2001) *Confidential Inquiry into maternal deaths 1996–1999*. London: Department of Health.

Department of Health (2002) *Why mothers die 2000–2002: Report on confidential enquiries into maternal deaths in the United Kingdom*. London: Department of Health.

Department of Health (2005) *Responding to Domestic Abuse: A handbook for health professionals*. London: Department of Health.

Dobash, R.E. and Dobash, R.P. (1992) *Women, Violence and Social Change*. London: Routledge.

Edleson, J. (1999) 'Children's witnessing of adult violence', *Journal of Interpersonal Violence*, 14: 839–70.

Epstein, C. and Keep, G. (1995) 'What children tell ChildLine about domestic violence', in A. Saunders with C. Epstein, G. Keep and T. Debbonaire, *'It Hurts Me Too': Children's Experiences of Domestic Violence and Refuge Life*. Bristol: Women's Aid Federation of England/ChildLine/NISW.

Farmer, E. (2006) 'Using research to develop practice in child protection and child care', in C. Humphreys and N. Stanley, (eds) *Domestic Violence and Child Protection: Directions for Good Practice*. London: Jessica Kingsley Publishers.

Farmer, E. and Pollock, S. (1998) *Substitute Care for Sexually Abused and Abusing Children*. Chichester: John Wiley and Sons.

Forman, J. (1995) *Is there a correlation between child sexual abuse and domestic violence? An exploratory study of the links between child sexual abuse and domestic violence in a sample of intrafamilial abuse cases*. Glasgow: Women's Support Project.

Gielen, A., O'Campo, P., Faden, R., Kass, N. and Xue, X. (1994) 'Interpersonal conflict and physical violence during the childbearing year', *Social Science and Medicine*, 19: 781–7.

Gill, A. (2004) 'Voicing the silent fear: South Asian Women's Experiences of Domestic Violence', *The Howard Journal*, 43: 5.

Gill, A. and Sharma, K. (2005) 'No access to justice: Gender, violence and immigration law', *Safe: the domestic abuse quarterly*: 15–18.

Golding, J. (1999) 'Intimate partner violence as a risk factor for mental disorders; a meta-analysis', *Journal of Family Violence*, 14 (2): 99–132.

Griffiths, S. (2000) 'Women, anger and domestic violence: the implications for legal defences to murder', in J. Hanmer and C. Itzen, (eds) *Home Truths about Domestic Violence*. London: Routledge.

Hague, G., Kelly, L., Malos, E. and Mullender, A. with Debonnaire, T. (1996) *Children, Domestic Violence and Refuges: a Study of Needs and Responses*. Bristol: Women's Aid Federation of England.

Harne, L. (2004a) 'Violent fathers – good enough parents?' *Safe, the domestic abuse quarterly*: 19–21.

Harne, L. (2004b) *Violence, power and the meanings of fatherhood in issues of child contact*. Ph.d Thesis, Bristol: Bristol University.

Harrison, C. (2006) 'Damned if you do and damned if you don't: the contradictions of public and private law', in C. Humphreys and N. Stanley (eds) *Domestic Violence and Child Protection: Directions for Good Practice*. London: Jessica Kingsley Publishers.

Hester, M. (2006) 'Asking about domestic violence: implications for practice', in C. Humphreys and N. Stanley (eds) *Domestic Violence and Child Protection: Directions for Good Practice*. London: Jessica Kingsley Publishers.

Hester, M. and Pearson, C. (1998) *From Periphery to Centre: Domestic Violence in Work with Abused Children*. Bristol: The Policy Press.

Hester, M. and Radford, L. (1996) *Domestic Violence and Child Contact Arrangements in England and Denmark*. Bristol: Policy Press.

Hester, M. and Scott, J. (2000) *Women in abusive relationships: group work and agency support*. London: Barnardos.

Hester, M. and Westmarland, N. (2005) *Tackling Domestic Violence: Effective interventions and approaches. Home Office Research Study 290*. London.

Higgins, G. (1994) 'Children's accounts', in A. Mullender and R. Morley (eds) *Children Living with Domestic Violence: Putting Men's Abuse of Women on the Child Care Agenda*. London: Whiting and Birch.

Home Office (2000) *Domestic Violence: revised circular to the police 19/2000*. London: Home Office.

Home Office (2003) *Safety and Justice: the government's proposals on domestic violence*. London: Home Office.

Humphreys, C. (2000) *Social Work, Domestic Violence and Child Protection: Challenging Practice*. Bristol: Policy Press.

Humphreys, C. (2006) 'Relevant Evidence for Practice', in C. Humphreys and N. Stanley (eds) *Domestic Violence and Child Protection: Directions for Good Practice*. London: Jessica Kingsley Publishers.

Humphreys, C. and Thiara, R. (2002) *Routes to Safety: Protection Issues Facing Abused Women and Children and the Role of Outreach Services*. Bristol: Women's Aid Publications.

Humphreys, C. and Thiara, R. (2003) 'Mental Health and Domestic Violence: I call it symptoms of abuse', *British Journal of Social Work*, 33: 209–26.

Humphreys, C., Regan, L., River, D. and Thiara, R. (2005) 'Domestic Violence and Substance Use: Tackling Complexity', *British Journal of Social Work*, 35: 1303–20.

Imam, U. and Acktar, P. (2005) 'Researching Asian children's experiences of domestic violence: the significance of cultural competence and shared ethnicities of participants in the research process', in T. Skinner *et al.* (eds) *Researching Gender Violence*. Cullompton: Willan.

Jaffe, P.G., Lemon, K.D. and Poisson, S.E. (2003) *Child Custody and Domestic Violence: A Call for Safety and Accountability*. Thousand Oaks, CA: Sage.

Jaffe, P.G., Wolfe, D.A. and Wilson, S.K. (1990) *Children of Battered Women*. Thousand Oaks, CA: Sage.

Keilty, J. and Connelly, G. (2001) 'Making a Statement: an exploratory study of barriers facing women with an intellectual disability when making a statement about sexual assault to police', *Disability and Society*, 16 (2): 273–91.

Kelly, L. (1988) *Surviving Sexual Violence*. Cambridge: Polity Press.

Kelly, L. (1999) *Domestic Violence Matters: an evaluation of a development project*. London: Home Office.

Kelly, L. (1994) 'The interconnectedness of domestic violence and child abuse: challenges for research, policy and practice', in A. Mullender and R. Morley (eds) *Children Living with Domestic Violence: Putting Men's Abuse of Women on the Child Care Agenda*. London: Whiting and Birch.

Kelly, L., Lovett, J. and Regan, L. (2005) *A Gap or a Chasm: attrition in reported rape cases*. London: Home Office.

Koss, M., Koss, P. and Woodruff, J. (1991) 'Deleterious effects of criminal victimization on women's health and medical utilization', *Archives of Internal Medicine*, 151: 342–47.

Leeds Inter-Agency Project (LIAP) (2005) *Disabled Women Experiencing Violence from Men they Know. Leeds Inter-Agency Project Working with Disabled Women 1996–2003*. Leeds: Leeds Inter-Agency Project.

Littlechild, B. and Bourke, C. (2006) 'Men's use of violence and intimidation against family members and child protection workers', in S. Humphreys and N. Stanley (eds) *Domestic Violence and Child Protection: Directions for Good Practice*. London: Jessica Kingsley.

Mama, A. (2000) 'Violence against black women in the home', in J. Hanmer and C. Itzen, (eds) *Home Truths about Domestic Violence*. London: Routledge.

Mathias, J., Mertin, P. and Murray, A. (1995) 'The psychological functioning of children from backgrounds of domestic violence', *Australian Psychologist*, 30: 47–56.

McCarthy, M. (1999) *Sexuality and Women with Learning Disabilities*. London: Jessica Kingsley.

McCarthy, M. and Thompson, D. (1997) 'A prevalence study of sexual abuse of adults with intellectual disabilities referred for sex education', *Journal of Applied Research in Intellectual Disability*, 10 (2): 105–24.

McGee, C. (2000) *Childhood Experiences of Domestic Violence*. London: Jessica Kingsley.

McWilliams, M. and McKiernan, J. (1993) *Bringing it out in the open: Domestic Violence in Northern Ireland*. Belfast: HMSO.

Mertin, P. (1995) 'A follow-up study of children from domestic violence', *Australian Journal of Family Law*, 9: 76–85.

Mezey, G. and Bewley, S. (1997) 'Domestic Violence and Pregnancy', *British Journal of Obstetrics and Gynaecology*, 104: 528–31.

Mirrlees-Black, C. (1999) *Domestic Violence: Findings from the BCS Self-Completion Questionnaire. Home Office Research Study 191*. London: Home Office.

Mullender, A. and Hague, G. (2000) 'Women survivors' views', in J. Taylor-

Browne, (ed.) *What Works in Reducing Domestic Violence?* London: Whiting and Birch.

Mullender, A., Hague, G., Imam, U., Kelly, L., Malos, E. and Regan, L. (2002) *Children's Perspectives on Domestic Violence*. London: Sage.

Nazroo, J. (1995) 'Uncovering gender differences in the use of marital violence: the effect of methodology', *Sociology*, 29: 475–95.

O'Hara, M. (1994) 'Child deaths in the context of domestic violence: implications for professional practice', in A. Mullender and R. Morley (eds) *Children Living with Domestic Violence: Putting Men's Abuse of Women on the Child Care Agenda*. London: Whiting and Birch.

Parker, B., McFarlane, J. and Soeken, K. (1994) 'Abuse during pregnancy: effects on maternal complications and birth weight in adult and teenage women', *Obstetrics and Gynaecology*, 84 (3): 323–8.

Parma, A. and Sampson, A. (2005) *Tackling Domestic Violence: providing advocacy and support to survivors from Black and other minority ethnic communities*. Home Office Development and Practice Report. London: Home Office.

Patel, P. (2003) 'Shifting terrain: old struggles for new,' in R. Gupta, (ed.) *From homebreakers to jailbreakers: Southall Black Sisters*. London: Zed Books.

Plichta, S. and Abraham, C. (1996) 'Violence and gynaecological health in women less than 50 years old', *American Journal of Obstetrics and Gynaecology*, 174: 903–7.

Pringle, K. (1998) 'Men and childcare: policy and practice', in J. Popay, J. Hearn and J. Edwards (eds) *Men, Gender Divisions and Welfare*. London: Routledge.

Quinlivan, J. and Evans, S. (2001) 'A prospective cohort study of the impact of domestic violence on young teenage pregnancy outcomes', *Journal of Paediatric and Adolescent Gynaecology*, 14: 17–23.

Quinton, D., Selwyn, J., Rushton, A. and Dance, C. (1998) 'Contact between birth parents and children placed away from home', *Family Law Quarterly*,10: 1–13.

Radford, J., Harne, L. and Trotter, J. (2005) *Good Intentions and Disabling Realities* Middlesbrough Domestic Violence Forum and Teesside University.

Radford, L. and Hester, M. (2006) *Mothering through Domestic Violence*. London: Jessica Kingsley.

Radford, L., Sayer, S. and AMICA (1999) *Unreasonable Fears? Child Contact in the Context of Domestic Violence: A Survey of Mothers' Perceptions of Harm*. Bristol: Women's Aid Federation of England.

Ross, S. (1996) 'Risk of physical abuse to children of spouse abusing parents', *Child Abuse and Neglect*, 20 (7): 589–98.

Rossman, R. (2001) 'Longer term effects of children's exposure to domestic violence', in S. Graham-Burton and J. Edleson, (eds) *Domestic violence in the lives of children: the future of research, intervention and social policy*. Washington American Psychological Association.

Saunders, H. (2003a) *Failure to protect? Domestic Violence and the Experiences of Abused Women and Children in the Family Courts*. Bristol: Women's Aid.

Saunders, H. (2004) *Twenty-nine homicides lessons still to be learnt on domestic violence and child protection*. Bristol: National Women's Aid Federation (England).

Siddiqui, N. and Patel, M. (2003) 'Sad, mad or angry? Mental illness and domestic violence', in Gupta (ed.) *From homebreakers to jailbreakers: Southall Black Sisters*. London: Zed Books.

Stanko, E., Crisp, D., Hale, C. and Lucraft, H. (1998) *Counting the Costs: Estimating the Impact of Domestic Violence in the London Borough of Hackney*. Swindon: Crime Concern.

Stark, E. and Flitcraft, A. (1995) 'Killing the beast within: Woman battering and female suicidality', *International Journal of Health Services*, 25: 43–64.

Stark, E. and Flitcraft, A. (1996) *Women at Risk: Domestic Violence and Women's Health*. London: Sage.

Statistics Canada (2003) *Family Violence in Canada: A Statistical Profile, 2003*. Ottawa: Canadian Centre for Justice Statistics, Ministry of Industry.

Suderman, M. and Jaffe, P. (1999) *A handbook for health and social service providers and educators on children exposed/to woman abuse/family violence*. Ottawa: Minister of Public Works and Government Services.

Taft, A. (2002) *Violence in pregnancy and after childbirth. Issues Paper* No 6. Sydney: Australian Domestic and Family Violence Clearing House.

Taft, A. (2003) *Promoting Women's Mental Health*. Australian Domestic and Family Violence Clearing House. Issues Paper 8. Sidney, Partnerships against Domestic Violence.

Thoennes, N. and Tjaden, P. (1991) 'The extent, nature and validity of sexual abuse allegations in custody/visitation disputes', *Child Abuse and Neglect*, 14: 151–63.

Thompson, D. (2000) 'Vulnerability, dangerousness and risk: the case of men with learning disabilities who sexually abuse', *Health, Risk and Society*, 2 (1): 33–46.

Walby, S. and Myhill, J. (2004) *Domestic violence, sexual assault and stalking: Findings from the British Crime Survey: Home Office Research Study 276*. London: Home Office.

Walker, L. (1979) *The Battered Woman*. New York: Harper and Row.

Wolfe, D. A., Zak, L., Wilson, S. and Jaffe, P. (1986) 'Child witnesses to violence between parents: critical issues in behavioural and social adjustment', *Journal of Abnormal Child Psychology*, 14 (1): 95–104.

World Health Organisation (1997) *Violence against women: health consequences*. Geneva: World Health Organisation.

World Health Organisation (2002) *World Report on Violence and Health: summary*. Geneva: World Health Organisation.

World Health Organisation (2005) *WHO Multi-country Study on Women's Health and Domestic Violence against Women*. Geneva: World Health Organisation.

Yazdani, A. (1998) *Young Asian Women and Self-harm. Mental Health Needs Assessment of Young Asian Women in Newham*. Newham Asian Women's Project.

Young, M., Nosek, M., Howland, C., Chanpong, G. and Rintala, D. (1997) 'Prevalence of abuse of women with disabilities', *Archives of Physical Medicine and Rehabilitation, Special Issue 78*.

3 Legal responses to domestic violence

This chapter explores the legal responses to domestic violence.[1] It is another story of struggle, waged by feminists, for women's voices to be heard and women's situations and circumstances to be recognised, in law. Appreciation of this history leads to some engagement with jurisprudence, the philosophy or theory of law, and its relationship to justice and society (Freeman, 1994).

The chapter begins with a brief theoretical engagement with the nature of law in liberal democratic societies. It examines both classical liberalism, which identifies the legitimacy of law through ideologies of justice and fairness, and more critical perspectives, which recognise how the power relations of society are reproduced in law. These debates frame the context in which the law relating to domestic violence has developed and offer understandings of contemporary legal responses to domestic violence and why it has been such a contested issue for over 200 years. The chapter proceeds by outlining contemporary law and identifies some issues which continue to be unresolved, despite the changes of recent years. It explores questions relating to the efficacy of introducing specific domestic violence legislation in a more integrative approach in respect of criminal and civil law. It also addresses questions relating to domestic homicide and women who kill in the context of domestic violence, and discusses the problematic nature of family law in the context of domestic violence and the protection of children.

The nature of law in liberal democratic theory

Liberal democratic theory is rooted in the philosophy of the late 17th century, the period known as the 'Enlightenment' or the beginnings of 'modernism' when, following the turbulence of English civil war and the restoration of the monarchy, a new, if famously unwritten, liberal constitution was formed, redefining power relationships between the monarchy, parliament and the citizen. This gave rise to the classical liberal model of law and society that generated the fundamental principles of liberty and equality and, according to McPhearson (1962), a new belief in the rights of the individual. These principles became central to the rule of law, often seen as a defining characteristic of liberal democratic society. The contemporary liberal democratic model of law as a just, neutral, impartial, objective, intellectually rigorous system for resolving conflicts dates back to this period. It finds expression in the idea of equality of all before the law, irrespective of class, race, gender or religion.

In this perspective the role of the criminal law is to arbitrate conflicts between the state and the citizen through 'due process'; that is, according to legal rules and procedures known as fair and seen to be just, weighted neither against the accused nor in favour of those with power. The presumption of innocence (Gelsthorpe, 2001) and the restraint of arbitrary state power, by separating government powers into the executive, legislative and judiciary, following the ideas of the 17th century and 18th century philosophers Locke and Montesquieu, are central to this perspective.

In this model, the role of civil law is to resolve disputes between individual citizens, again following legal rules that guarantee fairness and equality. Like the criminal law, civil law has developed through a mixture of common law or 'judge made' law; that is, by following 'precedent' as settled by senior judges in previous cases and statute law made by elected politicians in parliament.

Critical perspectives

While the classical liberal model of law, grounded in ideas of justice and equality, accounts for the legitimacy of law in democratic societies, it is increasingly accepted that it is an 'ideal type' model, describing how the system should work, rather than how it always works in practice (Gelsthorpe, 2001). Further, Gelsthorpe notes that formal legalism, the mere adherence to legal rules, cannot deliver justice in societies characterised by substantial inequality, since equal treatment of people who are not equal in terms of wealth or power produces greater inequalities not fairness. This was identified, over 100 years ago, by the writer Anatole France, who famously said: 'the law, in its magnificent equality, forbids rich and poor alike from sleeping under bridges and begging for bread in the streets' (France, 1894:3922).

Hall and Scraton (1981), in introducing Marxist theories of law and state, made a similar point when they stated:

> The pursuit of legal equality in a society based on uneven divisions of wealth, property and power has meant that the law legitimises and legalises precisely those inequalities.
>
> (Hall and Scraton, 1981:468)

As Hall and Scraton note, while Marxist critiques became increasingly complex, they basically hold that the class-based nature of all capitalist societies is reflected in law and the classical liberal notions of justice and fairness are merely mystifying ideology which masks the role of law as an oppressive and coercive instrument of the ruling class, which serves to maintain their power and as such is far from being neutral or value free.

While Marxist analysis has remained primarily economic, emphasising the class relations of capitalism and more recently the dynamics of globalisation, critical criminology identified other key power structures reflected in law including the structural relations of neo-colonialism. Murji (2001), for example, critiqued the imperial legacy of law and the pervasiveness of institutional racism.

Feminist perspectives

Feminist attention turned to law in the 1970s as part of the struggles for equality for women and justice and protection in respect of domestic and sexual violence. This formed the basis of a feminist jurisprudence, which examined the ways gender power relations, in addition to those of race and class, are embodied in law. Initially attention focused on the history of law as a man-made institution or as Sachs and Wilson (1978) described it 'the male monopoly of law'. These authors highlighted that despite the claims of equality of all before the law, women historically were totally excluded from law and law making. At the beginning of the 19th century, married women were denied the status of legal subjects and were unable to own their own property, including their own wages, and were unable to initiate legal actions.

Blackstone (1765) defined the common law legal position of married women thus:

> By marriage, the husband and wife are one person in law; that is the very being or legal existence of the woman is suspended during marriage, or at least is incorporated . . . into that of the husband; under whose wing, protection and cover she performs everything . . .
>
> (Blackstone's commentaries, 1765, cited in Hoggett and Pearl, 1987:32)

Divorce was also illegal for wives, and husbands could only get a divorce if they could prove adultery and pay enough to get a divorce through an act of parliament, hence the origins of the phrase one law for the rich and one law for the poor. Separation was only possible if the husband agreed to it – that is, if he chose to desert his wife, or if life-threatening cruelty could be proved, but generally women had no legal means of compelling their husbands to provide any maintenance for them if they were deserted and the husband could retain his wife's earnings and property (Holcombe, 1983).

'First-wave feminism'

The 19th century witnessed a wave of feminist struggle for women to gain legal rights in marriage, for separation and divorce, rights to access and custody of their children and legal rights to protection from domestic violence for women. The latter part of the century and the early 20th century also saw the struggle for equal access to education, employment and the professions and for the vote, as well as struggles around the sexual exploitation of women and campaigns to outlaw the sexual assault and rape of girls. In undertaking their campaigns women had to combat one major aspect of masculinist ideology which was used against them; that is, that they were incapable of the rational thought on which Enlightenment philosophy was based and so were considered to have weaker intellects than men. They therefore frequently used writings in pamphlets, letters and magazines to combat such ideologies (Shanley, 1989).

Mary Wollstonecraft

Mary Wollstonecraft led the way in her critique of the patriarchal nature of law in her essay 'A Vindication of the Rights of Woman', a direct response to the 'Rights of Man' (Thomas Paine, 1791), which was celebrated in Enlightenment philosophy. She compared married women's position to slavery and challenged the idea that a woman's place is only in the home, under the protection and control of husbands or fathers. Rather than rely on the rhetoric of 'protection', she championed women's rights to education and, on the basis that women are equally capable of reason, argued for citizenship rights for women, including married women, who were legally the property of their husbands. Defenders of the status quo argued that because women were 'protected' by their fathers or husbands, and because they were incapable of rational thought, they were excused the burden of civic responsibilities (Poovey, 1989). The hollowness of such claims was nowhere more apparent than in relation to what today would be called 'domestic violence' where husbands had the legal right, 'within reason', to beat their wives, control their actions and take their earnings, imprison and recapture them if they attempted to leave and, because they legally owned women's bodies, to rape them with impunity. Married women also had no legal rights to custody of their children and married fathers' rights were absolute in this respect (Blackstones' Commentaries: 1765).

'As a woman I have no rights; I have only wrongs': Caroline Norton, 1853

The story of writer Caroline Norton (1808–1877), an upper middle-class woman with influential social connections, illustrates the legal plight of married women in the early 19th century. Her father had died when she was a child leaving the family in debt. Fearing for their welfare, she had reluctantly agreed to marry George Norton, MP, when she was 16 years old. The family had, however, been misled about Norton's financial position and the couple became reliant on Caroline's earnings as a writer and her family connections with Lord Melbourne. The marriage had been unhappy from the beginning and Caroline had been subjected to brutal beatings. In 1836 George removed the children from their London home to punish Caroline for refusing him access to her own money and for going to her family for protection from his violence (Poovey, 1989). The culminaton of George's actions was to sue Lord Melbourne (who at the time was prime minister) for adultery with his wife (the preliminary step to divorce) and to demand damages of £10,000.

Changes to child custody laws

Although Lord Melbourne won the case, Caroline had been branded a scandalous woman. Following the trial, she could not divorce George because the law held that only a husband could sue for divorce. George retained ownership rights to the royalties from her writings and complete legal custody of their children, whom he refused to allow Caroline to see. However, Caroline continued to campaign through her writing for mothers to have custody on the grounds that they were the 'natural' carers of children. She had some limited success in the passing of The Infant Custody Act 1839, which allowed mothers to apply for custody of their children under seven, and access to children under 16 (Shanley, 1989). Although this law was very limited, in that mothers who were accused of adultery could be refused an application, it did represent a milestone for women and the beginning of the 'tender years' doctrine in custody applications – a legal assumption that young children should be with their mothers (Harne and Radford, 1994). It did not, however, benefit Caroline as George took the children to Scotland, where English law did not apply.

Caroline continued to campaign for the law to protect wives when George later failed to pay her an agreed allowance, arguing that deserted women should be allowed to keep their own property and earnings. She complained to Queen Victoria in a letter of 1855 about 'the grotesque anomaly, which ordains that women shall be "non-existent" in a country governed by a female Sovereign' (Norton, 1855).

At the same time, a new feminist movement was emerging which took up the issue of women's property rights through petitioning parliament on married women being able to keep their own earnings and property (Petition for

From a Letter to the Queen on Lord Chancellor Cranworth's Marriage and Divorce Bill (Norton, 1855)

. . . An English wife has no legal right even to her clothes or ornaments; her husband may take them and sell them if he pleases, even though they be the gifts of relatives or friends, or bought before marriage.

An English wife cannot make a will. She may have children or kindred whom she may earnestly desire to benefit; she may be separated from her husband, who may be living with a mistress; no matter: the law gives what she has to him, and no will she could make would be valid.

An English wife cannot legally claim her own earnings. Whether wages for manual labour, or payment for intellectual exertion, whether she weeds potatoes, or keep a school, her salary is the husband's . . .

An English wife may not leave her husband's house. Not only can he sue her for 'restitution of conjugal rights', but he has a right to enter the house of any friend or relation with whom she may take refuge, and who may 'harbour her' – as it is termed – and carry her away by force, with or without the aid of the police.

If the wife sue for separation for cruelty, it must be 'cruelty that endangers life or limb', and if she has once forgiven, or, in legal phrase, 'condoned' his offences, she cannot plead them; though her past forgiveness only proves that she endured as long as endurance was possible.

If her husband take proceedings for a divorce, she is not, in the first instance, allowed to defend herself. She has no means of proving the falsehood of his allegations. She is not represented by attorney, nor permitted to be considered a party to the suit between him and her supposed lover, for 'damages'.

the Reform of Married Women's Property Law, 1856). This group differed from Norton's demands for the protection of the law when husbands failed in their matrimonial duties to protect women, since their goals were similar to those of Wollestonecraft. Like Wollestonecraft, they wanted women to have equal rights in law, including equal rights to divorce and equal rights to citizenship, which included the vote (Shanley, 1989).

In 1857 a new civil divorce law was passed by parliament, which for the first time allowed women to apply for divorce. It did not, however, equalise the grounds for divorce, since it allowed men to apply on the grounds of their wives' adultery alone and claim criminal damages from the other man. Women, however, could only sue if they could prove aggravated adultery, which included incest or bigamy, desertion or cruelty. Thus the sexual double standard was maintained and the women's committee for property reform considered it a failure (Shanley, 1989). It did, however, allow women to gain a judicial separation but only when they had been deserted. In line with

Caroline Norton's demands for deserted women, the law allowed them to keep their own earnings and property and enter into legal contracts.

However, the operation of this law did not make divorce or separation much easier for women. The costs of divorce were often prohibitive and women were not allowed to give evidence against their husbands in court. Deserted women could apply to a magistrates court to have their earnings protected but they had to prove desertion and, as another 19th century feminist later pointed out, if their husbands returned within a fixed period, the courts would not accept desertion (Cobbe, 1868).

Hoggett and Pearl (1987) argue that this law was designed to secularise divorce and allow moderately wealthy men to divorce their wives. It illustrates how, despite appearances, formal legal gains often bring no real benefit to women because they are undermined in legal practice. While creating the illusion that the problem is resolved, and further protest is therefore unnecessary, in fact male power and privilege is preserved. In addition, since the act only allowed deserted women to keep their own earnings, it created problems for women still in marriages. It was to take another 30 years of feminist campaigning for married women to finally get equal rights over their earnings and property.

Domestic violence and the Married Women's Property Acts

As has been seen earlier, the very limited gains that had been made in relation to their legal status, earnings, divorce and separation were often connected to women's experiences of domestic violence. Nineteenth century feminists were well aware of the difficulties of escaping a violent marriage if women did not have the economic means of survival. The first women's petition on the reform of property laws (1856) mentioned 'wife-beating' as one reason why married women should be able to retain their own earnings, so that they could survive and support their children (Shanley, 1989).

In the late 1860s feminists such as Frances Power Cobbe cited domestic violence as a reason why women should be able to retain their own earnings and property, even if they had not been deserted. She gave as an example a well-publicised case where a violent husband who, though he had been repeatedly imprisoned for his violence, once released, returned to smash up his wife's home and rob her of her means of livelihood (Cobbe, 1868).

This led to the first Women's Property Act (1870), where wives were allowed to keep their own earnings and savings in marriage, without being deserted by husbands.

In 1878, Cobbe published a detailed analysis of domestic violence in her pamphlet 'Wife-torture in England' and this was quoted in parliamentary debates leading to the passing of the Matrimonial Causes Act 1878. This Act empowered magistrates to grant a separation order with maintenance to be paid to the wife, but only if her husband had been convicted of life-threatening aggravated assault against her. It also allowed her to keep custody of her children until the age of seven. This represented another theoretical legal victory as it enabled women, who had previously feared destitution, to separate from violent husbands. However, as Hammerton (1992) noted, following the Act local magistrates courts increasingly took a more paternalistic role:

> . . . eager to intervene in an attempt to make the wife forgive, the husband reform and the family reunite, and thus avoid the fragile division of slender economic resources. Magistrates, together with a growing army of police, court missionaries, probation officers and clerks of the court came to see themselves as marriage menders.
>
> (Hammerton, 1992:39)

By adopting this paternalist stand, local magistrates undermined these formal legal gains. Although significant as the first piece of English civil law to specifically address domestic violence, the potential benefits of the Matrimonial Causes Act 1878 were undermined in legal practice and acted as another example of the limited and contradictory nature of law reform in respect of domestic violence.

Legal change in the 20th century

The 20th century saw further amendments to the divorce laws, for example the Matrimonial Causes Act 1923 equalised the grounds on which women and men could apply for divorce, which for the first time led to more applications from women than men (Phillips, 1988). The Guardianship of Infants Act (1925) finally gave women equal rights to apply for custody or access to their children, but did not make women equal guardians of their children in marriage, and this did not happen until 1973 (Harne and Radford, 1994).

Other significant changes included the introduction of legal aid in 1949 and the Divorce Reform Act 1969 which made it much easier to get a divorce. However, it was not until the revival of feminism in the late 1960s/1970s that domestic violence resurfaced on the political agenda.

1970s feminist campaigns against violence against women

Feminist interventions in respect of law relating to domestic and sexual violence in the late 20th century had two interconnected strands, one activist and one more academic. The activist strand, led by organisations like Women against Violence against Women, supported by Women's Aid and the Rape Crisis movement, campaigned for violence against women to be recognised and treated as a crime. Domestic violence, for example, had by this time, despite the earlier feminist campaigns, come to be regarded by the police as 'just a domestic' – that is, a private affair between partners, in which they need not interfere (Hague and Malos, 2005). Campaigning strategies included marches through Leeds, London and other major cities, pickets of law courts and the Home Office, drawing press and public attention to the prevalence of domestic and sexual violence and the failure of the law, police and the criminal justice system to respond effectively, thereby denying protection and justice to women (rhodes and McNeill, 1985). The second strand, initially grounded in women's studies, engaged in feminist research, for example into the nature and extent of sexual and domestic violence, and the complicity of law through its failure to respond. Historical studies rediscovered the legal struggles of earlier generations of women, outlined above, which had become in Rowbotham's (1977) words 'hidden from history'. The interconnectedness of the two feminist strands ensured that an emergent feminist jurisprudence was grounded in 'feminist praxis'; that is, was informed by women's experiences of law, theorising and activism.

Feminist jurisprudence

As Naffine (1990) noted, rather than theorising specific legal issues, feminist jurisprudence theorised women's relation to the law as a whole. Naffine identified three distinct but intersecting and overlapping approaches in feminist jurisprudence. The first picks up on Sachs and Wilson's study of the male monopoly of law and explores women's struggle to achieve equality, against male efforts to preserve male dominance both of law and in the public sphere more generally. This approach has a long history, reaching back to the 18th and 19th century struggles of Wollstonecraft, Norton and Cobbe and the 19th and early 20th century feminist movements. Here the challenge focused on the ways man-made law (as practised by the men of law) operated on sexist principles to further their interests to the detriment of women. As Naffine notes, the feminist challenge was directed specifically at the male bias in law, by exposing liberal claims of legal fairness and impartiality. While, as outlined above, in the 18th and 19th centuries, male dominance of law and the public sphere was absolute, as women were denied any legal standing, by the 20th century women had secured some limited legal gains, although, as illustrated above, many proved to be 'hollow' victories. Nevertheless, as later campaigns demonstrate, law remains a site of struggle as male dominance in law continues into the 21st century.

This is evidenced by considering who, in terms of gender, are the lawmakers. Statute law is made through the Parliamentary political process. While the 20th century saw women entering Parliament as MPs, they remained in a small minority until the closing years of the 20th century. Their numbers increased markedly to 121 out of the 635 MPs in the 1997 election, fell slightly in the election of 2001, but rose again to 128 (20 per cent of MPs) in the election of 2005 (House of Commons, 2005). Despite this increase in the number of women in Parliament, it continues to be heavily male dominated even into the early years of the 21st century. In respect of the common law, where the greatest influence lies with senior judges, statistics also point to a continuing male dominance as the following table illustrates:

Table 1 Gender breakdown of the judiciary in England and Wales

Rank	Women	Men	% Women
Lords of Appeal	1	11	8
Heads of Division	1	3	25
Lord Justices	2	25	7
High Court Judges	7	100	7
Circuit Judges	60	550	10
District Judges (inc. Family Division)	82	354	19
District Judges (Magistrates)	21	85	20
Recorders	181	1220	13

(Centre for Advancement of Women in Politics, 2004)

These figures demonstrate that, even in the 21st century, male dominance persists in law making, and consequently the 'male monopoly' position still has considerable purchase. It is, as Naffine argues, an essentially liberal feminist position, as it assumes that the law could operate fairly, if a more equal number of women were to be involved in law making, as politicians or members of the judiciary.

The second approach in feminist jurisprudence rejected the above liberalism, arguing that male dominance encompasses every aspect of law. Not only is law man-made and consequently operates to the detriment of women, it has a deep-seated masculinist nature demonstrated in legal culture (wigs, robes, complicated legal language and rituals) and its adversarial style of law, which focuses on winning cases, rather than truth seeking, for example. This critique holds that the law's claim to impartiality and objectivity is mere ideology, which serves to mask its inherent maleness. Polan (1982) wrote:

> The judiciary remains overwhelmingly male. Judges have grown up in a patriarchal culture; their attitudes are inevitably shaped by their life experiences and their powers as beneficiaries of male supremacy . . . the whole structure of law, its hierarchal organisation, its combative adversarial format; and its undeviating bias in favour of rationality

over all other values – defines it as a fundamentally patriarchal institution.

(Polan, 1982:302–3)

The proposition that law is imbued with male culture and represents 'a paradigm of maleness – a symbol and vehicle of male authority' (Rifkin, 1980) is deeper than the 'male monopoly' position. McKinnon, for example, holds that 'the law sees and treats women the way men see and treat women' (MacKinnon, 1983:644) arguing that not only are the law, legal culture, legal institutions and legal methods not impartial, but that they represent a male viewpoint, which is masked by the law's claims to be detached and disinterested. She argues that at every level the law reproduces sexual experience from a male, not female, perspective and thereby legitimates male control over the bodies of women. Thus the law defining rape, domestic violence, prostitution and obscenity legislation has little to do with women's safety, but is primarily concerned with men's rights over women's bodies.

As this analysis holds that the law is not just man-made, but inherently masculinist, and has been actively engaged in sustaining the dominance of men through the oppression of women, it creates tensions for feminists looking to law for progressive change. Polan (1983) argues that it is pointless looking to existing law for meaningful change, but rather what is needed is a completely new legal system, centred on women's values and inclusive of the experiences and circumstances of women. Against this, other feminists, while recognising the deeply masculinist nature of law, nevertheless have argued that law has to remain a site of struggle because like it or not some women need to resort to law. Radford and Kelly (1990–1) examining the dissonance between women's meanings and legal understandings in the context of incidents of sexual and domestic violence noted:

> When women say 'nothing really happened' they are making statements about how much worse it could have been. When the law says 'nothing really happened' it implies that a woman has not been violated/abused.

(Radford and Kelly, 1990–1:51)

Although this quotation can give rise to questions over whether there can be any space in legal discourse for women's understandings of sexual and domestic violence, the authors concluded that while the scope of law in the control of sexual and domestic violence is limited, it remains a necessary site of struggle:

> The law cannot eliminate patriarchal attitudes and behaviours . . . Despite this, however, we do not think that feminists should abandon

> legal reform, rather this strand of activism must begin from a recognition that gains will be extremely limited if our campaigns are not informed by an understanding of how the law functions to limit what 'counts' as violence against women and children. Campaigns for legal reform, must, therefore, be directed at creating more inclusive definitions, and attempts at exclusion . . . must be resisted.
>
> (Radford and Kelly, 1990–1:52)

This quotation, in its recognition of the complexity of legal reform, moves well beyond the equalities arguments of the first position, although it does not abandon law as a site of feminist struggle and in this respect is close to a third approach. Naffine (1990) argues that the third approach recognises the law as being male dominated and reflective of the priorities of the dominant patriarchal social order in constituting women as the subordinate sex, but it also acknowledges the complex and contradictory nature of law and like Radford and Kelly (1990–1) holds that law remains an important site of feminist struggle because of how it constrains and controls women's lives.

Contradictions in legal reform: 1970s domestic violence legislation

Smart (1986), as a proponent of the third approach, recognised the oppressive nature of law and legal practice for women, but argued that there have been historical moments when the law has favoured women. This is illustrated in her analysis of the uneven development of the 1970s civil law around domestic violence.

As a consequence of campaigning by feminists in the 1970s, legislation was introduced to provide civil law protective remedies for those victimised by domestic violence. The Domestic Violence and Matrimonial Proceedings Act 1976 and the Domestic Proceedings and Magistrates' Courts Act 1978 represented the first legislation in this area for almost 100 years and as such, according to Smart (1986), was an important symbolic gain for women.

However, this legislation, which offered injunctive remedies, non-molestation and ouster orders (excluding the perpetrator from the home), was limited in its scope, since not all provisions applied to unmarried women and they were generally not enforcible, as two-thirds lacked powers of arrest if they were breached. Further, magistrates tended to interpret them restrictively, often accepting undertakings from perpetrators rather than making orders and these were largely ineffective. Judges were also reluctant to use ouster orders against perpetrators, viewing it as a step too far to override a man's rights to his property (Edwards, 2000). If an order was breached the applicant could apply for the perpetrator to be committed to prison, but the courts were very unwilling to use this measure. For example, in 1987 only 274 men were committed to prison for breaching injunctions (Edwards, 1989).

This ineffectiveness led Barron (1990) to conclude that the injunctions were 'not worth the paper' they were written on.

This illustrates Smart's argument about moments in law favouring women being undermined by uneven developments in legal practice, a conclusion which could also be applied to the previous domestic violence legislation, a hundred years earlier. Not only did the 1970s reforms not lead to progressive change in practice, in some ways they left women in a more difficult position because the very fact that reforms had been introduced was used to take the edge off further protests. Consequently, despite the widespread recognition that the 1970s legislation was extremely difficult both to use and enforce, it was another 20 years before the issue was revisited.

Family Law Act 1996 – Part 4

Continuing pressure from feminists led to the Family Homes and Domestic Violence Bill 1992 being introduced into Parliament, but this was quickly abandoned, following criticism from the Conservative right wing. On this occasion, pressure from women's organisations led to measures being reintroduced into Part 4 of the Family Law Act 1996, which revised, rationalised and consolidated the previous nightmare of legislation governing injunctions, providing a single set of remedies available in all family courts. This more comprehensive legislation was intended to make civil law protection against domestic violence effective. As in the previous legislation, it had two main orders, the non-molestation order and the occupation order. The occupation order is, however, more retrogressive than the previous ouster order as the court has to consider the conduct of both parties, which includes the victim, and the impact on both parties, including the perpetrator, before an order is made. But the court does have to consider the safety of children if an order is not made against the perpetrator (Women's Aid, 2006).

A key factor regarding the effectiveness of the legislation was in relation to a presumption of power of arrest being attached to an order (Section, 47:2) if it was breached, in contrast to the previous legislation where the power of arrest was discretionary. Effectiveness in relation to power of arrest was demonstrated by Edwards (2000) who found that they were attached to occupation orders in 75 per cent of cases and to 80 per cent of non-molestation orders in 1997/8 (Edwards, 2000). Nevertheless, problems with the power of arrest remained, since the police were reluctant to enforce them, as breaches were not regarded as criminal offences, although this has since in part been remedied in the Domestic Violence, Crime and Victims Act (DVCVA, 2000). Another problem with the Act was that the courts were reluctant to make non-molestation orders against harassment unless this also included physical violence, and this was remedied in the Protection from Harassment Act (1997).

The advantages and disadvantages of civil legislation

One major advantage of the 1996 legislation as amended by the DVCA (2004) is that it provides a single set of remedies available to a wide range of adults in family-type or intimate relationships, including cohabiting and non-cohabiting couples and lesbian and gay partners. Breach of a non-molestation order is also now a criminal offence, and the penalties for such breaches, where the perpetrator is found guilty, have been raised from a fine to imprisonment for five years. The DVCA (2004) did not, however, criminalise the breach of an occupation order and this and the time limits placed on such orders have been of concern to organisations like Women's Aid (Women's Aid, 2005). Further, although the 1996 Act was supposed to stop the courts accepting undertakings 'where a perpetrator has threatened or used physical violence', Edwards found that undertakings were still being widely used in looking at the early implementation of the Act (Edwards, 2000:193).

Another advantage is that the orders are free-standing and do not have to be attached to any other proceedings such as divorce proceedings and can be applied for in either magistrates or county family courts (Women's Aid, 2006). Nevertheless, although the provisions can be seen to be stronger than previous civil legislation, a major bar to their use has been reductions to legal aid. Generally, unless women are on a very low level of income, equivalent to basic income support benefits, they are liable to pay solicitors legal costs of taking out an order. These costs run to several thousands of pounds and are therefore prohibitive for many women, although self-help guides have been produced to enable women to take out the orders themselves (Rights of Women, 1997). Some support and advice centres for women experiencing domestic violence also give free legal help in this regard.[2]

A further problem is that there is very little recent research currently available on the effectiveness of civil orders. Some small-scale research which has looked at the benefits of individual support and legal advocacy projects in assisting women to take out civil orders in two local areas found that a substantial minority of orders with a power of arrest were breached and whether the police acted on these breaches was dependent on good inter-agency contacts (Hester and Westmarland, 2005).[3] There is also evidence that the courts are reluctant to attach powers of arrest to ex-parte occupation orders (that is emergency orders, where the perpetrator is not present) and this can place some women at greater personal risk (Edwards, 2000; Women's Aid, 2006).

Thus, on the one hand, the civil legislation empowers women, in theory, to take their own independent action against perpetrators without having to rely on the decisions or intervention of criminal justice agencies. On the other, women are still affected by the limitations of the law in practice and the prohibitive legal costs in taking civil action.

The Protection from Harassment Act 1997

Although the Protection from Harassment Act 1997 (PFHA) was introduced to address 'celebrity stalking', it has proved to be useful in dealing with post-separation harassment where women have lived with a partner and harassment and violence from a non-cohabitant boyfriend or partner.

Several elements in this legislation made it interesting and arguably progressive. Firstly, it combined provisions for civil law restraining orders with new criminal offences (causing fear of violence; causing harassment; and breach of a restraining order), marking a step towards the integration of civil and criminal law provisions. Also interesting was the decision not to define 'harassment', but to rely on a subjective understanding, namely a course of actions that 'a reasonable person' would consider harassment. This introduced an element of flexibility, not usually present in criminal law, and enables actions, like buying flowers, texting or sitting outside a property in a parked car, if committed more than once to count as harassment, even though in other contexts such actions are not illegal. As this legislation defines offences in terms of the cumulative impact of the behaviour on the victim, rather than the act per se, there is no requirement to prove intention to harass, just that the perpetrator knows or ought to know the effect of their behaviour. In these ways, the Act marked a significant new departure in the legislation available to deal with domestic violence. The DVCVA (2004) has also strengthened the provisions of the Protection from Harassment Act by extending the use of restraining orders to all criminal offences and to persons not convicted of a criminal charge. In the latter situation, a restraining order can be made where there may not be sufficient evidence for a criminal conviction but on the civil law level of evidence (the balance of probabilities) there is enough for a restraining order to protect the victim.

The flexibility of the PFHA may still make it a more appropriate legal option in some circumstances, given that it allows for a combination of civil and criminal measures, nevertheless early research into its implementation has shown it has been under-used by the police (Edwards, 2000).

The criminal law

The PFHA added to criminal law measures available in domestic violence situations, including psychological harassment, but only where a woman is not living with her partner. Although there is no single crime of domestic violence there are a range of offences which may apply to domestic violence, many of which are under-used by criminal justice agencies since they tend to focus only on physical assault (Edwards, 2000). The physical violence offences also allow for a range of charges from attempted murder, attempted strangulation, wounding, grievous bodily harm, actual bodily harm and common assault. Attempted strangulation is one offence which is not frequently used, but could usefully be applied more often, instead of a charge of actual bodily harm, because it is a form of violence that women frequently experience (Radford and Hester, 2006) and it carries a much heavier sentence than other offences.[4] 'Threats to kill' is also a charge which is under-used and is an offence which has grave implications for women's and children's safety. Other offences which are greatly under prosecuted in the context of domestic violence are sexual offences. There are also a range of other relevant offences which include criminal damage, kidnap and false imprisonment and a number of public order offences, which can be used in the context of domestic violence. Even traffic offences like dangerous driving can be committed in the course of domestic violence.

The Human Rights Act 1998 (HRA 1998)

The Human Rights Act (1998) came into force in 2000 and essentially brought the 16 fundamental rights and freedoms protected in the European Convention on Human Rights into domestic law. The relevant articles in respect of domestic violence are: the protection of life (Article 2); protection from torture, inhuman and degrading treatment (Article 3); and protection of the right to respect for private and family life (Article 8). The Act relates primarily to public authorities, as individuals cannot be accused of breaching each others' human rights. But, it places on the state a positive duty to protect women and children experiencing domestic violence and requires that reasonable preventative operational measures must be taken by public authorities to protect women and children at risk of violence. However, the Act, specifically Article 8, has been cited by domestic violence perpetrators in attempts to prevent police from acting effectively in respect of domestic violence investigations. Nevertheless, the Act does not prevent the police from using their lawful powers, in relation to entering private property to protect the safety of others, to prevent disorder or crime (Home Office, 2006).

The Domestic Violence, Crime and Victims Act 2004 (DVCVA)

Some of the significant provisions of the DVCVA have already been mentioned. Other key provisions included strengthening police powers by making common assault an arrestable offence, which was achieved through changes to the arrest provisions in the Serious Organised Crime and Police Powers Act 2005 (Section 10), and setting out the circumstances when reviews for domestic violence homicides should take place.

The Act was viewed by the government as the 'most radical overhaul of the domestic violence legislation for thirty years' and focused on improving legal and other protection for victims. Positively, it involved wide-spread consultation with the women's voluntary sector on domestic violence, as well as those in the statutory sector and feminist experts on domestic violence in academia and the law and meant that women who had an understanding of domestic violence were finally being heard. However, despite some important legal changes, many of those who were consulted felt that it had been a 'missed opportunity' to develop more comprehensive measures and address some of the injustices which still continue (Women's Aid, 2005).

Criticisms of the Domestic violence, Crime and Victims Act 2004

Despite the fact that there are some positive elements within DVCVA 2004, it has been the subject of criticisms relating to legal issues, which have been of concern and campaigning by women's organisations working to combat domestic violence during the 1990s. These relate to: the availability of legal defences to women who kill violent partners, or former partners, while attempting to defend themselves or survive the violence (see below); the failure to address the situation of migrant women experiencing domestic violence; and the failure to address the safety of children in family law, following separation. Both these latter issues have been highlighted in the previous chapter. Another issue of concern was a clause introduced into the Act which included a new offence where all adults in the household could be held liable for the offence of killing a child. This means that a victim of domestic violence can be held liable even if she was not involved in the injury and killing of the child (Women's Aid, 2005). Women's Aid had proposed that victims of domestic violence should not be included in this offence and such a proposal was connected to a new definition of domestic violence, which would include a recognition of children's safety (Hague and Malos, 2005).

Domestic homicide

The current law on domestic homicide has been an issue of campaigning by feminists for many years. It is perhaps the element of criminal law which highlights the continuing ideology of woman-blaming most acutely and which illustrates how 'man-made' law totally excludes the experiences of women (Griffiths, 2000). One key issue has been the lenient treatment of men who kill women, often as the culmination of a history of domestic violence against their partners. The other, as highlighted above, is the harsh treatment of women who kill their partners after experiencing a history of domestic violence in order to survive and/or preserve the lives of their children.

Men who kill women

The law on murder as it currently stands allows two defences, which can reduce a charge of murder to manslaughter and thus enable a much reduced lower sentence from the mandatory life sentence for murder. These are: provocation and diminished responsibility. A third defence – self-defence – is a total defence to murder and can only be used where it can be shown that the life of the defendant was immediately threatened.

The two defences of provocation and diminished responsibility have been used effectively for the last 15 years by violent men to reduce a charge of murder to manslaughter, as has been documented by Justice for Women. In this regard there appears to have been little change in the practices of judges and juries in excusing such men's killing of women on the following grounds:

- she nagged him
- she was unfaithful or he thought she was unfaithful
- she had left him or she was about to leave him, or he was afraid she would leave him
- he was depressed
- she was too drunk to go on holiday (Justice for Women, 2006:10).

Women who kill in the context of domestic violence

Women who kill who have experienced a history of domestic violence do so to preserve their own lives or those of their children, often as a result of escalating physical psychological or sexual violence, life-threatening attacks and/or threats to kill. Before the 1990s, these reasons were usually given no recognition in the law and most women who killed in these situations were convicted of murder.

Case study

In 1989 Kiranjit's husband, Deepack, attacked her with a hot iron but neither that nor the ten years of abuse she had previously suffered were taken into account at her trial. Kiranjit killed her abusive husband by pouring petrol over him and setting him alight; she was found guilty of pre-meditated murder and sentenced to life.

A sustained campaign by Southall Black Sisters, with the support of Justice for Women, led to the quashing of her murder conviction and a fresh trial was ordered. Two months later in September 1992 Kiranjit pleaded guilty to manslaughter on the grounds of diminished responsibility and was immediately released.

(Justice for Women, 2006:8)

As a consequence of the well-known campaigns by both Southall Black Sisters and Justice for Women, which highlighted the cases of Kiranjit Ahluwalia, Sarah Thornton and Emma Humphreys, the law on provocation, which had required 'sudden, temporary loss of control' to be proved before provocation could be used as a defence, was changed in the mid-1990s. This change recognised that there could be a gap between a perpetrator's final act of violence and the subsequent killing by a woman acting to save her or her children's life, and that the provocation could be cumulative over a period of time (Justice for Women, 2006). Nevertheless, these changes have other implications because they can also be used by violent men who kill their partners. Further, in practice most women who have gained a final verdict of manslaughter rather than murder have had to rely on a defence of diminished responsibility (Justice for Women, 2006). This defence, which has drawn on the controversial 'domestic violence syndrome', has been problematic because of its medicalisation of women's experiences and the implications of mental unbalance (Griffiths, 2000). At the time of writing, the use of the above defences for women remain precarious and some women who kill in this context are still being convicted for murder (Justice for Women, 2006).

Proposals for change

As Griffiths (2000) has highlighted, the difficulty for women has been to get legal changes that incorporate women's experiences and which challenge gendered assumptions of how women are supposed to behave. For example, even where women have killed immediately following serious life-threatening violence from their partners the law has not necessarily treated them in the same way as men, since it has been assumed that men have the right to respond but women do not (Edwards, 1989).[5] Some feminists had proposed that there should be a defence of 'self-preservation' which would reflect women's histories of domestic violence and a belief that they or their children were in danger (Radford, 1993; Griffiths, 2000). More recently it has been proposed that the law should recognise provocation as a defence 'where the defendant kills out of serious fear of violence from the deceased' (Justice for Women, 2006:4).

However, the Law Commission (2005) came forward with new proposals which, following the US law on homicide, would introduce the concepts of first and second degree murder. This meant that most of the cases involving women who kill as a result of domestic violence would be convicted of second degree murder, suggesting that some women would be treated more seriously than is currently the case. They would also still experience the stigmatisation of being defined as a murderer (Justice for Women, 2006).

Although no changes have yet been made to the law on homicide, these latter proposals continue to signal the ongoing institutional resistance to women's attempts at legal reform in this area.

Family law

> But the law of England has recognised the natural rights of a father, not as guardian of his children but as the father because he is the father.
>
> (Brett MR Re: Agar-Ellis v Lascelles Court of Appeal (1883)
> cited in Hoggett and Pearl, 1987:373)

Family law applies when parents seek contact or residence of their children on separation or divorce. It also operates when public agencies such as child protection agencies intervene to protect children. Private family law has been one of the most entrenched areas where changes have been resisted, which could protect children and their mothers from domestic violence. Some of the impacts of this resistance have been discussed in the previous chapter. Part of the history of family law has been to protect the 'inviolable rights' that fathers have traditionally held over children. Even when consideration of the 'welfare of the child' was introduced in the late 19th century, in custody law, this was always determined in reference to mother's behaviour, not fathers, since fathers' rights to children were unquestionable as the above quote indicates. It was also no coincidence that when women were finally given equal rights to guardianship of their children in marriage in the Guardianship of Minors Act (1973) this led to the beginning of a fathers' rights movement who felt that their traditional rights and authority over children had been eroded (Harne and Radford, 1994).

Moreover, although the language has changed, this movement, now most vociferously represented by groups such as Fathers4Justice and Families need Fathers, in the UK, has had a considerable impact on all subsequent legislation in preventing children from gaining safety from domestic violence in family law.

Canadian researchers Jaffe *et al.* (2003) have highlighted how fathers' rights movements internationally have managed to create a number of dominant discourses in relation to family law and domestic violence, which are profoundly gendered and have been generally accepted by judges and policymakers. These include discourses that the prevalence of domestic violence and its impacts on children are exaggerated and that the family courts are 'biased' against men (Jaffe *et al.*, 2003:12).

Children's human rights

One key piece of legislation which had and theoretically still has the potential to protect children from a violent perpetrator's violence and abuse is the Convention on the Rights of the Child passed by the UN Assembly in 1989. Article

19 made states responsible for protecting children from neglect, abuse and maltreatment by parents, and one innovatory provision gave children the right to have their voices heard in any legal proceedings which concern them (Article 12). But states have also to respect a child's family relations (Article 8) and not separate children from their parents unless this is in their best interests (Article 9). A child's best interest must be the primary consideration in legal proceedings concerning the child (Article 3) and it is this latter clause which allows a wide interpretation of what a child's best interest is.

The Children Act (1989)

The Children Act 1989 forms the basis of private and public law in decisions about children today. The Act replaced previous (private) law on what happened to children when parents separated. It also reformulated (public) child protection law. In its provisions, it was influenced by the fathers' rights movement and by some aspects of the European Human Rights Convention and the UN Convention on the Rights of the Child (Bainham, 1990).

One of its innovations was to introduce a welfare checklist, which the family courts must have regard to in considering the welfare of the child, as the primary consideration in contact and residence disputes. This checklist includes taking account of the wishes and feelings of the child (considered in the light of their age and understanding) (1.3.a); any harm a child might have suffered or is at risk of suffering (1.3.e); and the capabilities of each parent to meet a child's needs (1.3.f). Other provisions allow a court to order a welfare report (S.7) in private residence and child contact proceedings although it does not have to do so. Children may also be allowed to have their own representation but only if the courts grant leave. Problematically, the Act also gave each married parent 'parental responsibility' for the child following separation and made it much easier for non married fathers to gain parental responsibility. The term parental responsibility refers to parents' rights of legal ownership in the child, although it was also meant to place emphasis on parental duties (Bainham, 1990).

The best interests of the child

Although the Children Act was perceived as innovatory, particularly in enabling the possibility of giving a voice to children, as with other legislation its interpretation has relied on the views of judges and subsequent judge-made case law. Not long after the Act was implemented it became clear that the courts were defining the 'best interests' of the child as having contact with the non-resident parent (usually the father) in nearly all circumstances. This was despite any harm a child might have experienced from abusive and violent fathers and children's views on the matter (Hester *et al.*, 1994). By the mid-1990s, in two landmark judgments, the appeal courts ruled that children who were at risk from an violent and abusive father would suffer greater harm if they did not have an enduring relationship with both 'natural parents'.[6] They also stated that the family courts should not 'accord too much weight' to the distress of very young children in forcing them to have contact with a violent father. Such distress was regarded as transitory, and it was considered more important that children have ongoing contact with a violent father because this would benefit their 'long-term development'.[7] Thus, in effect, the case law had subsumed the best interests of children into fathers' rights to children, regardless of how these fathers had behaved. Instead the family courts chose to demonise abused mothers who raised concerns about their children's safety in contact disputes, defining them as selfish and irrational (Smart and Neale, 1997). As was seen in Chapter 2, in some cases mothers who defied contact orders were threatened with or were actually imprisoned by the family courts, and in other cases the courts punished them by giving violent and sexually abusive fathers residence of the children (Hester and Radford, 1996; Radford *et al.*, 1999).

Ignoring mothers' and children's safety

The two judgments described above have had considerable influence over the law in practice ever since, despite later case law and ongoing campaigning by the domestic violence movement and considerable research (discussed in Chapter 2) to get the law changed.

Later case law, known as the 'Re L judgment',[8] stated that the legal assumption of contact could be overturned in cases of 'serious domestic violence'. Following this judgment, non-statutory guidance was issued to the family courts about how they should take account of the impacts of domestic violence on children in decisions about contact and residence (DCA, 2001). An expert report was also published, which reviewed the research on the impacts of domestic violence on children. This report recognised that repeated exposure to domestic violence from a violent parent could have 'deleterious effects on children' and 'render contact inappropriate'. It also emphasised that children could be at risk where the contact parent escalated the climate of conflict around the child and criticised the resident parent to the children. Further, the authors argued that contact was inappropriate where the contact parent was unable to prioritise children's needs and stressed the importance of addressing children's wishes (Sturge and Glaser, 2000:618–20).

However, it has now been widely accepted that this case law and non-statutory guidance on domestic violence has generally been ignored by the family court professionals including family court advisors and judges, as well as by family lawyers advising their clients (Family Justice Council, 2006). This has resulted in children and their mothers being forced to endure several years of ongoing abuse and violence, as well as the killings of several children by revengeful violent fathers during contact visits (Saunders, 2004).

The law and child contact in cases of domestic violence

Case study

Mal, was only one year old when his parents separated and the violent father applied for contact. Whilst still living with Mal's mother, he had physically abused her two older children from a previous marriage and taken complete control over the care of Mal, refusing to allow the mother to breast feed or buy clothes for him and refusing to allow Mal outside of the family home. Mal witnessed severe physical violence towards his mother including a final incident where his father had stabbed her. Despite this incident, the family court initially ordered direct visiting contact, with pickup at a contact centre.

Following several incidents of post-separation violence and harassment, where Mal's father attacked his mother again at knife point, attempted to burn down her shop and threatened contact centre staff, the family court ordered that contact should move to a contact centre, but without close supervision. During this period of contact the child was terrified of seeing his father and refused to go into the fathers' room, resulting in several abduction incidents. Eventually after two years of this type of contact, where the child continued to demonstrate reluctance to see his father, the court ordered a psychiatric assessment to be undertaken on the father and he was also ordered to attend a perpetrator programme. After another few months where contact with the father was observed by a psychiatrist, and where a perpetrator programme report stated that Mal's father would not change his violent and abusive behaviour, contact was finally stopped. However, Mal had had to endure nearly three years of enforced contact, while his mother suffered further serious violence, before the family court recognised this father's unfitness to see his child.

(Harne, 2004b)

Contact by agreement and its impacts on children experiencing domestic violence

Since the presumption of contact in nearly all circumstances has been developed in the case law, there has been considerable pressure on abused mothers to agree to contact with a violent father, by family solicitors or by family court advisors through in-court conciliation,[9] without going through a full court hearing. In 2004 a new government green paper on child contact promoted contact by agreement, noting that only 10 per cent of cases were fully disputed, and proposed new legislation to further punish mothers who failed to comply with contact agreements, while at the same time stating that contact arrangements should not be made if they jeopardised children's safety (DfES, 2004). This was followed by another policy paper (DfES, 2005) further promoting contact through in-court conciliation in order to reduce the public cost of disputed court hearings. Following this policy, legal aid to mothers subjected to domestic violence who wish to dispute a father's contact on the grounds of children's safety has also been reduced and in some cases refused (Masson, 2006).

Connected to the above developments has been a reluctance to take account of the views of children experiencing domestic violence, particularly when they conflict with family court professionals' beliefs that children should have contact, as well as a reluctance by the family courts to allow separate representation of children in private law proceedings (Buchanan *et al.*, 2001; Harold and Murch, 2005).

Further, despite the government's assertions that contact should not be agreed where children's safety is at risk, research on the policy of in-court conciliation found that 43 per cent of participating mothers feared further domestic violence and physical abuse of their children by their ex-partner. In only 20 per cent of these cases had a welfare report been undertaken and mothers felt the issues of domestic violence and child abuse had been ignored due to pressure to reach an agreement over contact quickly in the conciliation meeting (Trinder *et al.*, 2006). Similar findings were made in a government inspection report on the practices of family court advisors (Cafcass officers) which stated that: 'The Cafcass focus on agreement seeking is out of balance because it does not pay proportionate attention to safety issues in domestic violence cases' (HMCS, 2005:19).

This latter report also found a catalogue of unsafe practices used by Cafcass, including a failure to check with the records of the police, health and social services to find out if there were risks to children and their mothers. Mothers were made to enter into joint meetings with perpetrators and set up contact visits at their home or in shopping centres so that officers could observe contact. Further, children were observed as being clearly distressed when asked about their fathers or observed in contact visits and these observations were not included in welfare reports. Interviews with children were also found to be conducted insensitively and not enough time was taken to seek children's views.

Further changes in policy to address children's safety

As a result of campaigning by women's organisations, a minor amendment to the Children Act extends the definition of harm in the welfare checklist. This states that the courts must have regard to 'the impairment suffered from seeing or hearing the ill-treatment of another' (S.120 Children and Adoption Act, 2002). This change was only implemented in 2005, through the new gateway forms for family court applications, so it is not yet known whether it will make any difference in practice. Initial evidence, however, suggests that changes are needed to the form to allow for women to fully disclose domestic violence and related child abuse (Family Justice Council, 2006).

A significant report by Lord Justice Wall in response to the Women's Aid research on the killings of 29 children during contact visits has also had some impact to later developments where he stated:

> It is, in my view, high time that the Family Justice system abandoned any reliance on the proposition that a man can have a history of violence to the mother of his children, but, nonetheless, be a good father.
>
> (L J Wall, 2006:66)

This has led to the Family Justice Council recommending that a direction (as opposed to guidance) is issued to the family courts, requiring them to consider a number of risk factors in relation to the violent father, and taking account of the welfare checklist, before any consent order on contact is made.[10] Other developments include changes in Cafcass policies in cases of domestic violence and the development of a risk assessment toolkit (Cafcass, 2005).

Whether, however, these changes will make any real difference to professional and legal practice remains to be seen, and it may well be that although family court professionals and judges will pay more attention to domestic violence, they will still decide it is safe for children to have contact.

At the same time, the government has passed further legislation (Children and Adoption Act, 2006) to penalise mothers who do not enforce contact on unwilling children. These penalties include criminalising mothers by making them do 'community service' if they do not comply with contact orders, and making them pay compensation to the father. However, this Act does include a clause which allows the family courts to refer a violent father onto a perpetrator programme and for an officer of the court to undertake a risk assessment where it is suspected a child could be harmed. Nevertheless, the overall message of the Act is to enforce contact whatever the circumstances, and this is another legal retrograde step that can only put mothers' and children's safety at further risk.

The need for new legislation to protect children and their mothers in private family law

While stating that current law and national plans are adequate to protect children (Home Office, 2005) and that 'contact arrangements where the safety of the child or the resident parent is put at risk should not be put in place' (Dfes, 2004), the government has consistently failed to introduce legislation which could make this more likely to happen. This would require a legal presumption against unsupervised contact and residence where there is domestic violence or child abuse, unless it could be shown to be safe, as has happened in New Zealand (Guardianship Act, 1995; S. 16B (4)). One of the key features of this Act is that it contains a statutory checklist for assessing safety in the domestic violence context. This includes addressing past violence, the likelihood of it reoccurring and the physical or emotional harm to the child, as well as the opinion of the child and the mother before contact is allowed to happen (Kaye, 1996). Moreover, although on occasion the New Zealand family courts have managed to circumvent the legislation (Jaffe *et al.*, 2003), the research indicates that children and their mothers have been far safer as a result of this legislation than under English law (Chetwin *et al.*, 1999).

Child protection (public law)

In contradiction to private law, the Children Act (1989) enables child protection services to intervene to protect children where children are suffering 'significant harm' or are at risk of suffering significant harm (S.47). The 2002 amendment to the Children Act (1989), discussed above, underlines the duty of local authorities 'to investigate whether there has been significant harm or risk of significant harm to a child' as a result of domestic violence (Humphreys and Stanley, 2006:11). In addition, an earlier amendment to the Children Act allowed local authorities, or the police, as a third party to obtain an exclusion order against a perpetrator, but only when an interim care order or emergency protection order was in place and the mother consented (S.38A [2]). However, this clause has never been implemented and this omission places considerable constraints on child protection services in being able to take effective action against violent perpetrators as fathers (Stanley and Humphreys, 2006). Ultimately, child protection agencies have the power to remove children and take them into care, in order to ensure their protection. Unlike in private family law, however, children who are subject to such child protection proceedings do have the right to their own representation and to having their own voices heard (Harrison, 2006).

The role of child protection agencies post-separation

As has been seen in Chapter 2, some mothers experience the intervention of social services as helpful when they have still been living with their partner, but unhelpful after separation in acting to protect children where the law still expects them to have contact with a violent perpetrator. The Children Act (1989) allows social services to undertake assessments where the children appear to be at risk of significant harm in private family proceedings for contact Children Act (1989: S.37). Social services could therefore play a much greater role in identifying the significant risks to children from a violent perpetrator, and undertake reports for the family courts, if they were called on by Cafcass.

Children Act 2004

The most recent legislation, Children Act (2004), changes the way services are delivered at local level through Children's Safeguarding Boards and the combining of different children's services. There is a renewed emphasis on multi-agency working through this Act and promoting partnerships to improve children's safety, as well as the better sharing of information about children through different agencies. As a result of this, revised guidance has been issued to different agencies with responsibility for children's safety, including schools and health services, as well as the procedures which should be followed in identifying and reporting children at risk, including those living with domestic violence. This does not mean, however, that such policies always work in practice, as was seen in Chapter 2.

Nevertheless, the new Act allows for the possibility of children's services to work more closely with the police to bring criminal prosecutions against violent abusive perpetrators, and with local perpetrator programmes. It also provides for the possibility of closer liaison with Cafcass services and for more funded support for children. However, one negative impact of the 2004 Act is that since it widens the net of agencies who have information on children and their mothers, it may reduce their confidentiality and therefore put them at greater risk from perpetrators. Another negative impact is that services to protect children and adults are still viewed separately and this could still work against abused mothers getting appropriate support when child protection issues are identified (Stanley and Humphreys, 2006).

Conclusions

This chapter has identified the problems with the law for women and children experiencing domestic violence, highlighting how – even where there have been some legislative improvements – the law in practice can still resist change and, in some areas, remain deeply patriarchal in its implementation. This emphasises the continued need for cultural change in organisations whose remit is to address domestic violence, particularly in regard to the judiciary, and this is a theme which is further addressed in the next chapter in looking at the implementation of the criminal law.

Notes

1   This chapter in general refers to English Law not Scottish Law, which historic-ally was more favourable to women in relation to divorce and property (Poovey, 1989).
2   Based on the authors' knowledge of local provision in some areas.
3   This research was undertaken before the implementation of the criminalisa-tion of breach of non-molestation orders under the DVCV Act (2004).
4   The significance of this offence was raised by a police officer attending one of the professional development courses on domestic violence run by the authors.
5   However, some women have been acquitted in this context. For example, in 2004, 18-year-old Emma Protheroe was acquitted in a few minutes by a jury after experiencing a prolonged attack before she killed her partner. The pros-ecution had offered a plea of manslaughter, which Emma had rejected. (Justice for Women, 2006).
6   (Re O (Contact: Imposition of Conditions) [1995] 2 FLR: 124)
7   (Re M (Contact: Supervision) [1998] Family Law: 71)
8   (Re L, V, M, H (Contact: Domestic Violence) [2000] 2 FLR: 334)
9   In court conciliation is a form of mediation where the parents meet to resolve the dispute with a family court advisor.
10   A consent order is given when partners reach agreement about contact or residence on divorce. This does however still have to be agreed by the court.

References

Bainham, A. (1990) *Children: the new law*. Bristol: Family Law.
Barron, J. (1990) *Not Worth the Paper*. Bristol: Women's Aid Federation.
Buchanan, A., Hunt, J., Bretherton, H. and Bream, V. (2001) *Families in Conflict: Perspectives of Children and Parents in the Family Court Welfare Service*. Bristol: Policy Press.
Cafcass (2005) *Domestic Violence Policy and Standards*. www.cafcass.gov.uk/policies
Centre for the Advancement of Women (2006) 'Women Members of the UK Judi-ciary'. www.qub.ac.uk/cawp/Ukhtmls/judges.htm
Chetwin, A., Knaggs, T. and Te Wairere Ahiahi Young, P. (1999) *The Domestic*

Violence Legislation and Child Access in New Zealand. Auckland: Ministry of Justice.

Cobbe, F. (1868) 'Criminals, Idiots, Women and Minors, Is the Classification Sound?' *Fraser's Magazine*, December: 380–397.

Cobbe, F. (1878) 'Wife Torture in England', reprinted in J. Radford and D. Russell (eds) *Femicide: the Politics of Woman Killing*. New York: Twayne Publishers (1992).

Cracknell, R. (2006) 'Women in Parliament and Government, House of Commons Library'. www.parliament.uk/commons/lib/research/notes/snsg-01528.pdf

Department for Education and Skills (2004) *Parental Separation: children's needs and parental responsibilities*. Green Paper. London: DfES.

Department for Education and Skills (2005) *Next Steps: Report of the Responses to the consultation and agenda for action*. London: DfES.

Department of Health (1999/2004) *Working Together to Safeguard Children*. London: The Stationery Office.

Edwards, S. (1989) *Policing Domestic Violence, Women, the Law and the State*. London: Sage.

Edwards, S. (2000) 'Domestic Violence and Harassment: an assessment of the civil remedies and New Directions in Prosecution', in J. Taylor Browne (ed.) *What works in reducing domestic violence*. London: Whiting and Birch.

Family Justice Council (2006) *Everybody's Business – How applications for contact orders by consent should be approached by the court in cases involving domestic violence. The Family Justice Council's Report and Recommendations to the President of the Family Division*. www.family-justice-council.org.uk/docs/reporton contact

France, A. (1917) *The Red Lily*. New York: Boni and Liveright, reproduced by The Project Gutenberg EBook of The Red Lily. http://www.gutenberg.org/files/3922/3922.txt

Freeman, M. (1994) *Lloyds Introduction to Jurisprudence*. London: Sweet & Maxwell.

Gelsthorpe, L. (2001) 'Due Process Model', in E. McLaughlin and J. Muncie (eds) *The Sage Dictionary of Criminology*. London: Sage Publications.

Griffiths, S. (2000) 'Women, anger and domestic violence: the implications for legal defences to murder', in J. Hanmer and C. Itzen (eds) *Home Truths about Domestic Violence*. London: Routledge.

Hague, J. and Malos, E. (2005) *Domestic violence: action for change* (3rd edn). Cheltenham: New Clarion Press.

Hall, S. and Scraton, P. (1981) 'Law, Class and Control', in M. Fitzgerald, G. McLennan and J. Pawson (eds) *Crime and Society: Readings in History and Theory*. London: Routledge and Kegan Paul in Association with the Open University.

Hammerton, J. (1992) *Cruelty and Companionship: Conflict in Nineteenth-Century Married Life*. London: Routledge.

Harne, L. (2004b) Violence, power and the meanings of fatherhood in issues of child contact. Ph.d thesis. Bristol: Bristol University.

Harne, L. and Radford, J. (1994) 'Reinstating Patriarchy: The politics of the family and the new legislation', in A. Mullender and R. Morley (eds) *Children Living with Domestic Violence*. London: Whiting and Birch.

Harold, G. and Murch, M. (2005) 'Inter-parental conflict and children's adaptation to separation and divorce: theory, research and implications for family law, practice and policy', *Child and Family Law Quarterly*, 17 (2).

Harrison, C. (2006) 'Damned if You Do and Damned if You Don't: the contradictions of public and private law', in C. Humphreys and N. Stanley (eds) *Domestic Violence and Child Protection: Directions for Good Practice*. London: Jessica Kingsley Publishers.

Hester, M. and Radford, L. (1996) *Domestic Violence and Child Contact Arrangements in England and Denmark*. Bristol: Policy Press.

Hester, M. and Westmarland, N. (2005) *Tackling Domestic Violence: Effective interventions and approaches. Home Office Research Study 290*. London: Home Office.

Hester, M., Humphries, J., Pearson, C., Qaiser, K., Radford, L. and Woodfield, K. (1994) 'Domestic violence and child contact', in A. Mullender and R. Morley (eds) *Children Living with Domestic Violence: Putting Men's Abuse of Women on the Child Care Agenda*. London: Whiting and Birch.

HM Inspectorate of Court Administration (HMICA) (2005) *Domestic Violence, Safety and Family Proceedings*. www.hmica.gov.uk/recpubs.htm

Hoggett, B. and Pearl, D. (1987) *The Family, Law and Society: cases and materials*. London: Butterworths.

Holcombe, L. (1983) *Wives and Property*. Toronto: University of Toronto Press.

Home Office (2006) *Lessons Learned from the Domestic Violence Enforcement Campaign*. Police and Crime Standards Directorate. London: Home Office.

Humphreys, C. and Stanley, N. (2006) 'Introduction', in C. Humphreys and N. Stanley (eds) *Domestic Violence and Child Protection: Directions for Good Practice*. London: Jessica Kingsley Publishers.

Jaffe, P.G., Lemon, K.D. and Poisson, S.E. (2003) *Child Custody and Domestic Violence: A Call for Safety and Accountability*. Thousand Oaks, CA: Sage.

Justice for Women (2006) *Justice for Women, men, women and murder. Summer Newsletter*. London: Justice for Women.

Kaye, M. (1996) 'Domestic violence, residence and contact', *Child and Family Law Quarterly*, 8 (3): 50–7.

Law Commission (2005) *A New Homicide Act for England and Wales? A consultation paper*. www.lawcom.gov.uk/murder.htm

MacKinnon, C. (1983) 'Feminism, Marxism, Method and the State: Toward Feminist Jurisprudence', *Signs: Journal of Women in Culture and Society*, 635: 8.

Masson, J. (2006) 'Consent Orders in Contact Cases: A survey of resolution members', *Family Law*, 36: 1042.

McPhearson, C. (1962) *The Political Theory of Possessive Individualism: Hobbes to Locke*. Oxford: Clarendon Press.

Murji, K. (2001) 'Racialization', in E. McLauglin and J. Muncie (eds) *The Sage Dictionary of Criminology*. London: Sage Publications.

Naffine, N. (1990) *Law and the Sexes*. London: Allen and Unwin.

Norton, C. (1855): 'A Letter to the Queen on Lord Cranworth's Marriage Bill' in *The Collected Writings Of Caroline Norton (1808–1877)*. London: Longman, Brown, Green & Longman, reproduced in Adam Matthew Publications. http://www.adam-matthew-publications.co.uk/digital_guides/norton_collected_writings

Phillips, R. (1988) *Putting Asunder: A history of divorce in western society*. Cambridge: Cambridge University Press.

Polan, D. (1983) 'Equal Rights in Retrospect', *Journal of Law and Inequality* 1.

Polan, D. (1982) 'Towards a theory of law and patriarchy', in D. Kairys (ed.) *The politics of law a progressive critique* (3rd edn). Basic Books.

Poovey, M. (1989) *Uneven Developments*. London: Virago.

Radford, J. (1993) 'Pleading for time: justice for battered women who kill', in H. Birch (ed.) *Moving Targets: Women, Murder and Representation*. London: Virago.

Radford, J. and Kelly, L. (1990–1) 'Nothing Really Happened: The Invalidation of Women's Experiences of Sexual Violence', *Critical Social Policy* 30. Reprinted in M. Hester, L. Kelly and J. Radford (eds) (1996) *Women, Violence and Male Power: Feminist activism, research and practice*. Buckingham: Open University Press.

Radford, L. and Hester, M. (2006) *Mothering through Domestic Violence*. London: Jessica Kingsley Publishers.

Radford, L., Sayer, S. and AMICA (1999) *Unreasonable Fears? Child Contact in the Context of Domestic Violence: A Survey of Mothers' Perceptions of Harm*. Bristol: Women's Aid Federation of England.

Rhodes, D. and McNeill, S. (1985) *Women Against Violence Against Women*. London: Onlywoman Press.

Rifkin, J. (1980) 'Towards a Theory of Law and Patriarchy', *Harvard Women's Law Journal* 3.

Rights of Women (1997) Domestic Violence DIY Injunction Handbook. London: Rights of Women.

Rowbotham, S. (1977) *Hidden from History, 300 Years of Women's Oppression and the Fight Against It*. London: Pluto Press.

Sachs, A. (1978) 'The Myth of Male Protectiveness and the Legal Subordination of Women', in C. Smart and B. Smart (eds) *Women, Sexuality and Social Control*. London: Routledge.

Saunders, H. (2004) *Twenty-nine homicides: Lessons still be learnt on domestic violence and child protection*. Bristol: National Women's Aid Federation (England).

Shanley, M. (1989) *Feminism, marriage and the law in Victorian England*. Tauris.

Smart, C. (1986) 'Feminism and law: some problems of analysis and strategy', *International Journal of the Sociology of Law*, 14 (2): 109–23.

Smart, C. and Neale, B. (1997) 'Arguments against virtue: must contact be enforced?', *Family Law*, 27: 332–6.

Stanley, N. and Humphreys, C. (2006) 'Multi-Agency and Muli-Disciplinary Work: Barriers and Opportunities Introduction', in C. Humphreys and N. Stanley (eds) *Domestic Violence and Child Protection: Directions for Good Practice*. London: Jessica Kingsley Publishers.

Sturge, C. and Glaser, D. (2000) 'Contact and domestic violence – the experts court report', *Family Law*, 30: 615–29.

Trinder, L., Connolly, J., Kellet, J. and Nortley, C (2005) *A Profile of Applicants and Respondents in Contact Cases in Essex*. London: Department of Constitutional Affairs. www.dca.gov/research/2005

Trinder, L., Connolly, J., Kellet, J., Nortley, C. and Swift, L. (2006) *Making Contact Happen or Making Contact Work*. London: Department of Constitutional Affairs. www.dca.gov/research/2006

Wall, L.J. (2006) *A report to the president of the family division on the publication by the Women's Aid Federation of England entitled twenty-nine child homicides: Lessons still to be learnt on domestic violence and child protection with particular reference to the five cases in which there was judicial involvement*. London: Royal Courts of Justice.

Women's Aid (2005) *Women's Aid Briefing Domestic Violence and Crimes Act, 2004*. www.womensaid.org.uk/briefings

Women's Aid (2006) *Protection from Violence under the Civil Law*. www.womensaid.org.uk

4   Policing, prosecution and the courts

This chapter examines the policing and prosecution of domestic violence. It begins by looking at the historical struggles for an adequate police response to domestic violence, waged by women, from the 1880s onwards. It reviews the consequent changes in policing policy and practice, including contemporary initiatives and identifies continuing issues in the police response to domestic violence in the 21st century. The chapter then moves on to consider the way domestic violence is prosecuted and dealt with by magistrates and judges and discusses recent innovations such as specialist domestic violence courts.

Policing domestic violence

Significance

In the UK, as in many countries, the police are the primary agency charged with maintaining civilian law and order, and protecting the public by preventing and fighting crime. They are a high profile, powerful and highly visible, uniformed service which, with the free 999 emergency phone number, is accessible 24 hours day, 7 days a week, 365 days per year. Although at present they are organised into 43 local constabularies, the police are comprehensive in their geographical coverage. Their organisation into 43 constabularies reflects the principle of local accountability which allows some autonomy to address local crime problems, albeit within the overall policing priorities, as settled by government and reflected in Home Office guidance.[1] One consequence of this localism is that police domestic violence policy and practice varies considerably between constabularies and, to some extent, within them. However, despite this variability, the police are one of the most visible, widely recognised, geographically comprehensive and accessible services.

The police are also a very powerful agency, with powers of arrest and detention and a gate-keeping role in respect of law enforcement and access to justice. This includes the power to define an incident as a crime or not, and to decide on whether and what action to take against suspected perpetrators.[2] They can also facilitate access to other voluntary sector and statutory services, thereby playing an enabling role in respect of community domestic violence, housing and health services. Although these services can be, and frequently are, accessed directly, it remains the case that not all women will be aware of their work or how to access their services, despite the increasing amount of outreach work undertaken by the Refuge movement, for example.

In respect of domestic violence incidents, the police response has a further significance, in that they may be responding to a first disclosure or attempt at help-seeking. How the police respond to such incidents carries important messages. A sensitive response is likely to reassure a survivor that her complaint is a legitimate one, which will be taken seriously and responded to with respect and professionalism. As well as providing protection through the criminal law, the police also have a role in enforcing civil orders, by arresting for a breach,[3] consequently a positive police response plays an important role in accessing justice and protection. Further, a positive police response may facilitate access to specialist domestic violence support services. Contrarily a poor response may deter future help-seeking and leave the victim unprotected and at risk of further violence. Given the figures for domestic homicide, it is no exaggeration to say a supportive response can save a life.

The police response also carries important messages to domestic violence perpetrators, regarding the non-acceptability, or otherwise, of domestic violence. Making an arrest and treating the domestic violence perpetrator as a criminal can come as a serious shock. For some, acquiring a criminal record has serious consequences in terms of their social standing and employment prospects. On the other hand, police inaction reinforces perpetrators' views that they have the right to use violence at home with impunity.

Further, police responses carry wider political and symbolic significance for society as a whole. Police inaction or ineffective action sends the message that domestic violence is not a matter of police or public concern. Such messages serve to condone men's use of violence against women and children, thereby effectively giving permission for, and increasing the risk of, further violence. This approach reinforces patriarchal assumptions regarding men's rights to use violence to discipline or control the behaviour of their wives or partners. Conversely, effective police action can indicate that domestic violence is taken seriously as violent crime, which itself can be a deterrent against further violence and as such contribute to reducing or eliminating it, and increasing the safety of women and children.

Historical background

Although the issue of police responses to domestic violence is a very contemporary one, it has a long history reaching back to the 19th century to a period when men were deemed to be the head of the family and law, policing, politics and government were held to be exclusively male preserves. As was seen in the previous chapter, since the 1830s feminists have petitioned for law changes to protect married women subject to domestic violence. This, together with later concerns for the plight of women held in police custody, being tried in court, or giving evidence as victims of rape or sexual assault, led women's organisations to call for the appointment of 'police matrons' in the 1880s, to ensure 'propriety and protection' in the police response to women, whether as offenders or victims of crime (Radford, 1989; Woodeson, 1993).

The response from men in authority, like the role of police matron itself, was limited. In 1914 a militant suffrage organisation, The Women's Freedom League, resorted to direct action in support of their demand for the appointment of women as police officers. Their concerns directly turned on women's rights, specifically the rights of women and children exploited in prostitution and those victimised by domestic and sexual violence (Radford, 1989). Not deterred by the refusal of government or the police authorities to allow women to join the police, even in the war-time emergency, the Women's Freedom League set up its own autonomous force of uniformed, paid, full-time Women Police Volunteers (WPV) in order to establish a police service for women by women (*The Vote*, 1915:566; Radford, 1989). Although the work of the WPV was highly regarded, it was dismissed as too radical when the then Metropolitan Commissioner of police appointed the first 100 women police officers in 1919. Nevertheless, the entry of women into the police service owes much to the pioneering work of the Women's Freedom League and the Women Police Volunteers (Allen, 1925; Lock, 1979; Radford, 1989; Jackson, 2006).

However, even after the Police Act 1919 and the Sex Discrimination Removal Act 1919, which permitted the employment of women as police officers, their future remained uncertain and insecure until the late 1940s (Lock, 1979). For most of the 20th century, the relatively small numbers of women officers were organised into separate women's sections, where they were accorded lesser powers, different working conditions and lower pay. Reflecting the sexism of the period, their duties were largely confined to working with women and children, perceived as low status work (Lock, 1979). The Sex Discrimination Act 1975 eventually brought this discriminatory situation to an end and women officers were absorbed into the general police structures. Arguably one of the costs of the equality agenda, in respect of the integration of women officers into the general police force in the 1970s, was a loss of expertise, experience and sensitivity in relation to policing domestic and sexual violence. Ironically this coincided in time with a renewed concern about the police response to gender crime on the part of a reawakened feminist movement.

Pressure for a changed police response: 1970–1990

In the UK, the reawakening of feminism in the 1970s' Women's Liberation movement led to a highlighting of the issues of domestic and sexual violence and the founding of Women's Aid refuges and the Rape Crisis movement. At that time there were very few options available to women experiencing domestic violence and in response Women's Aid groups formed and established refuges to provide safe accommodation for women and children fleeing domestic violence. Women's Aid also launched a powerful campaign for a wider recognition of the problem of domestic violence in law and social policy and challenged the trivialisation of domestic violence by the police.

Pioneering feminists working in academia struggled for domestic violence to be recognised as a legitimate subject of study in criminology and the social sciences. From the late 1970s onwards their research findings began to reveal more about the nature and extent of the problem. A series of research studies by Dobash and Dobash (1992), Pahl (1982, 1985), Hanmer and Saunders (1984), Radford (1987) and Edwards (1989) provided research evidence, which supported the experiential knowledge of Women's Aid in regard to the serious nature and widespread prevalence of the problem and the failure of the police to respond effectively. These studies revealed that domestic violence was accorded low police priority and officers failed to treat its survivors sensitively (Pahl, 1982). The research also found that domestic violence was characterised by a very low arrest rate and high levels of 'no-criming' with responses like 'No Cause for Police Action' (ncpa) or 'All Quiet on Arrival' (aqa) being recorded routinely in incident logs (Edwards, 1989). Further, these studies revealed significant levels of 'victim blame' in the attitudes of officers who frequently expressed the view that women provoked the violence or were in some other way blameworthy (Hanmer and Saunders, 1984; Radford, 1987). This body of research added to the pressure for a changed response and, in 1985, a government advisory body, the Women's National Commission (1985), in a report, criticised the police for their reluctance to intervene in domestic violence incidents, and specifically for their failure to arrest and prosecute perpetrators.

Changing policy – the 1980s–1990s

In response, the Home Office issued guidance to the police (Home Office Circular 69/1986), which was followed in 1987 by a force order to the Metropolitan police in London, encouraging positive action against domestic violence through a pro-arrest strategy. The Metropolitan Police set up a number of specialist police domestic violence units, a strategy followed by West Yorkshire and some Welsh police forces.

Explaining the 'U' turn

It is interesting to consider why such a major 'U' turn in the policing of sexual and domestic violence was instigated at this particular moment in time. It is certainly the case that by the late 1980s the women's movement had been campaigning actively on this issue for more than ten years. By this time, they were able to support their arguments about the inadequacy of existing police responses with testimony from the thousands of women who had approached Women's Aid for refuge, as well as being supported by findings from academic studies. However, it was also the case that the mid-1980s were characterised by a wider crisis in policing following their controversial roles in policing the miners' strike of 1984–5 (Fine and Millar, 1985) and the inner city uprisings of 1981 and 1985 (Scarman, 1981; Benyon and Salomos, 1987). These events were followed by a massive loss of public confidence in policing. Consequently, there was a recognised need to rebuild police community relations in the late 1980s, and it has been argued that the new response to domestic violence and sexual violence was part of a wider policy of re-establishing public support, by responding to demands from women (Dunhill, 1989). It is noteworthy that while criticisms of the police response to the miners' strike and in the inner cities related to excessive or 'heavy-handed' policing, feminist concerns, in respect of domestic violence, related to the police non-interventionist policy. Whatever the explanation, the reversal of this policy, confirmed in Home Office Circular 60/90 which extended the new approach across the UK, marked the beginnings of state intervention into what was previously seen as a private problem.

Home Office Circular 60/90

The publication of this circular promoted the new approach, which had been piloted in London and West Yorkshire, across the UK[4] marking the beginnings of a transformation in the policing of domestic violence. The circular advised police forces to introduce domestic violence policies, to recognise domestic violence as serious violent crime and to appoint dedicated domestic violence officers. It advised the police that their duty was to protect victims and to take positive action against assailants, i.e. to consider arresting and charging assailants, and not to be deterred by the fact that some women may withdraw charges, a long-standing excuse for police non-intervention in domestic violence incidents. In addition, they were encouraged to provide information and support to victims, including escorting them to a place of safety. For the first time, the police were advised to liaise with other agencies, including women's voluntary sector agencies, representing the beginning of a multi-agency approach. Other specific points in the guidance referred to recording complaints carefully, to avoid 'no-criming' and to ensure that all records are easily retrievable.

Innovative policing practice

Specialist domestic violence officers

Many, but not all, constabularies developed domestic violence policies, modelled on the circular, and established specialist domestic violence units or included dedicated domestic violence officers in community safety, child protection or vulnerable persons units and issued practice guidelines to their officers. The initial role of specialist domestic violence units was to provide support during the period between the incident and the completion of any criminal proceedings against the perpetrator, with a view to encouraging victims not to withdraw their complaints. Their precise roles were either specified in force policies or, as reported to one Domestic Violence Forum (Cleveland), developed by the officers appointed to this role, most of whom held the lowly rank of 'constable'. No training for this new role was provided either by the Home Office or the police themselves, possibly indicative of their lack of expertise at this time.[5] Given the very formal hierarchical structures of the police, according this level of responsibility to domestic violence officers was surprising and indicative of weaknesses in leadership and management in respect of the new policy. While, as will be discussed, implementation of the new policy had its difficulties, it should be acknowledged that its development owes much to the dedication and creativity of the police domestic violence officers themselves.

As the roles of the new police domestic violence officers were developed within local forces, implementation was characterised by local diversity. The approach developed within one constabulary, Cleveland, is drawn on here as an illustration.[6] As in many constabularies, domestic violence calls were now given a zero rating, i.e. top priority, and attended and initially dealt with by uniformed officers. Uniformed officers were briefed to treat domestic violence incidents like they would that of any crime scene, and to engage in 'enhanced' evidence gathering, drawing on forensic crime scene investigators, for finger prints, detecting forced entries and photographing injuries and criminal damage to the property. With the consent of the victim, they were encouraged to take statements from witnesses, like neighbours, and other family members. The officers attending completed a checklist domestic violence form, devised by the domestic violence officers to ensure key evidence was collected. The checklist also required officers to check on the welfare of any children in the residence. While they were not expected to be child protection specialists, they were required to note and respond to any visible injuries to the children and make a note if they were displaying distress.

The domestic violence form was to be passed on to domestic violence officers at the end of their shift.[7] In Cleveland, as in many constabularies, the role of the specialist domestic violence officers was primarily one of follow-up and support. Incidents were followed-up the next day, initially by visits, but as the numbers increased and safety issues assessed, visits were replaced by phone calls, unless it was very serious or complicated.[8] The aim of the follow-up was to provide advice and support and to ensure that best evidence was collected. It was considered that the victim would be better able to give a full statement, i.e. best evidence, and to accept advice and support on the following day, than during or in the immediate aftermath of the crisis incident. The different civil and criminal law options were explained by domestic violence officers, who through their involvement with the domestic violence multi-agency forum, were able to make informed referrals to other agencies, like the local refuges, housing, health and benefits services.

Safety planning with victims was another key role and, when appropriate, officers facilitated access to target hardening measures, which included the installation of panic alarms, small cctv cameras as well as door and window locks. An innovation developed by the Cleveland domestic violence officers was the production of pocket-sized domestic violence 'diaries'. Following a page of safety planning advice, the diary was structured to enable victims to record subsequent incidents, with prompts to ensure relevant information was collected, i.e. to record not only what had happened, but also dates, details of location and officers attending, things that women often overlooked. These 'diaries' proved particularly valuable in relation to civil law injunctions and proceedings under the harassment legislation. Following an instance when a domestic violence officer was called to court to explain these 'diaries', local courts allowed them to be used in evidence as 'contemporaneous notes'. Subsequently, constabularies in England, Scotland, Wales and Northern Ireland adopted these 'diaries' as a good practice innovation.

In Cleveland, as in many forces, instamatic cameras were made available to officers to record domestic violence injuries and criminal damage,[9] as an aspect of enhanced evidence gathering. These proved valuable in the interviewing of suspected perpetrators, serving to counter their strategies of denial and minimisation of the violence. Hertfordshire domestic violence officers developed the strategy of printing a double set of photographs, leaving one with the survivor, the intention being that they could be referred to if she was tempted to withdraw the complaint, in which case they served as a reminder of the seriousness of the violence.

In Cleveland, the domestic violence officer also played a key role in preparing cases for and making recommendations to the Crown Prosecution Service in relation to the decision to forward cases to prosecution. Their status as 'dedicated officers' allowed them time which, together with their developing expertise, enabled them to take detailed witness statements from the survivor and any other witnesses, for example neighbours, friends and or other family members. These statements not only referred to the incident in question but also included previous non-reported incidents as background history to indicate the seriousness and continuing nature of domestic violence.

In addition the Cleveland domestic violence officers were charged with taking withdrawal statements as it was considered that their specialist knowledge, together with the rapport struck up with victims would keep withdrawals to a minimum. Further, it was considered that they would be better able to assess whether or not the victim had been pressurised by the perpetrator or his family into making a withdrawal. This aspect of their role gave them a significant insight. They found that some, but not all, of the women wishing to withdraw were willing to be 'summoned' to court to give evidence because then the responsibility for proceeding with a case did not lie with them but with the police and Crown Prosecution Service (CPS), making it easier to explain to their children and family members. This strategy, supported by the local CPS, provided something of a negotiated solution to the dilemma presented by the pro-arrest positive policing strategy of taking forward prosecutions, where there is sufficient evidence, irrespective of the survivors' wishes. As will be explored there is a continuing dilemma over how much influence survivors should have in the new approach to domestic violence which is both 'victim centred' and committed to increasing arrest and prosecution rates.

In Cleveland the police were active members of the local multi-agency forums, joining voluntary sector activists and other statutory agencies on awareness raising events as well as regularly providing their statistics and keeping the forums up to date with policing policy developments and, from time to time, looking to the forum for guidance on difficult issues, whether relating to complicated cases or more general issues.

Impact of Circular 60/1990: the national situation

Nationally Women's Aid gave a cautious welcome to the new police approach, reporting that in some areas refuges were finding that the police were giving a higher priority to domestic violence, providing more information to women and they were beginning to follow-up incidents more carefully, with empathy replacing the old victim-blame attitude. However, they also reported that the new domestic violence units were often under-resourced and that their phonelines were on answer-phone for long periods. They also reported that the changes were unevenly developed across the country, and that some police forces had not developed new policies and so there was no evident change in policy or practice (Barron, Harwin and Singh, 1992). Rights of Women (ROW), a London based feminist legal organisation, while cautiously welcoming the new approach expressed similar concerns. They reported that the new specialist domestic violence officers had little status and were being marginalised within the police, while their very presence led other officers to believe domestic violence was not a concern for them. Other concerns raised by ROW were that although 'specialist' domestic violence officers were being appointed in some areas, they were given no training or job descriptions (Mavolwane and Radford, 1992). These rather mixed initial perceptions were confirmed in later research.

Early independent evaluations

Early independent studies reported some progress, as well as revealing difficulties in the implementation of the new policy. Mooney (1994) found that, in north London, police divisions with domestic violence units performed better in terms of victim satisfaction, incident reports, arrest rates, referrals to support agencies and to the Crown Prosecution Service. Hanmer (1990) reported similar findings from West Yorkshire, but also noted that women were dissatisfied with the length of time they had to wait to see a domestic violence officer. Walker and McNichol (1994) in a South Tyneside study similarly found the new approach was only partially successful. The authors concluded that, while the force policy looked good in writing, the critical question was how well it worked in practice. Interviews with uniformed officers revealed some positive attitudes but also some continuing prejudice against domestic violence survivors:

> They are the lowest of the low, they are low life . . . most of the times its in the poorest areas because they are just rubbish.

> Its just the boss's idea of quality of service . . . but in my eyes some of it is just very petty and you get called to just anything, and you walk in and you think 'oh here we go again' and its the same old story.

> We have got to intervene, it is quite simply a brutal crime. Domestic disputes, I would always attend. In my opinion, you have got to go back to the fundamental basic role of the police service . . . its about protecting people, protecting property.
>
> (Walker and McNichol, 1994:102, 106)

Interviews with survivors demonstrated appreciation of the domestic violence officers:

> If it were not for the domestic violence leaflets I would still be here doing nothing about it. I felt safe carrying the telephone numbers around with me.
>
> (Walker and McNichol, 1994:79)

However, many women while appreciating the respect, confidence, advice and information they received from the domestic violence officers, were critical of the lack of effective action against the perpetrator: 'It's funny because you don't need advice . . . what you want is for someone to do something' (Walker and McNichol, 1994:80).

A statistical analysis of the years between 1989 and 1992 revealed a significant increase in the number of women reporting domestic violence incidents to the police in South Tyneside, but a slight fall in arrest rate from 19 per cent in 1989–1990 to 17 per cent in 1991–2. This finding demonstrated a partial success in that significantly more women were reporting domestic violence incidents to the police but, despite this increase, the rate of arrests fell.

Innovative practice

Three evaluations of innovative policing practice, brought about by Circular 60/90, were also funded by the Home Office during this period.

Merseyside Domestic Violence Prevention Project

The innovations introduced in Merseyside included the issuing of quick response pendant alarms to those women identified as vulnerable. These aimed to deter the perpetrator and prevent imminent assaults through activation, which alerted the police to an emergency. These were positively received and increased the physical and psychological safety of women and children (Lloyd, Farrell and Pease, 1994). Similar measures were adopted in many forces, including Cleveland, where again the alarms were positively received,[10] but in this case the limited numbers of alarms available resulted in difficult decisions regarding their allocation and constraints on the length of time any one survivor could keep one.

In Merseyside a database on police attendance at domestic violence incidents was established, measures were put in place to improve the transfer of injunction details from the courts to the police, together with the provision of support and information to survivors of domestic violence. The construction of domestic violence databases has became a standard element in police response to domestic violence in many constabularies across the UK in the 1990s.

Domestic Violence Matters: North London

This initiative drew on a Canadian approach to policing domestic violence, where civilian workers worked alongside the police to deliver follow-up services, short-term support and advocacy within 24 hours of the police call-out. Through the provision of support, the aim was to increase the number of cases that went forward to prosecution. It also aimed to improve multi-agency co-ordination and highlight any gaps in service provision. The evaluation found that service users appreciated the quick follow-up and valued the practical and emotional support. They also appreciated the assurance that the violence was not their fault and that it was recognised as criminal violence. They liked the emphasis on women's right to justice and protection and referrals to other agencies, and confidence in the police was increased. Unfortunately, however, disputes arose between the police and the civilian workers. While the specialist domestic violence officers were comfortable working with civilians, problems between the attending officers and senior managers were not resolved and the project was discontinued Kelly (1999). Nevertheless, this project paved the way for later projects funded by the Crime Reduction Programme, such as Camden Safety Net, where civilian support workers based at the police station were successfully able to increase women's engagement with the criminal justice system (Hester and Westmarland, 2005).

The Killingbeck Project, West Yorkshire

This innovative project aimed to reduce domestic violence through a three-tiered programme of interventions which increased in intensity with each police call-out. Provision was made for the entry of particularly serious cases at levels 2 or 3. The interventions were intended to focus equally on demotivating the perpetrator and protecting the survivor in an interactive crime prevention model. This model involved the whole police force, rather than relying solely on the domestic violence officers. Level 1 interventions included the completion of full reports from uniformed officers, information letters being sent to both survivors and alleged perpetrators informing them that domestic violence was a crime and taken seriously by the police. Police watch or 'drive-bys' where marked patrol cars cruised the vicinities was a new element introduced at level 2. Other elements included second information letters, crime prevention target-hardening measures being installed in the property, if appropriate, and a visit from a community constable. Another new element at level 2 was 'cocoon watch' which, with the consent of the survivor, involved neighbours, friends and family in victim protection. If a prosecution was taken forward, the police opposed bail and passed a detailed case history to the Crown Prosecution Service. At level 3, further information letters were sent, 'police watch' and cocoon watch were maintained and similar measures were in place in respect of prosecutions. What was new at level 3 was the installation of panic buttons and a visit from the domestic violence officer.

The evaluation found a reduction in repeat victimisation and longer intervals between police call-outs and an improvement in the standard and consistency of police responses, although problems were identified in respect of prosecutions. Nevertheless, chronic and repeat offenders were identified and assessed, including those who had moved on to new victims. In this project there was also an improvement in multi-agency working, both between the police and other criminal justice agencies and some voluntary sector agencies (Hanmer et al., 1999). This project became very popular with the Home Office because it aimed to reduce costs by focusing on high volume crime, repeat victimisation and rationing of resources, and because it offered a standardised response. Although the project was not extended nationwide, aspects of Killingbeck such as having layered responses, cocoon watch and target-hardening measures, depending on the risk of repeat victimisation, have been adopted by some other police forces, for example in South Wales (Robinson, 2004).

In an overview of all three of these projects Hanmer and Griffiths (2000) concluded that good practice in respect of policing domestic violence required standardised definitions of domestic violence, consistent police interventions, clear leadership, robust accountability and good management support, together with domestic violence awareness training for all police officers and performance monitoring of officers, police attendance and effective use of resources. These three projects have also been central to the development of further initiatives by the police to protect victims in conjunction with other support agencies and to increase engagement with the criminal justice system (see below).

Home Office evaluations

The Home Office published a series of evaluations of the new and still evolving police responses to domestic violence. The elements of localism in police accountability structures resulted in differences in how the 43 constabularies interpret Home Office Guidance. Grace (1995) found that all but three of the English and Welsh constabularies had developed domestic violence policies and that 50 per cent of police forces had developed specialist domestic violence units or specialist community safety or vulnerable persons units with some responsibility for domestic violence. Interviews with uniformed police officers revealed that most thought the police response to domestic violence incidents had improved in that such incidents were taken more seriously with more positive police intervention and more advice being given, although a third had not heard of the new Home Office policy and half reported not having received new guidelines. Half of those who had received new guidelines stated that it was still a low priority issue. Grace found that the police domestic violence officers showed high levels of commitment to their work, providing support and advice on their options to victims. But she also found that few had received any training on domestic violence and all reported being seriously over-worked. Moreover, the appointment of domestic violence officers had had little impact on policing as they were marginalised from other officers. However, women victimised by domestic violence found their contact with the domestic violence officers positive, but their experiences of the uniformed officers were mixed, leading Grace to recommend that this was in need of improvement.

Grace concluded, five years after the circular, that more care was needed in the implementation of police domestic violence policy and more domestic violence officers were needed, with training and refresher training for domestic violence and uniform officers. Other recommendations turned on the need for more monitoring and improved recording of cases, and greater interaction between uniform and domestic violence officers to reduce the problem of marginalisation. She recommended a greater emphasis on the arrest of perpetrators and a more sympathetic approach to victims on the part of uniform officers. For example, she found that of the two police forces that did keep standardised databases on domestic violence incidents, the arrest rate in relation to recorded incidents was only between 12 to 14 per cent, which was an even lower rate than before the circular.

Three years later, a second Home Office evaluation undertaken by Plotnikoff and Woolfson (1998) focused not on the police response to victims or perpetrators of domestic violence, but on how forces are organised to deliver this service. The authors argued that this was significant as it impacts both on the quality of service and the working experiences of specialist domestic violence officers (Plotnikoff and Woolfson,1998). Their evaluation focused on the roles of domestic violence officers, their location within force structures, the monitoring of their performance, and information sharing between officers, with the aim of identifying good practice and areas where improvements are necessary. Their findings identified wide variations between police forces' policies in terms of where domestic violence officers were situated within the force, whether in specialist domestic violence units, community safety units, CID, child protection or vulnerable persons units; however, these findings did not identify any approach as more or less effective. Like Grace (1995) they found that irrespective of structures, domestic violence officers were perceived as being of low status, with limited or no job description, no training and subject to little systematic performance monitoring or supervision. Areas of work that were identified as undeveloped included links with child protection and addressing repeat victimisation. Recommendations from this influential study included training for domestic violence officers and improvements in their line management and supervision, as well as developing and sharing best practice. They also recommended standardisation in terms of the definition of domestic violence, the role of domestic violence officers and in how domestic violence incidents are responded to. They recommended that the role of domestic violence officers, initially a victim support role, be developed to include an investigative element and multi-agency working.

As illustrated above, the 1990s saw a major re-think of the police approach to domestic violence. New policies had been developed and, in many areas, dedicated officers had been appointed. Although the evaluations found survivors appreciated their work, they were undervalued in the police structure and weaknesses had been identified in their supervision and management. The evaluations also consistently found problems with the attitudes of many uniformed officers, which continued to impede effective policing. There was variation and uneven implementation of the new policy across the country, which meant that despite some improvements and innovations, even by the end of the 1990s the police response to domestic violence was still very much a postcode lottery.

A revised circular (HoC 19/2000)

To address these continuing problems, in 2000 the Home Office introduced a second, stronger and more detailed guidance circular, which recognised domestic violence as a human rights abuse, HoC 19/2000. It re-emphasised the need for clear force domestic violence policies, supported by strong management and leadership by senior police officers, within a multi-agency framework. It identified the protection of women and children and taking positive action against domestic violence perpetrators as key priorities in a positive policing model. It strengthened the pro-arrest policy by requiring officers to justify any decisions not to arrest if there was sufficient evidence and made the reduction of 'repeat victimisation' a police performance indicator. In respect of domestic violence officers, the circular called for more clearly defined roles, which balanced their victim support role with an investigative element and closer liaison with the Crown Prosecution Service. One of the aims of the new policy was to address the variability in policing practice identified above, within and between forces, in responding to domestic violence.

Nevertheless, more recent studies have found that there continued to be considerable inconsistency in arrest rates, recording of domestic violence incidents as crimes and investigations within and between forces, leading to considerable variability in the number of cases that are prosecuted and come before the criminal courts (Hester *et al.*, 2003; HMCPSI, 2004; Cook *et al.*, 2004a; Hester and Westmarland, 2005). This has combined with government concern at the high level of cases that fall out of the criminal justice system compared to most other crimes (HMCPSI, 2004). This is known as the attrition rate and has been the focus of later studies following the revised police circular.

Policing and attrition

The research has noted that cases can fall out of the system at a number of different stages in the criminal justice process from the reporting of domestic violence incidents, the recording of the incident as a crime, arrests, charges and through to convictions (HMCPSI, 2004). The police and the Crown Prosecution Service often cite the most common reason for attrition as being victims wanting no further action or withdrawing their statements. To a limited extent this view is supported through research, with fear of retaliation from the perpetrator or his family, shame, lack of financial resources, still wanting some kind of relationship with the perpetrator and needing to make arrangements for the children being common reasons why women withdraw (Hester et al., 2003; Gill, 2004). Other reasons may be satisfaction with the initial police action or survivors regarding a criminal prosecution as just 'not worth the candle', with regards to its deterrent effect or ability to protect them from further violence (HMCPSI, 2004). It is worth noting that a study by Women's Aid (Barron, 2002) found that staff working in refuges, advice and outreach services were more frequently sceptical of prosecution being a deterrent, with 64 per cent believing that it only deterred 'sometimes' and only 4 per cent viewing it as a total deterrent.

Nevertheless, the research evidence also suggests that attrition is affected by policing practice and this itself can have an impact on victim withdrawal. For example, later evaluation research of projects funded by the Home Office and developed to reduce 'the justice gap' evidenced by the high attrition rate, has found that some survivors are more prepared to give statements against perpetrators where there is photographic evidence of injuries or criminal damage, and are less likely to retract these statements (Hester and Westmarland, 2005). Thus survivors may be less willing to withdraw, if they see that the police are committed to investigating the crime and are taking it seriously. Research evidence also now exists to suggest that survivors may be more willing to engage with the criminal justice process in situations where they have ongoing individual support and advocacy from civilian support and advice workers, suggesting that, for some, it is fear and uncertainty of the criminal justice process that can impact on the decisions they make (Halt, 2004; Hester and Westmarland, 2005). These authors indicate that the attrition rate for victim withdrawals in areas where this kind of support has been offered is only about 10 per cent of cases, whereas other research where such support has not been available suggests a much higher attrition rate due to victim withdrawal of 44 per cent (see, for example, HMCPSI, 2004). This is discussed in more detail below when looking at the role of the CPS and specialist domestic violence courts.

Since the 19/2000 circular, the high attrition rate in relation to domestic violence was initially emphasised by a study in the North East of England carried out with the Northumbria police in three police districts (Hester et al., 2003). This study found three-quarters of incidents where there was a power of arrest actually led to arrest, indicating some improvement on previous policing practices, discussed above. Nevertheless, less than a third of arrests led to criminal charges, although in divisions where there was 'positive policing', which included substantive use of power of arrest and effective evidence gathering, criminal charges were more likely to follow.

One of the most comprehensive recent studies, which looked at how policing practice can be improved to reduce attrition, has been a joint review of policing and CPS practice by government inspectors (HMCPSI, 2004). One of the aims of this study was to examine attrition in response to government's renewed emphasis on the criminality of domestic violence and bringing more offenders to justice (Home Office, 2003). It looked in detail at the practices of six different police forces and examined 463 files of domestic violence incidents to which the police were called, in relation to attrition. It found that out of these 463 incident files only one in five (118) were recorded as crimes, although it noted, in reviewing the files, that 56 per cent of cases (260) should have been recorded as such, indicating a significant amount of 'no criming' at this early stage of attrition. It also found considerable variation between forces in recording, ranging from 10–66 per cent. At the charging stage, charges were brought in only a fifth of these cases. The report found that while the high fall out of some of these cases could possibly be accounted for by victim satisfaction with the initial police action, it noted that in some areas, it could be due to ineffective or no investigation to gather other evidence which would support victim statements. The overall attrition rate from recording to conviction indicated that only 3 per cent of cases ended up in criminal convictions, a figure which was similar to the Northumbria study discussed earlier (Hester *et al.*, 2003).

The report recommended that effective evidence gathering should be routine in domestic violence cases and should include not only the use of digital photographic evidence of injuries, but photos of the condition of the scene, scene of crime evidence, use of 999 tapes, use of medical evidence and neighbours' statements. It was also noted that some police officers were confused by counter-allegations from offenders and the lack of effective evidence gathering could contribute to this confusion. In addition, children's evidence was under-used and children's presence at the scene was often ignored, rather than being recorded for prosecution files, noting that violence in the presence of children is an aggravating factor in relation to sentencing.

It also noted a failure in 'intelligence gathering' in relation to previous history and breach of civil orders, information from other agencies and the under-use of the Protection of Harassment Act to pursue charges, with police in some areas having little understanding of this law. In addition, it found that the needs of minority women, refugees, asylum seekers and travellers were not adequately addressed in some areas, as is seen in the following quote from Geeta, a Bangladeshi woman.

> When I called the police out they came here and had a Pakistani interpreter on the phone to talk to me. I did not understand what she was saying and of course she must not have understood what I was saying.
>
> (HMCPSI, 2004:71)

In many of its recommendations in relation to policing, this report echoed earlier research. For example, some forces still lacked clear policies on arrest and 'effective' as opposed to 'enhanced' evidence gathering. In this regard, it emphasised that it should be routine practice to gather evidence to support victims' statements. Further recommendations included the need for a common definition of domestic violence for 'operational and monitoring purposes' nationally, accurate flagging of domestic violence incidents, training for all front-line and domestic violence officers and effective supervision of investigative practices, as well as giving all victims the opportunity to make impact statements for use in prosecution and sentencing.

Once again management issues were raised in relation to domestic violence officers, with the need for clear job descriptions reflecting their work, administrative support and clear line management. Nevertheless, the review found considerable areas of good practice in some forces with good local initiatives, multi-agency work and improving prosecution and conviction rates.

Other research with women has also found increasing satisfaction with police practice (Hester *et al.*, 2003; Hester and Westmarland, 2005) but less satisfaction with the Crown Prosecution Service (CPS) and the criminal courts in relation to prosecution and sentencing.

Further policing initiatives

Risk assessment

Risk assessment checklists are increasingly being used by different police forces when called to an incident of domestic violence (Home Office, 2006). In South Wales, where their use has been evaluated through research, they are used to structure police interviews with victims when attending a domestic violence incident and to inform actions to protect victim safety in the present and to implement further target-hardening measures in the short-term (Robinson, 2004). Those who are identified as 'very high risk' will trigger a multi-agency risk assessment conference (MARACS). The factors used in such checklists have been identified from research and reviews of domestic homicides. They are intended to predict which women and children are most at risk from very serious or potentially lethal violence.

However, such factors do not have very high predictive value in anticipating further serious violence, over and beyond the well-known factors of the frequency and escalation of violence: the point of separation and the young age of the offender (Robinson and Tregidga, 2005). The research has indicated that they work far better when they are combined with victims' own judgements of the dangers they are in from perpetrators (Robinson, 2006). Although a minority of women may underestimate the danger they are in, US research has indicated that victims' own views on the dangers are more accurate than other types of predictive risk assessment (Wiesz *et al.*, 2000).

One of the major disadvantages of the use of risk assessment checklists, given that they are not very accurate, is that it can result in police actions and resources such as 'police watch' only being targeted at those who have been identified as 'high' or 'medium' risk, depending on the number of ticks the police make against different boxes. The value of the information they elicit also depends on the sensitivity of front-line police in the way they deal with victims at the scene. Consequently, some may be left without their safety needs being adequately addressed. On the other hand, it has been argued that the checklists assist the police in paying attention to factors in their interviews with victims, which previously might have been ignored, because of the focus on physical violence, such as the level of power and control used by the perpetrator (Robinson, 2004).

Another problem has been the wide variety of risk assessment models used by police forces around the country. Recently ACPO (Home Office, 2006) has issued a list of key factors which should be used in all checklists (see below). This checklist includes asking survivors about their own perceptions of harm from the perpetrator, with a rider emphasising that although some victims may underestimate the dangers, they rarely 'overestimate' them. The model also stresses that children should always be seen by an officer attending a domestic violence incident and police responsibilities to protect children must be considered (Home Office, 2006:47).

Risk factors identified by ACPO (Home Office, 2006:47–8)

- Separation or child contact dispute
- Pregnancy or recent childbirth
- Escalation of the violence, including: worsening and frequency of the violence; previous convictions; injury and previous injury; use of a weapon; access to firearms; harm or threatened harm to pets or other animals; and attempts to choke, smother or strangle the victim
- Suspect's child abuse or threats to children
- Victim's isolation or barriers to help-seeking. This includes isolation arising from being prevented from seeing family or friends, or living in an isolated rural community. Barriers due to language difficulties or disability, ill health or substance misuse, forced marriage and families being involved in the abuse
- Suspect's attempts or threats at suicide or homicide
- Controlling behaviour, jealousy, stalking and harassment
- Fear of the suspect (victim's perception of harm)
- Sexual abuse
- Substance misuse and mental health of suspect

Call-handling, evidence gathering and targeting of prolific offenders

> While the protection and support of the victim and any children are critical to the success in multi-agency working, it is important to remember that the police function in partnership arrangements, after the initial action to protect life and property is to prosecute offenders.
> (Home Office, 2006:14)

Further police enforcement campaigns have introduced initiatives focused on improving evidence gathering and increasing the arrest rates and prosecution of prolific offenders, thus emphasising a renewed focus on the prosecuting role of the police. Checklists, for example, have been introduced for those who handle emergency 999 calls involving domestic violence and ensuring that calls are taped for use as evidence. Trials have also taken place of the use of 'head-cams' (head or body worn video cameras). These are particularly valuable when they capture evidence of the extent of a perpetrator's violence, as they can graphically counter defence strategies of minimisation or denial in court.

Through the use of a national intelligence model, prolific offenders have also been identified and targeted for arrest. The enforcement campaigns identified the lack of arrest of offenders who had already left the scene and highlighted this as a problem which needed to be addressed by the police, through concerted efforts to find and arrest the offender at the earliest opportunity. It was recommended that all prolific offenders should be monitored regularly, as well as breaches of bail conditions, where offenders had been arrested (Home Office, 2006).

As has been seen in the quotation above, these latest initiatives re-emphasise the police shift back to a prosecution, rather than a support role. This raises questions about the changing role of domestic violence officers, whose work has been focused as much on supporting victims as on prosecution. It also raises questions about the wishes of survivors in terms of pursuing prosecution since, as has been highlighted in earlier chapters, survivors tend to be more concerned with securing their own and their children's safety, than with the police goal or target of successful prosecutions. Many survivors are concerned that a prosecution will aggravate the violence and decrease their safety or believe that it is not in their interests for their (ex)partners to receive a criminal conviction. This is highlighted later when discussing further initiatives and research on the prosecution of domestic violence.

Prosecution and the courts

The police only have partial responsibility for enabling offenders to be brought to justice. The CPS was created in 1985 as the national criminal prosecution service. It employs solicitors who decide which cases to take forward for prosecution. Until 2004, the police had responsibility for charging suspects and the Crown Prosecution Service's (CPS) role was to review the evidence and decide whether there was sufficient evidence to take a case through the criminal courts. Subsequently, the CPS has had responsibility for decisions on charging in all but minor cases (Criminal Justice Act, 2003). Many CPS prosecutors are now located in police stations to facilitate decision-making in respect of charging. However, it remains to be seen whether this new arrangement is improving prosecution practices for victims. There is already some evidence that it is creating problems for the police in holding offenders overnight and charging offenders at a time when the CPS are not available and when most crimes associated with domestic violence occur. In these circumstances, the police have to consult a CPS service by phone (CPS Direct) and there appears to be some disagreements with the police over charging in these circumstances (Home Office, 2006).

New guidelines were issued on the prosecution of domestic violence cases in 2001. These put greater emphasis on using evidence other than that supplied by the survivor and on the more frequent use of S.23 (b) of the Criminal Justice Act, 1988. This provision allowed survivors' written evidence to be given where women were too fearful to attend court and give evidence in person. This provision has been replaced by Section 116 (2.e) of the Criminal Justice Act (2003) which allows for similar provisions, at the discretion of the judge hearing the case. The guidance also emphasised improved information giving to victims. At the same time, a network of domestic violence co-ordinators were created in each local CPS area, with responsibility for prosecution, strategic issues and training and working with local domestic violence forums (Home Office, 2003).

The HMCPSI review (2004) found in general that the police and CPS needed to work more closely together to facilitate better evidence gathering and to improve witness care in relation to retaining survivors' support for criminal prosecution, including the better use of special measures for vulnerable witnesses, such as the use of screens in court and the taking of victim impact statements to present to the court before sentencing. Clear guidance was also issued to the CPS on witness summons and warrants when victims were reluctant to give evidence. The review also identified the need to take the safety of children more seriously in prosecuting cases and in setting bail conditions. Inaction on the breach of bail conditions, where the offender could attempt to influence the survivor, was identified as a problem and the report recommended that further charges should be brought where this occurred. Since this review a revised CPS domestic violence policy incorporating these recommendations has been developed (CPS, 2005).

Specialist domestic violence courts

Specialist domestic violence courts have been developed in several local areas on a multi-agency basis as an attempt to address survivor dissatisfaction with the prosecution and court process, as well as to 'narrow the justice gap' by increasing the conviction rate and improve sentencing options. Significantly, other goals have been to reduce the costs of prosecuting domestic violence cases through speeding up the process (fast-tracking) and increasing efficiency by hearing all domestic violence cases on the same day (clustering) (Cook et al., 2004a).

Some initiatives have been operating for a number of years (for example, Leeds and West London)[11] others are more recent (Derby, Cardiff, Croydon and Caerphilly. Although the operation of these initiatives has varied considerably, reflecting different local multi-agency practices, evaluation studies have identified some common features. A key aspect has been the concentration of multi-agency resources in order to provide independent support and advisory services to survivors referred by the police. Originally called advocacy, these are now called independent domestic violence advisory services (IDVAS). There has also been a concentration on training key personnel such as CPS lawyers, domestic violence officers and, in some cases, magistrates and clerks and on developing improved information sharing protocols between key agencies. Most have aimed to improve survivor safety in the courts through having separate waiting areas and a few have been able to provide vulnerable witness facilities, such as the provision of screens, when victims are giving evidence. Most have been concentrated in the magistrates courts, although in a few the multi-agency protocols developed have been extended to Crown Court hearings, for example in Cardiff (Cook et al., 2004a).

One project in Croydon aimed to have an integrated domestic violence court (IDVC), which combined criminal and civil practice, including family law practice. The aim was to use the law more effectively by hearing all matters relating to the case at the same time, so that decisions were made in full possession of all the evidence. However, the difficulties in getting this set up has meant that, at the time of writing, there is no evaluation evidence to indicate whether this has actually improved practice to protect survivors, including children, when contact applications are made.

The effectiveness of specialist domestic courts (SDC)

Increasing the conviction rate
Evaluations of the effectiveness of these specialist magistrates courts have generally shown an increase in the conviction rate, which has in turn led to fewer

victim withdrawals and more guilty pleas (Cook *et al.*, 2004a and b). This has led to the government rolling out more of these courts in 25 police and CPS areas. By the end of 2005, areas with an SDC had a conviction rate of 71 per cent of defendants, whereas those with no SDC had a conviction rate of 53 per cent – a difference of nearly 20 per cent. However, the Crown Courts where more serious offences are tried also had a fairly high conviction rate of 68 per cent (CPS, 2006).

Survivor satisfaction

Nevertheless, survivors' satisfaction with criminal justice processes and outcomes has proved to be mixed, with some being less satisfied with the role of the police and the CPS and in the outcomes of prosecutions in relation to convictions and sentencing. The most detailed information from survivors was contained in two detailed evaluations of the SDCs in Caerphilly (Gwent) and in Croydon (Cook *et al.*, 2004b). Both these initiatives were set up specifically to address the needs of diverse groups of women including women from rural areas, in the case of Caerphilly, and black and minority ethnic women in Croydon. The study found that victims were most satisfied with the support and advice given by the Independent Domestic Violence Advice services and these services were credited as being a key factor in preventing many women from withdrawing from the criminal process. This finding has been confirmed in other research (Halt, 2004; Hester and Westmarland, 2005).

> It wasn't until I contacted Croydon Domestic Violence Advice Service that I got support and it was then that I made a statement. They encouraged me to file the report and they explained the process to me.

> The woman from the advice service encouraged me she told me that he needed to have this on his record and that it would be good for women in the future.
>
> (Cook *et al.*, 2004b:28)

Most women were also very satisfied with the support and information they were given by the Court Witness Services and welcomed the fact that they were offered pre-court visits and had separate entrances and facilities in the specialist courts to wait to give evidence, without having to see the perpetrator. Most were also informed about special measures that were available if they requested them, such as being able to give evidence behind a screen in the courts.

However, they were less satisfied with the quality of evidence sought and provided by the police and the fact that, with the exception of four women, victim impact statements[12] had been not taken.

> I think they should have taken photos of my injuries though because they were pretty bad, by the time I attended the court hearing the bruises and scratches had obviously disappeared.
>
> I was only told about these (impact) statements after I had given my evidence. The witness service asked me if I had been given the opportunity to complete one but I hadn't got the chance.
>
> (Cook *et al.*, 2004b:27–8)

The above examples indicate that despite all the guidance discussed above, there can still be a wide variation in practice, which can affect the outcomes of cases for survivors.

Child witnesses

The evaluations also highlighted the under-use of child witnesses and that the police should be trained to take statements from children. It emphasised that where children were willing to be witnesses, this could assist their own recovery from the impacts of the violence (Cook *et al.*, 2004a).

The prosecution process

Women remained dissatisfied with the prosecution process in relation to the lack of information from the police about the progress of their cases, bail conditions, and the releasing of suspects, which they felt jeopardised their safety. There was also dissatisfaction with crown prosecutors about changes to charges, without any consultation, and not knowing who the prosecutor was when they came to court to give evidence. 'I only gathered which (lawyer) was mine because I had been told by the witness service that the prosecuting lawyer would question me first' (Cook *et al.*, 2004b:31).

This lack of communication between the CPS and survivors is of considerable concern and although prosecuting lawyers cannot discuss the evidence, they can introduce themselves to victims. As a consequence, the new CPS policy on domestic violence states that they will consult with survivors if charges are changed or lowered as a result of a guilty plea (CPS, 2005).

Sentencing

Victims were most dissatisfied with sentencing, whether this was based on a change in charges or on the original charges. Many victims expected that sentences would provide them with some immediate protection through the perpetrator being sent to prison, but this was usually not the case, and there was a feeling that the courts had failed them.

> I wasn't satisfied with the outcome I wanted to see him punished for threatening to kill me but he was just punished for the criminal damage and he got a fine.
> I wanted to see him imprisoned. I was not told about the sentencing outcomes although the police thought that because of his history of abuse he would probably receive a custodial sentence. This hasn't happened and now he might just get an order that makes him paint a fence for a couple of hours.
>
> (Cook *et al.*, 2004b:32)

The problem regarding sentencing has been raised in other research (Hester and Westmarland, 2005; Hester *et al.*, 2003) and raises the key question for some survivors about whether it was worth going through the criminal justice process at all. Overall, the evaluations of the five specialist courts found that 59 per cent of domestic violence perpetrators were fined or had to pay compensation, 30 per cent were given a conditional discharge, 29 per cent were ordered to attend perpetrator programmes, 10 per cent were given a community punishment order and only 4 per cent were imprisoned (Travis, 2006). There was, however, some increase in custodial sentences where magistrates were given training about the dynamics of domestic violence. For example, in West London, where magistrates had received training, custodial sentences rose to 14 per cent. In addition, the training of magistrates also resulted in improvements in some areas on the setting of bail conditions and dealing with breaches (Cook *et al.*, 2004a).

Referral onto perpetrator programmes
Following the training of magistrates, there was also an increase in perpetrators being ordered to attend programmes through community rehabilitation orders. This, however, is problematic because there is little evidence that these programmes work in stopping the violence for the majority of perpetrators and this is discussed further in the next chapter.

New sentencing guidance

New sentencing guidelines have been published as a response to evidence that the courts have been giving lower sentences for domestic violence assaults than those carried out on strangers (Sentencing Guidelines Council, 2006). However, these guidelines are criticised as another missed opportunity to demonstrate that domestic violence is taken seriously and that sentences should take into account the need for victim protection. For example, although they indicate that serious violence should be reflected in custodial sentences, they also allow offenders who have 'just' crossed this sentencing threshold to be referred onto a perpetrator programme in the community, if there is no 'proven' previous pattern of violence. Since a previous 'proven pattern' is likely only to be recognised by the criminal courts as previous convictions or cautions,[13] this means an offender who has been convicted of grievous bodily harm can still get a non-custodial sentence, even though he may actually have a considerable history of previous violence towards his partner.[14] This guidance fails to recognise the continuing nature of domestic violence, the difficulties survivors experience in reporting it and the high levels of attrition in respect of reported incidents.

Another example of the failure of the guidance to take domestic violence seriously is the contradiction between aggravating and mitigating factors, particularly in relation to children. For example, perpetrating violence against a partner that is witnessed by the children is regarded as an aggravating factor. Yet at the same time, a perpetrator can argue that his relationship with his children would be disrupted if he is sent to prison, and claim this as a mitigating factor to lessen his sentence (Sentencing Guidelines Council, 2006).

After the criminal justice process

The majority of victims whose views were sought in the evaluations of the Specialist Domestic Violence Courts discussed above felt they were left unprotected after the criminal justice process, regardless of whether or not the perpetrator was found guilty. Women feared an aggravation of the violence as a result of their going to court when a custodial sentence had not been obtained. Further, even where a short custodial sentence was given, women were offered no information about the dates of release of their ex-partners, and this also raised concerns about their own safety.

> I am not satisfied with the support I have received. I feel very unprotected, he was found guilty. I did that to him and am therefore fearful of any repercussions.

> Probably some protection as he was found not guilty – what was I supposed to do after that, knowing he is still around, he could have done anything.
>
> (Cook *et al.*, 2004b:33)

Conclusions

This chapter has discussed the struggle for the recognition and treatment of domestic violence as criminal violence and the responses of government, police, prosecution and the courts. It has reviewed the hundred years' history of this struggle from the 1880s to the 1980s. It examined the 1990 shift in police policy, the introduction of specialist domestic violence police officers and the shift towards multi-agency working. It also reviewed the post-2000 changes, the shift to 'positive' policing, the introduction of specialist domestic violence courts and of independent specialist advisors (now being rolled out throughout the country). It notes that these changes have improved the arrest and conviction rates but survivor satisfaction has been less favourable, particularly with the outcomes of criminal prosecution, where women and children have continued to feel unsafe.

One problem that has been highlighted is the failure of the criminal courts to protect mothers and children when violent fathers' contact with their children are put before survivor safety in sentencing. Another problem is that sentencing practices often fall short of providing any protection from chronic perpetrators who are likely to re-offend again.

Performance targets

The post-2000 managerial focus on performance targets for criminal justice agencies is also proving problematic, as these targets still fail to meet the government objective of putting victims at the heart of the criminal justice system. For example, the target of increasing the number of 'sanction detections', i.e. the number of cases which result in a caution or criminal prosecution, while attempting to ensure effective policing, fails to consider survivor perspectives and the extent to which such outcomes protect survivors and their children. Further anecdotal evidence is emerging which suggests that a second policing target, the reduction of re-victimisation, is resulting in police being less receptive to repeat call-outs from these victims.

These issues continue to raise questions about survivors' confidence in the criminal justice system to increase their safety over the intermediate and long term. Nevertheless, there is some evidence that multi-agency interventions for those women who are identified as being at highest risk has improved their protection and this is discussed further in the final chapter.

Notes

1   At the time of writing, a controversial proposal to restructure the police into 12 'super' forces was under consideration. Her Majesty's Inspectorate of Constabulary (HMIC) 'Closing the Gap' report September 2005 argued that larger forces are better placed to respond effectively to major incidents, serious and organised crime, public disorder and counter terrorism (Protective Services), whilst at the same time maintaining an effective local policing service. Chief Constables and Police Authorities throughout England and Wales were invited

by the then Home Secretary, Charles Clarke, to consult on and review a series of options to restructure the police service (HMIC, 2005).

This review has proved to be controversial. Concerns turn on the principle of local police accountability, costs of re-organisation and job losses (Hansard, House of Lords debates, Tuesday, 7 February 2006).

2   However, they no longer have responsibility for charging decisions (Criminal Justice Act, 2003).

3   Subsequent to the full implementation of the Domestic Violence, Crime and Victims Act 2004, breaching of a civil non-molestation order becomes a criminal offence, further strengthening police powers in this context.

4   Equivalent circulars were issued in Northern Ireland (1990) and Scotland (1991).

5   Cleveland constabulary approached the University of Teesside for domestic violence education and training, which led to the development of the University Certificate in Professional Development (Domestic Violence) in the 1990s, a module which has been delivered to many UK police forces and still recruits from police and other professionals with a remit to respond to domestic violence.

6   This discussion is based on discussions of their emerging role as presented to and recorded in the minutes of Cleveland Domestic Violence Forum (until 1996) and subsequently Middlesbrough Domestic Violence Forum.

7   A frequent complaint of the domestic violence officers was that they never received all the forms, so they had to spend hours trawling through the computers to identify missed cases.

8   Women who could not be contacted this way received domestic violence advice leaflets and letters informing them of the new police approach and inviting them to contact the domestic violence officer.

9   These supplemented, rather than replaced, those taken by scenes of crime officers.

10   According to reports to Middlesbrough Domestic Violence Forum from both the domestic violence officers and survivors' groups.

11   Through the Standing Together project founded in 1998.

12   Victim impact statements are an opportunity for victims to describe the impacts of the violence on themselves and their children (CPS, 2005).

13   The Criminal Justice Act (2003) now allows previous bad character and misconduct to be taken into account in sentencing.

14   As seen in Chapter 1, on average, women may experience up to 35 incidents of violence before they report to the police.

References

Allen, M. (1925) *The Pioneer Policewoman*. London: Chatto and Windus.

Barron, C. (2002) *Five years on: a review of legal protection from domestic violence.* Bristol: Women's Aid Federation England.

Barron, J., Harwin, N. and Singh, T. (1992) *Report to Home Affairs Committee Inquiry into Domestic Violence.* Bristol: Women's Aid Federation England.

Benyon, J. and Solomos, J. (eds) (1987) *The Roots of Urban Unrest.* Oxford: Pergamon.

Cook, D., Burton, M., Robinson, A. and Vallely, A. (2004a) *Evaluation of specialist domestic violence courts/fast track systems.* CPS Policy Directorate.

Cook, D., Burton, M., Robinson, A., Tregidga, J. and Vallely, A. (2004b) *Evaluation of Domestic Violence Pilot Sites at Gwent and Croydon 2004/2005.* Interim Report. CPS Policy Directorate.

Crown Prosecution Service (2005) *CPS Policy on Prosecuting Cases of Domestic Violence.* London: CPS Policy Directorate.

Crown Prosecution Service (2006) *More domestic violence offenders convicted.* www.cps.gov.uk/news/pressreleases/archive/2006/139_06html

Dobash, R.E. and Dobash, R.P. (1992) *Women, Violence and Social Change.* London and New York: Routledge.

Dominy, N. and Radford, L. (1996) *Domestic Violence in Surrey: developing an effective inter-agency response.* London: Surrey County Council and Roehampton Institute.

Dunhill, C. (1989) (ed.) *The boys in blue: women's challenge to the police.* London: Virago.

Edwards, S. (1989) *Policing Domestic Violence, Women, the Law and the State.* London: Sage.

Fine, B. and Millar, R. (1985) *Policing the Miners' Strike.* London: Lawrence and Wishart.

Gill, A. (2004) 'Voicing the silent fear: South Asian Women's Experiences of Domestic Violence', *The Howard Journal*, 43: 5.

Grace, S. (1995) *Policing Domestic Violence in the 1990s. Home Office Research Study 139.* London: Home Office Research and Planning Unit.

Hanmer, J. and Saunders, S. (1984) *Well-founded Fear.* London: Hutchinson.

Hanmer, J. (1990) *Women, violence and crime prevention: a study of changes in police policy and practice in West Yorkshire. Research Paper No.3.* Violence, Abuse and Gender Relations Unit. Bradford: Bradford University.

Hanmer, J. and Griffiths, S. (2000) 'Reducing Domestic violence . . . What works?' *Policing Domestic Violence, Crime Reduction Series, Policing and Reducing Crime Briefing Note.* London: Home Office.

Hanmer, J., Griffiths, S. and Jerwood, D. (1999) *Arresting Evidence: Domestic Violence and Repeat Victimisation.* Police Research Series Paper 104. Policing and Reducing Crime Unit, London: Home Office.

Hanmer, J., Radford, J. and Stanko, B. (1989) (eds) *Women, Policing and Male Violence: International Perspectives.* London: Routledge.

Her Majesty's Inspectorate of Constabulary (HMIC) (2005) *Closing the Gap* report. London: HMIC.

Hester, M. and Westmarland, N. (2005) *Tackling Domestic Violence: Effective interventions and approaches. Home Office Research Study 290.* London: Home Office.

Hester, M., Hanmer, J., Coulson, S., Morahan, M. and Razak, A. (2003) *Domestic Violence: Making it through the criminal justice system.* University of Sunderland.

HMCPSI (2004) *Violence at Home: a joint thematic inspection and prosecution of cases involving domestic violence.* www.hmcpsi.gov.uk/reports

Home Office (2003) *Safety and Justice: the government's proposals on domestic violence.* London: Home Office.

Home Office (2005) *Domestic Violence: a national report.* London: Home Office.

Home Office (2006) *Lessons Learned from the Domestic Violence Enforcement Campaign,* Police and Crime Standards Directorate. London: Home Office.

Jackson, L. (2006) *Women police: Gender, welfare and surveillance in the twentieth century.* Manchester: Manchester University Press.

Kelly, L. (1999) *Domestic Violence Matters: An evaluation of a development project, Home Office Research Study 193,* The Research Development and Statistics Directorate. London: Home Office.

Lloyd, S., Farrell, G. and Pease, K. (1994) *Preventing Repeated Domestic Violence: a demonstration project on Merseyside,* Police Research Group Crime Prevention Series Paper 49. London: Home Office.

Lock, J. (1979) *The British Policewoman: her story.* London: Robert Hale.

Mavolwane, S. and Radford, J. (1992) 'Police Domestic Violence Units', *Rights of Women Bulletin,* Summer 1992. London: Rights of Women. www.rightsofwomen.org.uk

McWilliams, M. and McKiernon, J. (1993) *Bringing it Out into the Open: Domestic Violence in Northern Ireland.* Belfast: HMSO.

Mooney, J. (1994) *The Hidden Figure: Domestic Violence in North London.* London: Islington Council, Police and Crimes Unit.

Pahl, J. (1982) 'Police response to battered women', *Journal of Social Welfare Law,* November, 337–43.

Pahl, J. (1985) *Private violence and public policy.* London: Routledge.

Plotnikoff, J. and Woolfson, R. (1998) *Policing Domestic Violence: Effective Organisational Structures.* Policing and Reducing Crime Unit. London: Home Office.

Radford, J. (1987) 'Policing Male Violence: Policing Women', in J. Hanmer and M. Maynard (eds) *Violence and Social Control.* London: Macmillan.

Radford, J. (1989) 'Women and Policing: Contradictions Old and New', in J. Hanmer, J. Radford and B. Stanko (eds) *Women, Policing and Male Violence: International Perspectives.* London: Routledge.

Robinson, A. (2004) *Domestic Violence MARACS (Multi-Agency Risk Assessment Conferences) for Very High Risk Victims in Cardiff, Wales. Cardiff,* A Process and Outcome Evaluation. Cardiff: Cardiff University. www.cf.ac.uk/socsi/whoswho/robinson.hmtl

Robinson, A. (2006) 'Advice, Support, Safety and Information Services Together

(Assist)' *The Benefits of Providing Assistance to Victims of Domestic Abuse in Glasgow*. Cardiff: Cardiff University. www.cf.ac.uk/socsi/whoswho/robinson.hmtl

Robinson, A. and Tregidga, J. (2005) *Domestic Violence MARACS (Multi-Agency Risk Assessment Conferences) for Very High Risk Victims: Views from Victims*. Cardiff: Cardiff University. www.cf.ac.uk socsi/whoswho/robinson.hmtl

Scarman, Lord (1981) *The Brixton Disorders 10–12 April 1981: Report of an Inquiry*. London: HMSO.

Sentencing Guidelines Council (2005) *Sentencing Guidelines on Domestic Violence: a consultation paper*. London: Sentencing Guidelines Council.

Sentencing Guidelines Council (2006) *Sentencing Guidelines on Domestic Violence*. London: Sentencing Guidelines Council.

The Vote: The origin of the Women's Freedom League. (9.4.1915). London: Fawcett Library.

Travis, A. (2006) 'Domestic attackers escaping with a fine', *Guardian* 15/4/06.

Walker, J. and McNichol, L. (1994) *Protection, prevention or prudence?* Newcastle Centre for Family Studies, University of Newcastle upon Tyne.

Weisz, A.N., Tolman, R.M. and Saunders, D.G. (2000) 'Assessing risk of severe domestic violence: the importance of survivor predictions', *Journal of Interpersonal Violence*, 15 (1): 75–89.

Women's National Commission (1985) *Violence Against Women, Report of an Adhoc Working Group*. London: Cabinet Office.

Woodeson, A. (1993) 'The First Women's Police: a force for equality or infringement', *Women's History Review*, 2 (2).

5   Preventing domestic violence

The need for primary prevention

Primary prevention is based on the idea that domestic violence is not inevitable but can be explained through hierarchical and gendered social relations of
power. Thus, as highlighted in earlier chapters, domestic violence can be seen
as a social problem which does not occur in a vacuum but is a common feature
of male-dominating societies. Earlier chapters have also demonstrated that,
despite according some formal equality to women and improving legislation
to address domestic violence, western societies continue to tolerate and excuse
domestic violence and fail effectively to punish the perpetrators. They therefore continue to reinforce broader social relations of male power and women's
subordination, which allows domestic violence to flourish. Primary prevention (stopping the violence before it happens) involves challenging the institutional acceptance of male dominance as well as challenging social attitudes
towards domestic violence itself.

The first half of this chapter looks at young peoples' attitudes towards
violence against women and the difficulties in addressing these, through public awareness campaigns and school-based prevention programmes. Secondly
it outlines the problems in attempting to change perpetrators, and in examining different approaches, it discusses whether community-based programmes
are effective in increasing the safety of women and children experiencing
domestic violence.

Young people's attitudes

The ongoing toleration of domestic violence is illustrated through attitude
surveys undertaken with young people in the UK. These surveys indicate that
such violence is still regarded as acceptable by large numbers of teenagers
(Mullender *et al.*, 2002; Burton *et al.*, 1998b). One study of 1400 children
between the ages of eight and sixteen found that a third of teenage boys and a

fifth of teenage girls still thought that women 'deserved to be hit' in some situations (Mullender *et al.*, 2002:219). This study also indicated that teenage boys' attitudes towards the acceptability of violence towards women became more entrenched as they got older. Earlier research undertaken with over two thousand young people in Scotland for Zero Tolerance found that one in two young men and one in three young women considered physical violence or forcing sex on women as being acceptable in certain circumstances. These circumstances included if a woman had had sex with someone else, if she 'nagged,' and if she was disrespectful towards her partner/boyfriend. Attitudes blaming women for the violence were even more extensive in this study with 78 per cent of young men and 53 per cent of young women believing that women are 'often' or 'sometimes' to blame for the violence perpetrated against them (Burton *et al.*, 1998a).

Further, although these studies suggest that young women are less tolerant of domestic violence than young men, a recent survey which targeted the readers of *Sugar* (a girls' teen magazine) about their experiences suggested that over 40 per cent of those responding to the survey believed it was acceptable for a boyfriend 'to get aggressive' in some situations. These included where the girl cheated on him, flirted with someone else, screamed at him or dressed in an outrageous manner. More than 40 per cent also thought they would give a boyfriend a second chance if he hit them, although there were wide regional variations in responses in this area; with far less young women from London and the south east believing this than young women in other geographical areas (NSPCC, 2005).

Nor are such views confined to teenagers. Earlier ethnographic studies indicate that some boys may acquire these beliefs at a very young age. For example, Connelly, in studying the social construction of masculinised identities in an inner city primary school found that boys of between 4 and 6 years old described their relationships with girls 'overwhelmingly' in terms of 'power, violence and domination' (Connelly, 1995:185–6). Further, studies with nursery and primary school teachers have found that such behaviour by boys may be regarded as 'natural' and tolerated within the ideology of 'boys will be boys' where there is an underlying assumption that nothing can be done about their violent behaviour (Walkerdine, 1981). However, Connelly found that the sexually violent behaviour of very young boys towards girls in primary school was affected by these children watching violent videos and video games at home, indicating that the role of the media and its impacts on very young children cannot be underestimated. This is a theme that will be returned to later in this chapter when looking at the effectiveness of primary prevention.

The findings discussed above suggest the importance of preventative education with children beginning in the early years. Such education is perceived as primary prevention, since its goal is to prevent the violence from happening in the first place, through changing the values, attitudes and beliefs that maintain gendered inequality and violence. In addition, for children and young people who are already living with or have contact with a parent who is domestically violent, or who are already experiencing domestic violence from a boyfriend, such education has the purpose of letting them know that it is wrong and helping them to find sources of help. Acknowledging the importance of changing social values and attitudes towards domestic violence has led to initiatives around primary and secondary prevention through public awareness campaigns and school-based and youth education.

Public awareness campaigns

Several public awareness campaigns on domestic violence have been run in different areas of the UK, using public posters and billboards, newspaper articles and local radio, television and cinema adverts. The most extensive of these were first run in Scotland by the Zero Tolerance campaign initiated by Edinburgh Council in 1992. More recently there has been the National Strategy to address domestic violence in Scotland with specific campaigns targeted at young people (Gillan and Samson, 2000).

The original Zero Tolerance campaign run in Edinburgh, which incidentally first coined the term 'zero tolerance', aimed to challenge the government crime prevention strategies of the time, which were blaming victims for their experiences of crime. It emphasised that violence against women in all its forms was a gender problem and wanted to move this problem up the public policy agenda. Prior to the launch of the campaign, research with young people had found that tolerance of gender violence could be challenged by providing information about violence against women. Posters highlighted the extent of different forms of gender violence and confronted the ideology that women were to blame, through slogans such as 'no man has the right', which stressed that violence against women should be regarded as a crime and not be tolerated (Gillan and Samson, 2000).

Since then there has been increasing emphasis on the unacceptability of domestic violence in public awareness campaigns in local areas and some campaigns have been targeted at specific audiences. In 2005, for example, the Metropolitan Police launched a campaign aimed particularly at perpetrators of domestic violence, which included targeting pubs and using slogans on beer mats. These stated that perpetrators would be arrested even if victims refused to make statements against them (Metropolitan Police, 2005).

Evaluations of such campaigns indicate that they appear to have most impact in informing victims/survivors that domestic violence is a crime, as well as informing them where they can get help and support. As a consequence, they frequently result in increased reporting to the police and greater demand for domestic violence services in local areas (Hester and

Westmarland, 2005). However, their impact on challenging social attitudes is less clear. McCarry (2007) found that despite having been exposed to several public campaigns about domestic violence aimed specifically at young people, students in Glasgow secondary schools continued to believe that it was legitimate for boyfriends to be dominant and dictate the terms of intimate relationships, including using violence to get girlfriends to conform to their wishes. She suggests that such attitudes are deeply embedded in the culture and unless these norms of masculine behaviour are challenged, there is unlikely to be any change in beliefs that women 'deserve' their experiences.

Preventative programmes in schools

One of the positive messages from the research with children and young people cited above is that the majority wanted education on domestic violence in schools (Mullender *et al.*, 2002; Burton *et al.*, 1998a). In the last few years numerous programmes have been run in schools, although these have often been short-term and not been an ongoing part of the school curriculum (Ellis, 2004).

The effectiveness of school preventative education depends on a number of factors including the content of such programmes, how they are taught and, most significantly, how far they are prioritised and supported in whole school policies and practices. Schools themselves may be seen as approving gender violence through their failure to address sexual harassment of girls and women teachers and the lack of recognition of gender violence in policies in schools on bullying and harassment (Harne, 2000).

Evaluations of projects undertaken within the Home Office Crime Prevention Programme, which looked at student attitudes prior to and up to two years after interventions, found that those projects which were not just one-off initiatives and aimed to take a whole school approach were more successful than others (Hester and Westmarland, 2005). The training of teachers in understanding the gendered dynamics of domestic violence and in dealing with disclosures from pupils who may be living with a domestically violent parent or experiencing domestic violence in a 'dating' relationship were also crucial to the relative success of such programmes in changing attitudes and assisting students who were already victims (known as secondary prevention). Further, the use of multi-agency resources and the development and piloting of pupil-centred materials were key factors in the most successful projects in sustaining changes in attitudes in primary and secondary schools (Hester and Westmarland, 2005). This evaluation found that one-off initiatives such as drama workshops were far less successful in changing attitudes but could have some value in increasing students' factual knowledge about domestic violence. Further, even where projects were less successful, they did raise the awareness of teachers and highlighted the need for work on gender inequalities in intimate relationships, an issue that was often missing from the mainstream curriculum. Another in-depth evaluation study, which looked at the effectiveness of a domestic violence prevention programme delivered in schools in a run-down inner city area, also stressed the importance of taking a gendered approach to domestic violence and how this enabled pupils after the programme to understand it as 'mostly men bullying women' (Ellis *et al.*, 2006). This research also indicated that boys were more likely to change their attitudes where the delivery of the programme included a male facilitator. However, attitudes were less likely to be sustained if students only received a one-off programme as the learning needed to be reinforced in later years. This evaluation found that the programme was helpful in enabling those who were already living with domestic violence to seek help from others, as well as enabling other students to provide appropriate peer support to their friends in this situation (Ellis *et al.*, 2006).

Overall the evaluation research suggests that programmes in schools do have a value in both primary and secondary education and can be effective in producing some attitude change, if they take a gendered approach, are an ongoing part of the school curriculum and are supported by whole school policies and teacher training.

The influence of the media

At the same time it needs to be recognised that school programmes alone cannot be an overall solution to preventing gender violence. Research has indicated that media influences are a far more important factor in influencing the attitudes and behaviour of young people, particularly the behaviour of young men in this area. For example, the Zero Tolerance research discussed earlier found that young men used media representations from pornography and 'lads mags' to inform their behaviour and make sense of their experiences (Burton *et al.*, 1998a). Earlier research has indicated that most boys obtain their sex education from viewing pornography (Measor, 1996) and easy access to increasingly violent pornographic images on the internet has been fuelled by a lack of state control over internet service providers and sexually violent computer games, and the growing market in lads mags (Gillespie, 2000). Girls too may feel pressurised to view and tolerate pornographic representations and fear social rejection if they express disapproval (Burton *et al.*, 1998a). Access to pornography and violent pornography, except in its most extreme forms, has been regarded by government as a right to freedom of expression under human rights legislation in the UK (Home Office, 2005). But unless there is stronger control over this kind of easily available material, school programmes are likely to be far less effective.

Perpetrator programmes – tertiary prevention

Perpetrator programmes for violent men have proliferated in the last few years in the UK and have come to be viewed as a key means of rehabilitating domestically violent offenders within criminal justice policy (Home Office, 2003). They are also increasingly being regarded as the main method in family law policy to make violent and abusive fathers safe to have contact with children post-separation (Children and Adoption Act, 2006). In the UK until the late 1990s most but not all were run in the voluntary sector (Humphreys *et al.*, 2000). Many of these programmes included men who volunteered to participate, although they also took men who had been ordered to attend by the criminal courts. With a renewed focus by New Labour on the rehabilitation of offenders in the criminal justice system and the need to have different sentencing options for the courts, apart from the usual fine, many new probation-led programmes have been set up in local communities and the intention is to have at least one programme in each probation area in England and Wales (Home Office, 2005). Unfortunately, however, this massive growth in programmes has not been accompanied by any substantial evidence that they work for the majority of offenders who come in contact with the criminal justice or family court systems, and there is therefore a problem with regarding them as the main solution for dealing with chronic perpetrators. Alongside this is a significant concern that they may actually put women and children at further risk, since they may fuel some men's resentment about having to attend a programme. There is also a fear that they are reducing the resources available to providing refuges and other services to survivors of domestic violence. These are issues which are discussed later in this chapter.

Perpetrator behaviour and the problems facing perpetrator programmes

There are considerable difficulties in changing entrenched attitudes and behaviour for the majority of perpetrators who are chronic offenders and who, by the time they have been arrested and convicted by the criminal courts, usually have well-established careers of domestic violence (Hearn, 1998). A further part of this problem is that for most of these offenders, domestic violence is regarded as a normal way of treating women and a normal aspect of their masculine identities and thus their motivation to change is often very low (Hearn, 1998; Dobash and Dobash, 1998).

For those who have worked with groups of domestically violent men, contempt for women and the belief that women are inferior beings and exist only to service men's sexual and domestic needs are commonly expressed attitudes by programme participants (Wilson, 1996). At the same time, research with perpetrators shows that they use highly effective verbal strategies to deny and minimise the violence and deflect blame when they are confronted by professionals (Harne, 2004b; Cavanagh *et al.*, 2001; Hearn, 1998). Hearn (1998), drawing on the ground-breaking work of the US researcher Ptacek (1988), has described these strategies of accounting for their violence as 'denials', 'minimisations', 'justifications' and 'excuses' and demonstrates that it is important to understand how these strategies are used by perpetrators to diminish the seriousness of their actions.

Denial and minimisation

Offenders' strategies of denial may involve outright denial or the use of various tactics such as saying they cannot remember what happened, or denying that what they have done is 'real' violence within their own definitions. For example, it is common for such perpetrators to regard only hitting or punching someone as 'real violence' and anything else as something less, as is illustrated in the following example. *'I wasn't violent, but she used to do my head in . . . I picked her up and threw her against the wall. I've never struck a woman and I never will'* (Hearn, 1998:117).

Minimisation may include trivialising violent events as well as claiming it was reciprocal violence. Hearn has highlighted that the word 'just' is often used in the process of minimisation, as can be seen in the following example from a man convicted of multiple assaults on his partner: *'just a few little arguments, just slaps, where she's digged me and I've digged her back'* (Hearn, 1998:120).

Excuses and justifications

Justifications and excuses may be combined with partial denial and minimisation. Hearn argues that justifications involve accepting responsibility for the violence but not the blame, while excuses involve accepting blame but not responsibility. A common excuse used by perpetrators is to suggest that the violence is beyond their own control and they just cannot help losing their tempers because they have a 'short fuse', which is triggered by their partners' or children's behaviour. These accounts, however, do not hold up when it is recognised that women's experiences frequently indicate that the violence is often highly controlled and does not explain why, for most perpetrators, their short tempers are only 'triggered' by women's or children's behaviour and does not occur in other contexts.

Another familiar type of excuse is to blame alcohol for causing the violence. But again this is not substantiated by the research, which indicates that the majority of offenders are not intoxicated when they use violence, although alcohol can act to make the violence far worse (Finney, 2004). As Hearn (1998) has noted excuses are particularly hard to work with on perpetrator programmes because they allow offenders to evade responsibility for their violence and are often supported by popular psychological and medical discourses.

Excuses can also be combined with justifications because it is women who are viewed as triggering the 'explosion of violence' and therefore it is women who are to blame. As has been seen in Chapter 3, one of the most common justifications in this regard is the socially constructed idea of the 'nagging' wife. In every day terms, such a concept is used against women who argue back and who refuse to do what the perpetrator wants, as can be seen from the following example.

> What winds me up about her is that I have actually raised my voice to my other two girlfriends and once they'd seen me raise my voice – it was enough to make them shut up – it was enough to frighten them, but not this one – she pushes and pushes and I will snap and go and hit her.

> (Harne, 2004b:235)

Related to this are constructions of women partners as merely possessions. Women who assert their autonomy, who make decisions and have their own friends can all be seen as 'provoking' the offender's violence. Thus, jealousy of not only contacts or suspected contacts with other men but also any contacts with family or friends and even attention given to children can all be viewed as justifying the violence because women are not constantly focused on meeting the needs of the perpetrators themselves (Hearn, 1998; Mullender *et al.*, 2002).

Other common forms of justification include women not meeting the expectations of how they should behave as defined by perpetrators. These include not doing the housework, or not doing the housework in the correct way, not controlling the children correctly, not having the 'right' appearance (for example, being too fat, not wearing the 'right' clothes), not restricting their movements and friends (Hearn, 1998). In collective family systems women's perceived failures to act as good wives may be interpreted as bringing shame on the whole family and therefore can also be used to argue that they deserved the violence because they have not conformed to cultural codes of honour (Gill, 2004). The restrictions and boundaries on women's behaviour that may be used to justify domestic violence can vary cross-culturally, within cultures and over time. But as Hanmer (2000) has argued, the cultural restrictions on women's behaviour, although they may vary, all have in common that they are used to protect men's privileged social status, where their own behaviour is usually not questioned. Part of the problem therefore in attempting to bring about change with domestically violent offenders is about challenging their beliefs and expectations about women, which may be commonly held in wider communities and cultures of men (Connell, 2002; Walklate, 2001).

Different approaches to rehabilitating violent perpetrators

Although work and research with perpetrators as discussed above indicates that most offenders regard it as their right to control women through violence, a number of different explanations and therefore ways of trying to change violent perpetrators have developed, which do not necessarily recognise domestic violence as a gendered problem of power and control. Many of these approaches originated in the US, which has a much longer history of working with violent perpetrators. The approaches were critiqued by Adams (1988) for failing directly to address why men were being violent towards their partners and instead of regarding domestic violence as a crime, located the problem as a mental health one, in need of 'treatment'. For example, some psycho-therapeutic approaches locate the problem in unhappy childhood experiences, while social learning approaches see it merely as a problem of perpetrators learning to manage their anger. Despite these shortcomings, such approaches may still be offered to perpetrators in the UK through individual or group counselling, or referral onto anger management courses, and it is important to understand why they are ineffective.

Psycho-therapy

By locating the problem of domestic violence in some kind of psychological disorder, psycho-therapeutic approaches often feed into the commonly accepted excuses that perpetrators use to explain their violence. Psychological discourses of dependency or co-dependency, poor ego functioning, low self-esteem, insecurity, unresolved conflicts with parents, and 'emotional repression' are amongst numerous psyche discourses which serve to focus the problem away from violent men's responsibility for their violence and the benefits they gain from it. The way this type of explanation assists men to evade their responsibility is illustrated in the following interview (cited by Adams) with a client who had been in therapy for three years.

> Counselor: What do you think causes you to hit your wife?
> Client: Insecurity. I guess it goes way back . . . I've always been insecure around women.
> Counselor: This is helping me understand why you're insecure but not why you hit your wife.
> Client: Sometimes I take things the wrong way . . . I overreact I guess you could say, because of my insecurity . . .
> Counselor: A lot of people are insecure but they are not violent. What I am interested in finding out is how you make the decision to hit your wife – and to break the law – even if you are feeling insecure.
> Client: I never really thought of it that way, a decision.
>   (Adams, 1988:176)

One of the main dangers with using psycho-therapeutic approaches either in groups or in individual counselling is that they tend to reinforce the 'poor me syndrome' where violent men redefine themselves as the main 'victims' and as the ones who need help and the focus moves away from their responsibility and the impact of their violence on women and children (Harne, 2004; Hester *et al.*, 2006).

Such approaches can also be specifically woman-blaming and reinforce ideologies that women are responsible for the violence they receive.

Couple counselling

In couple counselling drawn from family systems theory, both partners are considered as equal victims and equally responsible for the violence (Adams, 1988). Thus, a woman may be regarded as contributing to the violence through various aspects of her behaviour such as 'refusing sex' and 'nagging' and she can be accorded partial responsibility for bringing her partner's violence under control. Further, although couple counselling aims to improve communication and negotiation skills between partners it implicitly supports the violence by seeing it as an 'unfortunate' outcome of the interaction process (Adams, 1988:185). Couple counselling can be particularly dangerous to women because it does not hold men responsible for their violence and can put victims at much further risk. In the US, the use of couple counselling as a method of dealing with domestic violence has largely ceased as a result of therapists being sued and held responsible for the deaths of women killed by their partners following counselling sessions (Hart, 1988). In the UK, voluntary national standards for organisations using domestic violence interventions also state that 'couples work' and 'mediation' are not an 'appropriate' response to 'men's abusive behaviour towards women' (Respect, 2004:16). Nevertheless, family systems theory, which holds that interactions between partners is the cause of violence and abuse, can still be a part of social work and mental health training and research has indicated that there are still professionals who believe that domestic violence is a product of the relationship, and not the responsibility of individual perpetrators (Hester *et al.*, 2006). The current authors have also come across practice where couple counselling is still used as a means of addressing domestic violence, without any understanding of the risks this poses to survivors.

Social learning approaches and anger management programmes
These approaches are based on the principle that since violence is learnt behaviour, it can also be unlearnt. Adams (1988) argues that, on their own, social learning approaches are limited because they allow violent men to rely on the excuse that their behaviour is a product of their social conditioning. Cognitive behavioural programmes also often known as 'anger management'

courses are based on the principles of social learning and include exercises to change thought patterns and behavioural techniques to control violent behaviour. For example, participants are encouraged to use anger logs to identify negative thoughts and feelings so that they can recognise circumstances when their violence is 'triggered' and control their reactions. These can be combined with basic behavioural techniques such as using 'time-outs' to prevent violent outbursts. In general, however, anger management courses do not recognise domestic violence as being connected to male dominance nor that it is used by perpetrators as a deliberate means of imposing their will on women in intimate relationships. They therefore feed into some of the excuses highlighted above where men may state that they 'have uncontrollable tempers'. In contrast, the experience of victims in this regard is that the violence is often highly controlled, directed towards specific parts of the body or used deliberately in front of the children, in order to humiliate women and lower their resistance. The UK voluntary national standards referred to above state that anger management courses are not appropriate ways of addressing men's domestic violence because, although they may reduce the physical violence in the short term, they do not deal with the control element, which can shift to more subtle methods of control (Respect, 2004). However, at the time of writing, both the criminal and family courts continue to mandate attendance on this type of programme.

Pro-feminist approaches

In contrast to the other approaches, the philosophical principles underlying pro-feminist programmes are to hold offenders wholly responsible for their violence. They also regard the violence as purposeful and their aim is to get perpetrators to recognise that they can make the decision not to be violent. Thus, they stress the importance of not colluding with offenders' denials, minimisations, excuses and justifications through directly confronting and challenging their rationales for their violent behaviour. As with social learning models, feminist approaches recognise that violence is socially learnt, but they also incorporate understandings of patriarchal power structures and ideologies, which reinforce individual men's beliefs about the acceptability of their violence. In practice they generally use a combination of cognitive behavioural techniques and educational approaches to directly confront behaviour and attitudes. The well-known Duluth programme typifies this approach and uses examples from the power and control wheel to challenge strategies of dominance and control and to develop men's understanding of the impacts of their violence on their partners and children. Some programmes use re-enactments of violent events for each participant in the group to get them to analyse how power and control operates. They may also get individual men to use control logs (in contrast to anger logs) or checklists of violent, intimidatory and controlling behaviour so that they can monitor their own behaviour. In the early stages of programmes the emphasis is often on stopping the physical violence. At later stages attitudes such as lack of respect for women are challenged. Programmes drawing on the Duluth model are now being widely used in the UK, this approach having been adopted for the path-finder probation-led programmes (Bilby and Hatcher, 2004).

Women's and children's safety

Most significantly pro-feminist approaches emphasise that women and children's safety must be the first priority of programmes and confidentiality is therefore not guaranteed to programme participants, since there is a clear risk of further violence and abuse. Information provided by perpetrators may therefore be given to partners and other agencies where there are indications of dangerousness or further risk. Other principles also recognise that programmes can be relatively ineffective and can put women and children's safety at further risk. For example, the Respect standards (2004) state that women need to be informed that their partners may not change and they can be at increased risk if they decide to stay with perpetrators on the basis that the programme will stop the violence. They also need to be aware that being on a programme can lead to an increase in violence and that perpetrators can use programmes as a further form of control of their partners, using language learnt on the programme to tell women they are at fault and pretending they are attending when they are not. For these reasons one of the key minimum standards is that a women's support service should be in place alongside any programme, and that the support service should be pro-active in contacting women whose partners or ex-partners are referred or mandated to attend a programme. Support services should also handle the flow of information between the programme and women partners and offer women individual safety planning sessions, including assisting them to decide whether they want to leave partners, if they are still living with them. Some women's support services also offer support and confidence building sessions for groups of survivors. Another basic principle linked to the safety of survivors is the need for ongoing monitoring of a perpetrator's behaviour to assess his level of risk whilst on the programme, which can include obtaining feedback from his partner or ex-partner if it is safe to do so. Programmes should also ensure that they are accountable to the local community and work in conjunction with other local services and agencies such as domestic violence partnerships and domestic violence fora (Respect, 2004). Although many of the principles above reflect best practice in relation to standards for perpetrator programmes, at the time of writing, these remain voluntary and apply only to organisations that are members of the Respect organisation. However, it is hoped this will be rectified in the future through the introduction of national accreditation for those running perpetrator programmes, in the voluntary sector at least.

Do perpetrator programmes work?

Despite the now widespread use of Duluth-type programmes in the UK, there remain serious questions about whether they work in stopping perpetrators' violent and controlling behaviour and whether they are more effective than other criminal justice sanctions in increasing women's and children's safety. As was highlighted in the last chapter, referral onto a perpetrator programme in the community is now being used for serious offences and can be used as an alternative to a custodial sentence, as well as for more minor offences, instead of a fine.

Effective evaluation

Assessing whether perpetrator programmes work requires effective evaluation, undertaken by external researchers, where the views of partners and ex-partners are sought and where the outcomes in terms of changes in perpetrators' behaviour are compared with other forms of criminal justice sanction. Very little of this kind of the evaluation has been undertaken in the UK and most programmes have relied on perpetrators' self-reports, which are not a reliable indication of change because many perpetrators learn to 'talk the talk' and manipulate the system (Burton *et al.*, 1998b). Alternatively, some probation-led programmes rely on re-offending rates to measure their success, but again these are not reliable, because of the low level of reporting domestic violence to the police (Harne, 2004b).

   One of the few published externally evaluated studies to date in the UK took place in Scotland (Dobash *et al.*, 1996) and looked at outcomes for women whose partners had been on Duluth-type programmes and compared them to outcomes for women whose partners received other criminal justice sanctions, mainly fines. Unfortunately, however, although this study indicated that women partners of men who had been on the programme experienced less violence than those whose partners had merely been fined, one year after the programme had ended, the numbers of women's reports were too small to be conclusive.

US evaluations of perpetrator programmes

The most effective evaluations have been undertaken in the US, where Duluth-model programmes have been running for much longer and have been more embedded within criminal justice systems in several states. One well-designed large-scale study in New York found that men who had been randomly assigned to attend 40 hours on a programme were slightly more likely to be violent, according to women partners' reports, than those randomly assigned to undertake 40 hours community service (Taylor *et al.*, 2001).

Another large-scale study which compared men from four different programmes found that only a fifth had stopped being physically violent or verbally threatening, 30 months after the programmes ended (Gondolf, 1998). Further, a meta-analysis of 40 evaluation studies found that there was 'no substantial evidence that most [perpetrator] programmes are effective or that any programmes are highly effective' (Gondolf, 2004:615).

Attendance on programmes

US research has also found that part of the problem is related to retaining violent men's attendance on the programmes and 55 per cent were found to drop out in the first two months (Gondolf, 2004). Nevertheless, one programme in Pittsburgh was far more effective in retaining attendance and in keeping perpetrators to the conditions of the programme, by making immediate imprisonment for 28 days a penalty for non-compliance (Gondolf, 1999). This finding provides significant lessons for programmes run in the UK, where breaches for non-attendance or for further violence frequently go unpunished, as was seen in the previous chapter.

A shift in tactics – partners' views

One problem with these types of evaluations is that very little detail is given of partners' views and few in-depth studies of this kind have been undertaken. One exception has been a study conducted by Gregory and Erez (2002) with 33 women whose partners had attended a programme in Ohio. The majority of these women reported that although the physical violence reduced while the men were on the programme, there was an increase in verbal abuse and threats such as threats to kill and an increase in blaming women for the violence. This was also a finding from one small-scale process evaluation undertaken in the UK (Burton *et al.*, 1998b).

Some women in the Ohio study felt that attendance had merely increased perpetrators' resentment and strategies to manipulate the system, as is reported in the following accounts

> It did not help. It was just something he had to do a couple of hours on a Saturday. It just taught him new manipulative tactics . . .

> They learn new ways. He was court-ordered, he was just playing along.

> He stated he felt it changed him, helped him control his temper. I feel it only taught him not to go beyond a certain stage because of getting into trouble with the police.

Others felt that the programme did not work because their partners were not motivated to change.

> Participation made him angrier because he never realised why he was there.
> He was not willing to change. [It] may help others, but not if they don't want to.

(Gregory and Erez, 2002:223)

Programmes as a soft option

Moreover, although almost half of the women in this study felt there had been some positive change, many expressed fears of further violence once the programme had ended. It was also felt that being referred onto a programme was not a severe enough sanction given the offences involved and that the programme was only effective when combined with the sanction of imprisonment for further violence. The following quotations indicate partners' views on what type of criminal justice sanction should be used.

> They need to be punished, not just let go with a fine. Need actual jail time to serve.

> Immediately put them in jail and don't let them have custody of their children.

> Repeat offenders should go to jail for a long time.

> Makes them think more about the consequences of their actions. [He] only went [to classes] because he could go to jail and understands if he does it again he'll go to jail.

(Gregory and Erez, 2002:224–5)

Key messages from US evaluations

These evaluations convey some important messages for the use of perpetrator programmes run in the UK where referral onto a programme is used as a criminal justice sanction.

- Programmes are more effective in keeping women safe, while partners are on the programme, if they are combined with further criminal justice sanctions, notably an automatic prison sentence if conditions are breached. The length of programme is less important than the real threat of further sanctions. This requires training for magistrates and judges in dealing with breaches as well as a review in sentencing in the UK.
- Men who tended to drop out at an early stage of the programme were

more socially excluded men, mainly from Black and minority ethnic communities, suggesting a need for specific courses for minority men from different ethnic groups, run by programme leaders from the same groups.

- Programmes tend not to work for chronic repeat offenders in keeping women and children safe, they therefore should not be used as an alternative to a custodial sentence.
- UK programmes need to be subjected to effective external evaluation, where the views of partners and ex-partners are sought – not only while the men are on the programme – but following programme completion. Only this kind of evaluation can demonstrate whether the significant investment in community programmes as a criminal justice solution is working in keeping women and children safe and in stopping perpetrators' violent and controlling behaviour.

Women's support services

One outcome of the US multi-site evaluation discussed above (Gondolf, 1999) is that despite most perpetrators' failure to change, some women felt safer and many made the decision to leave their violent partners. This can partly be accounted for by the fact that the provision of support services to women while men were on the programme gave them the space and support to make these decisions. A finding that has also been found in a small-scale evaluation study of one perpetrator programme in the UK (Burton *et al.*, 1998b).

Perpetrator programmes, violent fathers and children's safety

Earlier in this chapter it was pointed out that referral onto a programme was increasingly being regarded by the family court system as means of making violent fathers safe to have contact with their children, following separation. The Respect standards also view one of the aims of programmes as being to 'develop men's ability to have safe and appropriate contact with their children', despite also recognising that children are at greater risk of being directly abused by violent perpetrators and that children can be used as weapon of power and control against mothers (Respect, 2004:24). Very little evaluation research has been undertaken either in the US or the UK to date to assess specifically whether such programmes stop abusive parenting and are therefore improving children's safety. Nevertheless, some US evaluators have acknowledged that perpetrators often use their attendance on a programme as a means to enhance their position with the family courts in relation to access and custody applications, as well as to punish mothers and children, by pursuing contact and custody (Bennett and Williams, 2001; Rittmeester, 1993).

In the UK, Harne's (2004a) exploratory research on violent fathers attending perpetrator programmes found that although all the programmes were addressing aspects of abusive parenting, fathers' own accounts indicated little change. One of the most significant findings was violent fathers' persistent disregard of children's own fears of their violence, even though many admitted that their children were absolutely terrified of them. These fathers, while often stating that they 'loved' their children, believed their own rights to contact and ownership of their children should not take account of the fact that their children were very afraid of them. Their other reasons for wanting contact were also frequently suspect. Several fathers acknowledged that they used contact with their children to carry abusive and threatening messages to their mothers without any consideration of the impacts of such threats on the children themselves. Most also indicated that they wanted contact because the children would meet their own emotional needs, rather than giving any indication that they were prepared to prioritise children's needs and interests above their own. In addition, these fathers often acknowledged that they continued to behave abusively and threateningly towards very young children when they came for overnight or home visits and found it difficult to stop this abusive behaviour, even though many had been attending programmes for over six months or more. In this regard, in some cases, programme leaders stated that they had had to write reports, when asked by the family courts, stating that violent fathers attending their programmes were not safe to see their children.

Lessons for children's safety

As with the US research, the above UK study indicated that fathers could often use attendance on a programme as a means to pursue contact in a way that was unsafe for mothers and their children. It therefore becomes far more urgent that those providing programmes recognise children's real fears of violent parents and the serious risks posed to children during contact visits. They also need to aknowledge that violent fathers may never change enough for contact visits to be safe. On the other hand, as seen above, experienced programme workers can usefully contribute to safety or risk assessments to inform decisions being made on child contact by professionals, both prior to, during and after programme attendance. This is because such workers often have a good understanding of the tactics such perpetrators use to deny and minimise their own violence and abuse, and deflect blame onto mothers and present themselves as good parents (Harne, 2004b; Radford, L. *et al.*, 2006).

Such risk assessments need to take account of the following factors.

- The likelihood that the children will be very afraid of their violent fathers, through observing either directly or indirectly, physical and/ or sexual violence, intimidation and threats against their mothers, including threats to kill, and emotional abuse and humiliation of their mothers, as well as being directly abused themselves.
- Past abusive parenting practices by perpetrators and the likelihood that such abusive and neglectful parenting will continue during contact visits. (These considerations need to consider not just any direct physical or sexual abuse of children, but also acts of mental cruelty towards children and how far children are directly subjected to threats, intimidation, humiliation and extreme control by violent fathers, and how far they attempt to undermine mothers' parenting to the children (see Chapter 2).
- Violent fathers' reasons for wanting contact, including how far they demonstrate that they are able to consider children's own fears and feelings about their violence and their willingness and capacity to prioritise children's own needs and interests above their own.
- Violent fathers' shifting of blame onto mothers and children, for example in relation to children's fears of them and denial and minimisation of their own violence and abusive parenting practices (Bancroft and Silverman, 2002; Harne, 2004a,b; Radford, L. *et al.*, 2006).

Other initiatives in relation to perpetrator programme work and children's safety include undertaking risk and safety assessments when perpetrator referrals are made by social services, usually when violent fathers are still living with the family (Radford, L. *et al.*, 2006). Finally, if perpetrator programmes are to be able to adequately address children's safety, any effective monitoring and evaluation needs to address specifically this aspect of their work, including seeking children's views, either directly or indirectly, as well as taking mothers' views on their (ex-)partners' parenting into account.

Conclusions

In conclusion, a number of problematic aspects of perpetrator programmes have been highlighted, particularly in relation to how effective they are in practice as a criminal justice solution to addressing the problem of domestic violence. While some improvements can be made in terms of their operation to increase women and children's safety, particularly by using them in combination with more severe sanctions, they are not a panacea as has been noted by others (Dobash *et al.*, 2000). Further, in the view of some survivors they are a soft option, which neither provides adequate punishment for the violence they have experienced, nor protects them from further violence.

In contrast to the criminal justice approach, it has been argued that voluntary attendance and earlier referral onto programmes before violent perpetrators enter the criminal justice system would produce more success in achieving change (Hester *et al.*, 2006). Nevertheless, there is little evidence to date that indicates this latter approach is more successful – with US research, suggesting that volunteers on programmes,[1] are far more likely to drop out early on than those who have been mandated by the criminal courts, since there are no sanctions to keep them in attendance (Gondolf, 2004). Further, research on attendance on perpetrator programmes to change violent fathers and increase children's safety has been at the time of writing only exploratory, with little evidence of any real change (Harne, 2004b). More recent initiatives in this area need to be externally evaluated to see if they are making any real difference in safeguarding children, or are merely prolonging abusive parenting relationships.

Notes

1   Perpetrators volunteering to attend programmes are often motivated by threats from partners that they will leave them unless they change their behaviour. When women remain, there is often no further motivation for them to attend.

References

Adams, D. (1988) 'Treatment models of men who batter: a pro-feminist analysis', in K. Yllo and M. Bograd (eds) *Feminist Perspectives on Wife Abuse*. Newbury Park, CA: Sage.

Bancroft, L. and Silverman, J.G. (2002) *The Batterer as Parent: Addressing the Impact of Domestic Violence on Family Dynamics*. Thousand Oaks, CA: Sage.

Bennett, L. and Williams, O. (2001) *Controversies and Recent Studies of Batterer Intervention Program Effectiveness*. www.vawnet.org/domesticviolence/research/vaw

Bilby, C. and Hatchet, R. (2004) Early stages in the development of the Integrated Domestic Abuse Programme (IDAP): Implementing the Duluth Domestic Violence Pathfinder. Home Office Online Report. www.homeoffice.gov.uk/rds/pdf504.

Burton, S., Regan, L. and Kelly, L. (1998b) *Supporting Women and Challenging Men: Lessons from the Domestic Violence Intervention Project*. Bristol: The Policy Press.

Burton, S., Kitzinger, J., Kelly, L. and Regan, L. (1998a) *Young People's Attitudes towards Sexual Violence, Sex and Relationships. A Survey and Focus Group Study.* Edinburgh Zero Tolerance Trust.

Cavanagh, K., Dobash, R.E., Dobash, R.P. and Lewis, R. (2001) 'Remedial work: men's strategic responses to their violence against intimate female partners', *Sociology*, 35 (3): 695–714.

Connell, R.W. (2002) 'On hegemonic masculinity and violence: response to Jefferson and Hall', *Theoretical Criminology*, 16 (1): 89–99.

Connelly, J. (1995) 'Boys will be boys? Racism, sexuality and the construction of masculine identities among infant boys', in J. Holland, B. Blair and S. Sheldon (eds) *Debates and Issues in Feminist Research and Pedagogy*. Cleveland: Multilingual Matters and Open University.

Dobash, R.E. and Dobash, R.P. (1998) 'Violent men and violent contexts', in R.E. Dobash and R.P. Dobash (eds) *Rethinking Violence Against Women*. London: Sage.

Dobash, R.P., Dobash, R.E., Cavanagh, K. and Lewis, R. (1996) *Research Evaluation of Programmes for Violent Men*. Edinburgh: The Scottish Office.

Dobash, R.P., Dobash, R.E., Cavanagh, K. and Lewis, R. (2000) 'Confronting violent men', in J. Hanmer and C. Itzen, *Home Truths about Domestic Violence*. London: Routledge.

Ellis, J. (2004) *Preventing Violence against Women and Girls: a study of educational programmes for children and young people*. London: Womankind Worldwide.

Ellis, J., Stanley, N. and Bell, J. (2006) 'Prevention Programmes for Children and Young People', in C. Humphreys and N. Stanley (eds) *Domestic Violence and Child Protection: Directions for Good Practice*. London: Jessica Kingsley Publishers.

Finney, A. (2004) *Alcohol and intimate partner violence: key findings from the research.* London: Home Office.

Gill, A. (2004) 'Voicing the silent fear: South Asian Women's Experiences of Domestic Violence', *The Howard Journal*, 43:5.

Gillan, E. and Samson, E. (2000) 'The Zero Tolerance Campaigns', in J. Hanmer and C. Itzen (eds) *Home Truths about Domestic Violence*. London: Routledge.

Gillespie, T. (2000) 'Virtual violence? Pornography and violence against women in the internet', in J. Radford, M. Friedberg and L. Harne (eds) *Women, violence and strategies for action*. Buckingham: Open University Press.

Gondolf, E. (1998) *A 30-month Follow-up of Court-referred Batterers in Four Cities.* Durham, DA: Paper presented at Program Evaluation and Family Research: An International Conference.

Gondolf, E. (1999) 'A comparison of four batterer intervention systems: do court referral, program length and services matter?', *Journal of Interpersonal Violence*, 14:41–61.

Gondolf (2004) 'Evaluating batterer counseling programs: a difficult task showing some effects and implications,' *Aggression and Violent Behavior.* 9: 605–631.

Gregory, C. and Erez, E. (2002) 'The Effects of Batterer Intervention Programs: the battered women's perspective,' *Violence against Women*, 8: 206–236.

Hanmer, J. (2000) 'Domestic violence and gender relations: contexts and connections', in J. Hanmer and C. Itzen, *Home Truths about Domestic Violence*. London: Routledge.

Harne, L. (2000) 'Sexual violence and the school curriculum', in J. Radford, M. Friedberg and L. Harne (eds) *Women, Violence and Strategies for Action*. Buckingham: Open University Press.

Harne, L. (2004a) 'Violent fathers: Good enough Parents?' *Safe, the domestic abuse quarterly*, 9: 19–21.

Harne, L. (2004b) Violence, power and the meanings of fatherhood in issues of child contact. Ph.d thesis. Bristol: Bristol University.

Hart, B. (1988) 'Beyond the "duty to warn": a therapist's "duty to protect" battered women and children', in J.C. Campbell (ed.) *Assessing Dangerousness: Violence by Sexual Offenders, Batterers, and Child Abusers*. Newbury Park, CA: Sage.

Hearn, J. (1998) *The Violences of Men: How Men Talk about and How Agencies Respond to Men's Violence to Women*. London: Sage.

Hester, M. and Westmarland, N. (2005) *Tackling Domestic Violence: effective interventions and approaches*. Home Office Study 290. London: Home Office.

Hester, M., Westmarland, N., Gangoli, G., Wilkinson, M., O'Kelly, C., Kent, A. and Diamond, A. (2006) *Domestic Violence Perpetrators: Identifying Needs to Inform Early Intervention*. Bristol: University of Bristol in association with Northern Rock Foundation and the Home Office.

Home Office (2003) *Safety and Justice: the government's proposals on domestic violence*. London: Home Office.

Home Office (2005) *Domestic Violence: a national report*. London: Home Office.

Humphreys, C., Hester, M., Hague, G., Mullender, A., Abrahams, H. and Lowe, P. (2000) *From Good Intentions to Good Practice: Working with Families where there is Domestic Violence*. Bristol: Policy Press.

Measor, L., Tiffin, C. and Fry, K. (1996) 'Gender and sex education: a study of adolescent responses', *Gender and Education*, 8 (3):275–88.

Metropolitan Police (2005) www.metpolice.uk/campaigns/2005

Mullender, A., Hague, G., Imam, U., Kelly, L., Malos, E. and Regan, L. (2002) *Children's Perspectives on Domestic Violence*. London: Sage.

NSPCC (2005) *Teen Abuse Survey of Great Britain 2005*. www.nspcc.org.uk/home/informationresources/pateensurvey.htm

Ptacek, J. (1988) 'Why do men batter their wives?' in K. Yllo and M. Bograd (eds) *Feminist Perspectives on Wife Abuse*. London: Sage.

Radford, L., Blacklock, N. and Iwi, K. (2006) 'Domestic Abuse Risk Assessment and Safety Planning in Child Protection – Assessing Perpetrators', in C. Humphreys and N. Stanley (eds) *Domestic Violence and Child Protection: Directions for Good Practice*. London: Jessica Kingsley Publishers.

Respect (2004) *Statement of Principles and Minimum Standards of Practice*. London: Respect.

Rittmeester, T. (1993) 'Batterers' programs, battered women's movement and issues of accountability', in E. Pence and M. Paymar, (eds) *Education Groups for Men who Batter*. New York: Springer.

Taylor, B.G., Davis, R.C. and Maxell, C.D. (2001) 'The effect of a group batterer treatment programme in Brooklyn', *Justice Quarterly*, 18:170–201.

Walklate, S. (2001) *Gender, Crime and Criminal Justice*. Devon: Willan Publishers.

Wilson, M. (1996) 'Working with the Change men's programme', in K. Cavanagh and V.E. Gree (eds) *Working with Men: Feminism and Social Work*. London: Routledge.

6 Community responses to domestic violence

This chapter explores community responses to domestic violence, beginning with a brief look back into history before moving on to examine the responses stemming from the Women's Liberation Movement in the 1970s, with a specific focus on the work of Women's Aid. Still moving forward historically, the chapter then reviews the shift towards multi-agency and partnership working, initiated in the late 1980s, developed through the 1990s and into the new millennium, looking at whether this has improved local practice and thereby increased the safety of women and children.

Customary community responses

As noted earlier, domestic violence is not a new issue and community resistance against the extremes of 'wife-battering' took place in the form of public rituals such as pot-banging and chanting to try to shame husbands who brutalized women in the 17th and 18th centuries. In Nottinghamshire, for example, it was referred to as 'Ran Tanning', as illustrated in the popular rhyme.

> With a ran tan tan
> This man has been beating his good woman
> For What and Why?
> For eating so much when she was hungry
> And drinking so much when dry
> With a ran tan tan
> Set on fire.
>   (Anon, undated)

These forms of public shaming did not, however, challenge men's patriarchal authority or override their common law right to moderately 'chastise' wives, but only addressed the most severe violence against women (Dobash and Dobash, 1992).

Suffrage struggles

Although feminist campaigning for legal reform to address domestic violence began in the 19th century, the early 20th century saw feminist activism against domestic and sexual violence led by militant women in the suffrage movement, such as those in the Women's Freedom League. In the years between 1908 and 1918, feminists staged political protests in the courts for handing out derisory sentences for domestic violence, rape and sexual assault against women and girls. However, by the early 1930s this feminist movement had all but disappeared, and with it the issue of domestic violence once again became hidden (Jeffreys, 1985; Radford, 1987).

Women's Aid[1]

Origins

It was 60 years later, with the rise of the Women's Liberation Movement (WLM) in the 1970s that feminist attention returned to the issue of violence against women. At this time feminist voices were loud, angry and oppositional, as reflected in their numerous protests including pickets of courtrooms and the Home Office. 'Reclaim the Night' marches were organised in many towns by the activist group Women Against Violence Against Women, to protest both against men's violence and the failings of the police and criminal justice system, understood as complicity by the state in men's use of violence in the social control of women and children (rhodes and McNeill, 1985). Feminist press releases were often picked up by sympathetic journalists and supported by women MPs, which helped secure wider media and political attention, not just to the protests themselves but also to the problem of violence against women.

Against this context, from the early 1970s onwards, in the absence of any response to domestic violence by government or any state services, women's groups, women's centres and individual women began providing practical support, assistance and protection to women experiencing domestic violence (Malos, 2000). This took many forms, from minding each others' children, taking and collecting women from hospitals, staying overnight in each others' homes to provide protection and responding to women too scared to return to their homes. In respect of the latter, women's groups in many towns began squatting empty properties to provide safe houses for women and children fearing violence. In this informal way the Women's Aid Refuge movement was born (Hanmer, 2003).

Dobash and Dobash (1992) described it as 'one of the most important social movements of our time', which addressed:

> deeply held cultural beliefs, entrenched patterns of response and the struggle to move away from supporting male violence towards its rejection. It is a story that is at once personal and institutional, local and international, depressing and inspirational.
>
> (Dobash and Dobash, 1992:1)

By 1972 there were about six refuges in the UK, and three years later the number had increased to 38. These early refuges were located in squatted properties, run by volunteers and the residents themselves on shoe-string budgets. In 1975 the first national Women's Aid conference saw the formation of the first Women's Aid Network, which committed itself explicitly to the feminist principles of collectivism, mutual support and self-help. The same year saw the first Women's Aid pamphlet 'Battered Women Need Refuges', written incidentally in five different type faces, reflecting both the limited technology of the period and the very limited resources of Women's Aid.

As a consequence of this awareness raising work, a Parliamentary Select Committee on Violence in Marriage was established. In writing a submission to this Committee, Women's Aid made its first and very strategic intervention into policy development. In this way, what for so long had been perceived as a private trouble was transformed into a political issue, reflecting the Women's Liberation belief that the 'personal is political'. When the Parliamentary Select Committee reported later in 1975, it recognised the valuable work of Women's Aid in highlighting the previously 'hidden plight of the brave and desperate women, trapped in degrading and often life-threatening relationships through economic and sometimes emotional dependency on violent partners' (Parliamentary Select Committee, 1975:59). It accepted Women's Aid's argument that the major reasons why women were trapped in these relationships were: lack of independent income; lack of alternative housing; punitive state policies and practices; the negative attitudes of social services which held women responsible for the violence their husbands/partners inflicted on them; and the unequal power relations between men and women both in the family and wider society. The Select Committee concluded by recognising the need for refuges, recommending the establishment of at least one refuge per 10,000 households, a target which still has not been realised, despite the rapid growth in Women's Aid refuges through the 1970s, 1980s and 1990s (Hague and Malos, 2005).

Women's Aid was initially organised along WLM principles of collective responsibility with no leaders or 'stars'. The initial network was reorganised into the four UK Women's Aid Federations[2] of the present day. The Federations worked from grass roots upwards, rather than being centralised, with national offices playing liaison rather than leadership roles. All decisions whether in the refuges or at national conferences involved everyone, residents, volunteers and workers (Hague *et al.*, 2000). Children's meetings provided the opportunity for peer support as well as being a forum for children's voices and opinions to be heard and respected within the refuge. Hague *et al.* (2000) note, for example, that in one refuge their anti-smoking policy came directly from a children's meeting, illustrating how the women residents 'had to challenge their own ideas about the importance of children' (Hague *et al.* 2000:120).

Over the years, changes in structure and organisation of refuges occurred to keep pace with wider social and political change, although some like the Middlesbrough refuge held on to their collective structure until well into the 1990s. From the mid-1980s, the appointment of paid workers led to the development of new structures, with most refuges opting initially for management groups or steering committees, workers collectives and volunteers. However, as albeit very limited funding became available from mainstream statutory and local government sources, funding bodies began imposing conditions which forced many refuges into more traditional hierarchal structures.

The roles of Women's Aid refuges

The initial role of the refuges was to provide temporary, emergency accommodation for women and children fleeing domestic violence on request; this latter element being in contrast to the strict eligibility requirements characteristic of state welfare services. Refuges operated an open door policy which, in the early days, often led to their being overcrowded; although as the network of refuges grew, women could be referred on to other refuges when the local one was full. For some women security and safety concerns made referral out of area the preferred option. Unlike the more 'professional' shelter movement in the USA, the Women's Aid movement never placed limits on the length of time women could stay at the refuge or the number of times they could return.

The length of time women stayed at the refuge varied around the country, determined by the availability of alternative accommodation, which depended in part on the local housing situation and the extent to which the different Local Authority Housing Departments recognised women fleeing domestic violence as being in priority need. In areas like London, where pressures on housing were very high, the length of stay tended to be considerably longer than in areas of falling population, like Cleveland in the North East of England, for example.

Some women, partly as a consequence of the wait for alternative accommodation, chose to return to live with violent partners, hoping perhaps that their time away had given the perpetrator time to think about and change their behaviour. While this might be perceived as a negative choice, refuges always made it clear women could come back to the refuge when necessary. Longer-term studies showed that while women may return on several occasions, most eventually left the violent partner. Cleveland Refuge and Aid for Women and Children (CRAWC, 1985) found that 50 per cent of women who used their service never returned to the violent partner; of those who did return, only 20 per cent were still living with them two years later and they described themselves as 'unenthusiastic about their married lives' (CRAWC, 1988:32). Binney (1981) found that 14 per cent of women returned to violent partners but only 11 per cent were still with them at the time of the second interview, conducted 12–18 months after they left the refuge.

Although the provision of safe accommodation was a primary aim of the refuge movement, the service provided was much more than this. Refuges also offered a safe place where women and children could share experiences and gain support from others in similar situations as well as advice and support from workers and volunteers, reflecting the principle of mutual self-help. Sharing experiences helped women realise they were not alone and that domestic violence was a social issue rather than an individual problem. This awareness often helped women to deal with the guilt often experienced for breaking up the family home by moving to the refuge, or in countering perpetrator claims that the women were somehow to blame for the violence (Dobash and Dobash, 1992).

Underpinning the support provided for women fleeing domestic violence were the fundamental principles of Women's Aid: that is, that women had the right to be believed when they spoke of their experiences of violence; that they had a right to protection; and the right to live independently and be free from the threat of violence. Looking back at the early years, Hague *et al.*, noted that as a consequence of these principles:

> All the early groups had to struggle with invisibility, hostility, lack of interest or judgmental, woman-blaming attitudes on a level which is scarcely credible today (although these struggles do, of course, still occur).
>
> (Hague *et al.*, 2000:116)

In addition to providing support and promoting mutual self-help, refuge workers and volunteers also provided specialist advice in respect of subsequent problems, for example in making applications for state benefits and advice in respect of accessing the various legal options, for example seeking civil law injunctions or reporting to the police and accessing the criminal justice system, as well as registering with sympathetic doctors and new schools for the children, as necessary. This latter task was not an easy one as it often entailed educating teachers about the impact of domestic violence and safety issues associated with the collection of children from school (CRAWC, 1988).

Given that children consistently outnumbered women as refuge residents, Women's Aid was always aware that children, like their mothers, required escape from the violence. So from the outset, many refuges like Middlesbrough, for example, provided play and homework space for the children and organised activities for them, both after school and during holidays. This provision was informed by anti-sexist and anti-racist childcare principles and consistent with their anti-violence ethos, many refuges promoted 'no-smacking' and anti-bullying policies (Cleveland Refuge and Aid for Women and Children, 1988). As funding was secured for work with children in the 1980s, often from short-term grants from the BBC's Children in Need Appeal, refuges employed specialist children's workers. They worked with the children using creative play therapies to help them come to terms with the violence. Combating racism as well as violence was further developed by children's workers who used and developed anti-racist teaching materials, books and toys as they attempted to build a committed anti-racist child-work practice (Hague *et al.*, 2000).

In larger towns and cities like London, with significant minority ethnic communities, specialist black and Asian refuges were developed, which additionally provided support and solidarity in respect to racism, which sometimes became an issue in general refuges, for example over different cultural practices in relation to food, languages, childcare or faith issues (Mama, 1996).

Outreach services

In the 1980s Women's Aid refuges began to provide outreach services. These included providing legal advice and advocacy to women who did not want to or could not enter refuges, with some providing telephone helplines or drop-in centres. Outreach services also offered resettlement support for women who had left refuges and had been rehoused to help overcome problems of isolation, poverty and hardship, and some facilitated self-help groups amongst former residents, and indeed former residents of refuges who were concerned to 'give something back' were often welcomed back as volunteers or refuge workers (Kelly and Humphreys, 2000). By the turn of the century it was found that 77 per cent of refuges in England and 88 per cent in Scotland, Wales and Northern Ireland provided outreach services, although many of these services were not specifically funded (Humphreys *et al.*, 2000). Outreach services now provide an invaluable form of flexible support to individual women and children in local communities who do not use refuge provision, including women from 'hard to reach' groups. Many also provide resettlement services for ex-residents of refuges, which can include leisure activities for women and children, confidence building groups and ongoing individual support and advocacy.

Awareness raising and campaigning

As well as providing safe accommodation for women and children escaping domestic violence and support in resettlement into new lives, Women's Aid retained its political agenda and continued to engage in public education and awareness raising and challenged male violence and state policies, practice and legal judgments that condoned or excused that violence. A key theme here was campaigning for changes to policy and practice in relation to police, legal and welfare responses to domestic violence (Hague and Malos, 2005).

Although the Women's Aid refuge movement has had considerable success in supporting women and children escape violent relationships, it has confronted and survived a series of difficult issues and challenges over the years. Like many services within the women's voluntary sector, Women's Aid accepted funding from a range of statutory and charitable agencies. Such funding was not 'without strings' and in consequence Women's Aid had to adapt its structure, which often resulted in struggles to retain its independence and hold on to its women-centred ethos. Funding, however, has been a continuing problem and despite the various funding regimes over the years, Women's Aid services have survived on insufficient and insecure short-term grants, which has made continual searching for and writing applications for funding a necessary task for refuges. Thus, although the quality of accommodation is much improved in comparison to the squatted refuges of the 1970s, and these days women with their children will, at a minimum, have their own family room, purpose-built refuges with separate rooms for the children and adequate access for women and/or children with physical impairments is only available in some areas (Hague and Malos, 2005). Nowadays some refuges have one ground floor room adapted for use by physically disabled women but, in general, accessibility still remains a problem (Radford *et al.*, 2005).

Security has been another continuing concern for refuges and serious efforts have always been made to keep their location or address secret in order to protect the residents. However, given the thousands of women who have used refuge services and the number of taxi-drivers, police officers and tradespersons whose business takes them to refuges, total secrecy has never been possible. As a consequence it was not unusual for angry husbands or partners to turn up on refuge doorsteps, and dealing with such disturbances also became a part of refuge life. While these days most refuges can call for police protection, in earlier years such protection depended largely on the attitudes of individual officers. Sadly, over the years there have been a few tragedies in which women were killed while living at a refuge; for example, in 1985 Balwant Kaur was murdered by her husband in Brent Asian Women's Refuge (Southall Black Sisters, 1990). Although this tragedy was aggravated by careless press publicity, which required the immediate evacuation of the refuge, fortunately such incidents have been rare, itself a testament to the trust and loyalty of refuge residents and workers, which have made refuges safe for over 30 years.

Another challenge faced by refuges, as reflected in one of their more controversial policies, relates to teenage sons of women seeking escape from domestic violence. Women's Aid recognises that the presence of teenage boys and young men can create difficulties in women-only refuges and while each refuge has its own policy, all have an upper age limit for sons, usually between 14 and 16 years. While some mothers are able to make arrangements for their older sons to stay with friends or other family members, some may find themselves in the unfortunate position of not being able to stay in a refuge. This is, of course, regretted but refuges have to balance the needs of all residents and given the unease the presence of young men could generate, particularly for younger residents, hard decisions have to be made. This need to protect the well-being of all residents also means that refuges cannot accommodate some women presenting with multiple problems, for example women with drugs problems who are not on treatment programmes can pose risks to other women and children, and could expose the refuges to prosecution for allowing illegal drugs to be used. Without specialist staff some women with serious mental health issues are hard to accommodate, although there are some, but not enough, specialist refuges which cater for this group of women.

Women's Aid today

Women's Aid is now over 30 years old and remains 'the domestic violence charity' in the UK in terms of its scope, comprehensiveness, expertise and experience, despite the fact that there are now other statutory and local government agencies that have a remit to work on this issue. In light of their history of opposition and struggle, it is perhaps somewhat ironic that government, recognising their expertise, required professionals new to the issue to learn and take a lead from Women's Aid in relation to domestic violence in service provision and multi-agency approaches.

Women's Aid continues to operate the federated structure with national offices in England, Wales, Scotland and Northern Ireland. Women's Aid Federation of England currently provides support for over 500 refuges and other domestic and sexual violence services in England; Scottish Women's Aid supports 46 refuges; Welsh Women's Aid supports 35 agencies and Women's Aid Federation, Northern Ireland supports 11 refuges and related services. Each of the federations maintain comprehensive websites which detail their services and readers are encouraged to visit these websites for up-to-the-minute information about their services, detailed legal information, current campaigns and statistics about service users. Women's Aid Federation of England, for example, at the time of writing reported that they provide help and support for over 320,000 women and children each year (Women's Aid, 2006).

Women's Aid continues to advocate on behalf of survivors of domestic violence and to ensure their safety through the three 'P's: protection (by influencing policy and practice in respect of domestic violence); prevention (through raising awareness and developing education programmes); and provision of services needed to help women and children escaping domestic violence, including the UK-wide network of refuges and outreach services and the National Domestic Violence Helpline, which they support together with Refuge, another domestic violence agency. The current aims of Women's Aid Federation of England are listed below:

Aims of Women's Aid Federation of England

- Empower women who have been affected by domestic violence
- Meet the needs of children affected by domestic violence
- Provide services run by women, based on listening to survivors
- Challenge the disadvantages which result from domestic violence
- Support and reflect diversity and promote equality of opportunity
- Promote cohesive inter-agency responses to domestic violence and develop partnerships

(Women's Aid, 2006)

Despite this, funding for refuges and related outreach services continues to be inadequate to meet the demand for these services.[3] Further, many refuges still struggle to get funding year on year and funding for children's workers remains a problem in many areas. Another problematic development is that some organisations outside of the Women's Aid movement are gaining funding to set up their own refuge services, and this means that the basic principles of empowerment and support to survivors is being undermined (Hague and Malos, 2005).

Multi-agency responses

As shown above, the current aims of Women's Aid include promoting inter-agency responses to domestic violence which, as explored below, was heralded by government in the 1990s as the way forward in respect of domestic violence and a range of other 'social crime' problems (Home Office, 60/1990). The need for co-ordinated multi-agency approaches are, in some ways, obvious since no one service can meet all the needs of survivors (James-Hanman, 2000). In the late 1980s research showed women on average were having to make between five and twelve contacts with different services in order to get the help they required. In many cases this was because they received unhelpful responses or were just referred on to yet another agency (Binney *et al.*, 1985). However, multi-agency approaches are not without problems and some organisations including Southall Black Sisters have been highly critical of them because they can represent a false consensus and have not resulted in real changes in improving safety for survivors (Gupta, 2003). These issues are discussed in more detail below.

The origins of multi-agency working in the UK

Interestingly, it can be argued that multi-agency approaches were initially pioneered by Women's Aid and other women's voluntary sector organisations in the 1980s (Malos, 2000). For example, in setting up their management committees or steering groups, many Women's Aid groups recruited feminists from a range of strategic locations, including feminist lawyers, doctors and local government housing officers because of the valuable expertise they could offer in terms of knowledge of the workings of these services. This 'networking' proved invaluable both in promoting the welfare of their clients and the smooth running of the organisation.

Local refuges were also 'by necessity' engaging and challenging the police and other local services to improve their responses to survivors of domestic violence during this period. In the late 1980s women's committees and women in equalities units in some local authorities also began to take up the issue of domestic violence and began to organise local conferences to raise awareness and to develop co-ordination between services (Malos, 2000). Feminists were also influenced by the model which had been developed in Duluth in the US (Pence and McDonnell, 2000) where different agencies had developed and co-ordinated consistent reponses to domestic violence, which resulted in a considerable reduction in repeat offences as well as a reduction in the number of domestic violence murders (James-Hanman, 2000)

The other strand for developing multi-agency approaches came from the criminal justice system, with the Metropolitan Police in London arguing for such an approach in the mid-1980s (Patel, 2003). By the 1990s multi- or inter-agency working had been taken up by the Home Office and seen as a solution to reducing not only the crime of domestic violence but, as seen above, a solution to reducing crime in other areas. This, in turn, translated into Domestic Violence Forums being set up in many local areas, bringing statutory and voluntary services together in meetings to discuss strategies of co-ordination. Since then renewed impetus has been given to local partnership working to reduce domestic violence through the Crime and Disorder Act (1998) and further Home Office guidance on the importance of multi-agency approaches (Home Office, 1999).

Multi-agency and inter-agency approaches to domestic violence

In the absence of any comprehensive strategy for addressing crime reduction generally and domestic violence specifically, multi-agency, inter-agency and partnership working[4] have become the buzzwords of recent times. These approaches are presented as ground-breaking ways to turn policy or 'joined-up thinking' into best practice. Their appeal stems from the recognition that domestic violence is a multi-dimensional and complex problem, in terms of its nature and impacts, and as a consequence effective responses require the engagement of a range of agencies. As has been seen earlier, in terms of dealing with its impacts, survivors may need to contact a wide range of agencies in relation to the different aspects of their situations, including: Women's Aid; police; solicitors; family and civil court services; health services; the benefits agency; the local authority housing department; children's services; schools; and, possibly, a counselling service. To engage with so many agencies is a massive task for a survivor in the aftermath of traumatic domestic violence experiences. It requires significant energy and organisation in terms of making and travelling to keep all the appointments, dealing with the inevitable waiting times and balancing all this around school hours, childcare or taking younger children with her. In recognition of this, in introducing the multi-agency approach, Paul Boateng, as a Home Office Minister, stated:

> No one agency on its own can address the full range of problems created by domestic violence. To tackle domestic violence effectively, to reduce its incidence and to help its survivors, all the interested parties must come together to play their role.
>
> (Home Office, 1999)

This argument presented multi- or inter-agency working as an obvious good idea. But the reality was more complex because in the 1990s and still to a large extent today, the different agencies had very different levels of awareness and discourses or understanding of domestic violence. For example, policing policy in the 1990s had come to recognise domestic violence as serious violent crime, a human rights abuse and a criminal justice issue. In contrast, social services understood the problem within a familial welfare framework. The health services were dominated by a medical model, seeing domestic violence in relation to health and illness, inclusive of mental as well as physical health.

This plurality of discourses produced some quite fundamental contradictions that were more far-reaching than academic quibbles in multi-agency Domestic Violence Forums. For example, the police and criminal justice perspectives made clear distinctions between perpetrators and victims, with an onus to collect evidence against and prosecute offenders through the justice system, while protecting the victims from further harm. Holding perpetrators accountable for their criminal violence and protecting the victims and survivors, while consistent with a feminist and Women's Aid approach, stood in contradiction with the familial approach of social services.

Social services retained a model which rather than holding perpetrators accountable for their violence identified the problem in the dynamics of the family and particularly with women, who were deemed primarily responsible for the emotional well-being of the family, resulting in a victim blame perspective, in direct contradiction to the justice model. This 'family saving' discourse required 'work' with family members, namely the adults, through couple counselling or family therapy (see previous chapter). So, far from offering protection to victims from perpetrators, the welfare perspective involved bringing them together to work through the 'family' problem.[5] Rather than confronting this denial of protection, in this perspective the concept of domestic violence was minimised and held that woman must take some responsibility for the violence, a concept that has subsequently been favoured by the family courts responsible for civil orders. In this way a major tension resurfaced in the legal system between the justice and welfare perspectives in respect of understandings of domestic violence.

Other problems surfaced in defining the causes of domestic violence and in recognising it as overwhelmingly a gendered problem of men's violence towards women (James-Hanman, 2000). Although many forums eventually came to an understanding of the gendered nature of domestic violence in the 1990s, the promotion of a gendered neutral approach is an issue which continues to resurface (Malos, 2000; Hague and Malos, 2005).

Other tensions have surfaced in the shift to multi- or inter-agency working which reflect the power differential between some statutory and voluntary sector agencies. This issue was raised directly by Women's Aid in a statement that supports the multi-agency approach but with the key qualification that the central role accorded to them in consequence of their expertise and experience of working to combat domestic violence since the 1970s should be respected in practice:

> A co-ordinated multi-agency approach is needed at all levels of government (local and national) involving all key criminal justice and social welfare agencies. Independent women's advocacy and refuge organisations must be involved centrally in reviewing the law and planning and delivering services.
>
> (Women's Aid, 1998)

When the idea for partnership working was first mooted in the late 1980s, and was reflected in the Home Office guidance to the police to work in partnership with other relevant agencies, this essentially led the police to get involved with Women's Aid and in some areas support advocacy services provided by

Black women's groups, such as Southall Black Sisters, as these were the sole agencies who were working on domestic violence at the time. This shift brought together a very unlikely partnership, given Women's Aid's roots in feminism and their strident criticisms of government and police failings in respect of domestic violence. While this policy reflected a transformation of Home Office and subsequently police policy and practice in respect of domestic violence, the requirement that the police work collaboratively with strident critics from the women's movement was viewed with suspicion and scepticism by both the police and feminists. At one level this policy shift clearly represented a major success for feminist campaigns on domestic violence, as domestic violence was now recognised as serious violent crime, but there were also real concerns from Black and minority ethnic women's organisations stemming from the social control role of the police and, at that time, their limited understanding and experience of domestic violence (Gupta, 2003). Southall Black Sisters, for example, found that although they supported the idea of multi-agency working, in practice they were prevented from criticising the police or holding them accountable when the police failed to implement their own pro-arrest policies, and when breaches of confidentiality occurred which put individual women at further risk (Patel, 2003).

Despite these concerns, many women's voluntary sector agencies working in this area gave a partial welcome to multi-agency approaches and co-operated, reserving judgement until its practical impact on the lives of women and children could be assessed. Without doubt, there were reciprocated concerns on the part of the statutory agencies, including the police. These may explain the slow and reluctant implementation during the 1990s as revealed in Home Office studies, which identified some positive changes while highlighting the limited, partial and patchy implementation of policing policies and problems in terms of lack of leadership and positive management, as well as in the attitudes of individual officers, (Grace, 1995; Plotnikoff and Woolfson, 1998). The 1990s experience led to the Home Office issuing a stronger and more detailed revised circular in 1999.

As a whole, the research on effectiveness of Domestic Violence Forums during the mid-1990s found that practice varied widely with some remaining merely talking shops or information and network exchanges and others taking responsibility for monitoring local provision and initiating and transforming services in their local areas. Best practice included identifying and filling the gaps in provision, initiating preventative work including public awareness campaigns and preventative work in schools, and monitoring perpetrator programmes. But in some forums conflict and distrust between agencies was rife. Women's Aid and Black and minority ethnic women's organisations were marginalised and forums were dominated by the perspectives of statutory agencies. Such organisations often remained talking shops creating the illusion of collaboration without effecting real change and draining resources from women's organisations (Hague *et al.*, 1996; Malos, 2000).

Survivor consultation

Further, a notable lack of inclusion in many forums has been representation from survivor groups and a lack of consultation with survivors about the effectiveness of service provision. While survivors may not initially be in a position to be consulted, given that they are the main users of domestic violence services, individual agencies and multi-agency initiatives need to find ways of monitoring survivor satisfaction and seeking their views on service delivery and how it could be improved (Mullender and Hague, 2001).

Multi- or inter-agency practices today

In many ways the focus has moved away from the workings of Domestic Violence Forums specifically and has looked at the success or otherwise of specific 'multi-agency' or 'inter-agency' initiatives that have been undertaken in local areas to improve services to women and children and to reduce repeat victimisation, a number of which initially received some Home Office funding under the government Crime Reduction Initiative (Hester and Westmarland, 2005). Some of these have been described in earlier chapters and have included a variety of specific partnerships or multi-agency working, such as the specialist Domestic Violence Courts, and involved the co-ordination of services provided by a number of different agencies. Others have focused on the safety of the most high-risk victims, through the use of risk assessment and often identified initially, but not always, by the police, and have resulted in multi-agency risk assessment conferences (MARACS). In this approach, different agencies come together regularly to discuss what action each has taken and should take to improve the safety and protection of individual survivors and this is discussed further below. Other initiatives have involved closer liaison or partnership working with one particular agency. For example, some initiatives have included an independent support and advice service working closely with the police. Other initiatives developed in the health field have meant closer liaison between health services and Women's Aid or a women's advice and support service, which can provide advice and support when women disclose domestic violence. Many of these initiatives have also included the development of inter-agency protocols, which define ways of working between the agencies, and include the sharing of information (Robinson, 2004; Hester and Westmarland, 2005).

One-stop shops

Some of these projects have been described as 'one-stop shops', where services are grouped together so that women do not have to hunt around to get their needs met by different agencies. However, there are considerable variations to this concept. In some initiatives, for example, the police and an independent women's support and advice service have been based in one place, in others independent advice and support centres have acted as a liaison point between a survivor and different agencies and assisted them to negotiate the criminal justice system or civil law systems and other services such as housing.

Evaluations of multi-agency initiatives

Evaluations of these initiatives have produced mixed results, with inconsistencies in practice between and within agencies. As was seen in the Domestic Violence Courts projects, discussed in Chapter 4, many women were satisfied with the women's advice and support services and victim witness services and had greater satisfaction with police practice, but they felt let down by the CPS and the criminal courts. Further, although prosecution and conviction rates increased in line with the aims of the initiatives, these outcomes did not necessarily improve women's and children's safety, which must be considered the primary outcome measure.

Multi-agency risk assessment conferences (MARACS)

Case study: The use of multi-agency risk assessment conferences (MARACS)

Brenda, who had three children, was referred to the domestic violence officer by a social worker. She had recently been assaulted and had bruising to her face and body from her partner, Bill. On receiving the referral, it was arranged that Brenda would be visited by frontline officers, with the social worker present for support. A risk assessment checklist was filled out and Brenda made a statement. As a result of this, Bill was arrested and was charged with common assault. However, the police bailed him to his home address and because he lived very near Brenda, this put her at further risk and she was given a panic alarm and a warning marker was placed on her address. Two days later, when Brenda was visited by the social worker it was found that Bill had assaulted her again and had destroyed her panic alarm. Brenda had been too frightened to call the police. Another visit was made to her house by police officers and Bill was re-arrested because he had breached his bail conditions. An application was made to remand him in custody and this gave Brenda confidence to report earlier incidents of violence against her.

Due to Bill's repeated violence, this case was brought to the monthly MARAC conference, which was attended by all the relevant agencies, including the Crown Prosecution Service. As a consequence of this meeting, several actions were taken. Brenda and her children were supported by Women's Aid and social services, and housing services were required to review Bill's tenancy and the security on her home. The prison service was asked to monitor his letters and phone calls to ensure he did not further threaten Brenda, and probation were asked to monitor his progress in court.

As the case was likely to go to trial because Bill continued to plead not guilty, Brenda was supported by the Vulnerable and Intimidated Witness Service and given special measures including a screen and support at court. She was reluctant to give evidence because she was frightened of further repercussions from Bill, but did so and he was found guilty of assault and received a four-month custodial sentence. At this point, it was likely that Bill would have been released very soon due to his time on remand but since the CPS was aware that further offences were outstanding, he was remanded in custody until he came to trial for these other offences. Eventually he received a four-and-a-half year sentence and Brenda and her children were safe for a while. During the period of Bill's imprisonment the family continued to be supported by Women's Aid and Brenda requested rehousing to a different area, so that it would be less easy for Bill to find her on release. Housing services did, however, turn her down and because of this she asked for her case to be discussed again at a MARAC.

(Based on information provided by a domestic violence police officer, North Wales Police Force. NB some details have been changed in order to protect the survivor's anonymity and confidentiality.)

More success has been claimed in improving victim safety in the MARACs initiative, which focuses on survivors identified as being at highest risk (Robinson, 2004; Robinson and Tregidga, 2005). This type of intervention was pioneered in South Wales and was evaluated over a two-year period. The agencies initially involved included representatives from the police, probation, social services, health and housing services and the Women's Safety Unit (the survivor/victim advice and support service) and later a representative from education services. At first the group met fortnightly, and later monthly, to discuss actions to be taken by each agency to protect victim safety and document and monitor actions to be taken in the future.

One key finding from the evaluation was that it improved communication and co-operation between the different agencies who participated. However, notably absent was Cafcass (Child and family court advisory and support service) and this was found to be particularly significant because several high-risk women and children were experiencing further violence and abuse, through being forced by the family courts to have unsafe contact arrangements with perpetrators.

Nevertheless, one of the significant benefits was the sharing of information between the police and probation services, as is seen in the following account:

> With regard to a victim who suffered years of horrific abuse ... Through the MARAC process and discussing the issues, we discovered that the guy had breached his probation order. He turned up at probation and we were able to arrest him. In that way it opened up lines of communcation with agencies, whereby we have contact points within each agency.
>
> (Robinson, 2004:19)

However, although communication between agencies improved, important information was often not communicated to victims, and this was particularly the case in relation to criminal justice agencies when survivors were not informed about bail conditions, or prison releases; a finding that has also been confirmed from other research on specialist Domestic Violence Courts. This meant that, in some cases, and despite information-sharing between agencies, survivors failed to be protected.

> I needed to know about when he was going to be released from prison. Probation would not disclose any information to me about when he would be released. [I felt they were] very unprofessional, [this was] not handled properly. This has had a massive impact on my feelings of safety. I wasn't worried about his release until I knew that. I assumed I would be told everything.
>
> (Robinson and Tregidga, 2005:24)

A few survivors also found that individual agency intervention could be unhelpful and this was particularly the case in relation to social services and housing, as is seen in the following accounts.

> I feel that social services are bullies. I thought that they were there to help people like me. But they frightened and intimidated me. I have never hidden anything, but I think people may clam up and then not tell the whole truth about things.

> Housing has been rubbish, no help at all. The only options they could offer me was to go homeless or go to a refuge. I don't want to be put in a homeless situation. That feels unsafe to me and I don't want to leave my daughter who is agrophobic ... We own our own home.

> The housing people said if my name is on the mortgage then I cannot
> be put on the housing list. I feel let down.
>
> (Robinson and Tregidga, 2005)

On the other hand, some victims welcomed the support they received from the different agencies and the fact that the agencies were working together to support them and deal with the violence from perpetrators. Further, although some victims found most agencies helpful, the Women's Safety Unit was found to be the most useful in communicating information, supporting women in court, liaising with the other services and providing continuing support to victims after the various actions taken by other agencies had been completed. The service also had the responsibility of representing victims' views to the MARACS, and, like other one-stop shop type support services was the only agency 'whose sole mission was to provide a range of services and assistance to victims of domestic violence'. As the final evaluation stated, 'it is difficult to imagine how the MARACS could succeed let alone function without the existence of such an agency' (Robinson and Tregidga, 2005:23).

Reduction in repeat victimisation

The evaluation also found that forty-two per cent of the original 102 women included in the MARAC study had not experienced further violence at the end of 12 months, according to police data and additional information provided by other agencies. Although little information is given about those victims who continued to experience violence, child contact is identified as a significant factor in preventing women and children from moving on. Most of the few victims interviewed also stated that they felt more in control of their situation and that their safety and quality of life had improved. This is claimed as a 'considerable achievement' of the MARAC intervention, since all the survivors concerned were experiencing a high level of chronic repeat violence as identified at the initial risk assessment stage.

Unfortunately, what is not known from the evaluation is the level of repeat violence to victims who were not classified as very high risk and therefore did not receive this level of intervention. This was identified by one agency member as the biggest weakness of the approach.

> I think the bigger threat to women's safety is the numbers – we can
> only look at those who are very high risk as perceived by a risk assessment which is a crude tool . . . I think that is the biggest weakness but there is no solution – there are thousands to deal with.
>
> (Robinson, 2004:19)

Nevertheless, this kind of multi-agency approach did seem to work better than others, even though it was focused only on highest risk victims, because the agencies concerned were held accountable for their actions on a regular basis. The success of the MARAC initiative has meant it has now been adopted as a model in other areas of the country, and limited government funding has been given to independent advice and support services for women, in recognition that they play a key role in enabling the MARACs to work.

Conclusion

In conclusion, as the above example shows multi-agency working can operate to increase the safety of women and children, where there is a commitment on behalf of individuals in different agencies to co-operate and improve lines of communication, take appropriate action and monitor the outcomes. However, such initiatives need adequate funding and they do have their limitations, when they can only affect the lives of small numbers of those experiencing domestic violence. They are also limited when some services fail to participate, as was seen in the evaluations above in relation to Cafcass. Their effectiveness also depends heavily on the liaison work undertaken by independent women's support and advice services. Yet these are the services, which, while most valued by survivors, remain under threat from inadequate resourcing and the vagaries of local and national government decison-making on domestic violence.

Notes

1 Women's Aid Federation of England (Women's Aid) is the national charity working to end domestic violence against women and children. http://www. womensaid.org.uk/about/about_wafe.htm

2 Women's Aid Federation, England; Women's Aid Federation, Wales; Women's Aid Federation, Scotland; Women's Aid Federation, Northern Ireland.

3 Funding is now provided through the supporting people programme, which excludes funding for children.

4 Although these terms are often used synonymously in domestic violence discourses, crime reduction analyses have differentiated between multi-agency approaches, which involve agencies collaborating on certain work but retaining their own organisational identities, ways of working and core tasks, and inter-agency where there is a closer fusion of their work in specific projects (Crawford, 1998).

5 Although this perspective has now been challenged in current social work

training and practice (Hague and Malos, 2005), it still remains a perspective that can be used by different social work agencies, in the experience of the authors.

References

Anon (undated) 'With a ran tan tan' found in *Newark Advertiser*.
Binney, V., Harkell, G. and Nixon, J. (1981) *Leaving Violent Men: A Study of Refuges and Housing for Abused Women*. Bristol: Women's Aid Federation.
Binney, V., Harkell, G. and Nixon, J. (1985) 'Refuges and housing for battered women' in Pahl, J. (ed.) *Private Violence and Public Policy* London: Routledge & Kegan Paul.
Cleveland Refuge and Aid for Women and Children (CRAWC) (1988) *Private Violence and Public Shame*. Published by CRAWC in conjunction with Women's Aid Federation of England.
Dobash, R. and Dobash, R. (1992) *Women, Violence and Social Change*. London: Routledge.
Grace, S. (1995) *Policing domestic violence in the 1990s. Home Office Research Study No. 139*. London: HMSO.
Gupta, R. (ed.) (2003) 'Some recurring themes' in *Homebreakers to Jailbreakers: Southall Black Sisters*. London: Zed Books.
Hague, G. and Malos, E. (2005) (3rd edn) *Domestic Violence: Action for Change*. Cheltenham: New Clarion Press.
Hague, G., Malos, E. and Dear, W. (1996) *Multi-agency work and domestic violence: A National Study of Inter-agency Initiatives*. Bristol: Policy Press.
Hague, G., Mullender, A., Kelly, L. and Malos, E. (2001) 'Children, domestic violence and refuges', in C. Itzen and J. Hanmer (eds) *Home Truths About Domestic Violence*. London and New York: Routledge.
Hague, G., Mullender, A., Kelly, L., Malos, E. and Debonaire, T. (2000) 'Using Innovation: the history of work with children in UK domestic violence refuges', in J. Hanmer and C. Itzin (eds) *Home Truths About Domestic Violence*. London and New York: Routledge.
Hanmer, J. (2003) Interview in 'Never Give Up – Against Violence Against Women in West Yorkshire': directed by Al Garthwaite; Vera Media.
Hester, M. and Westmarland, N. (2005) *Tackling Domestic Violence: Effective interventions and approaches. Home Office Research Study 290*. London: HMSO.
Home Office (1999) *Break the Chain: Multi-Agency Guidance for Addressing Domestic Violence*. London: Home Office. www.crimereduction.homeoffice.gov.uk/dv/dv08d.htm
Home Office (2000) *Revised Police Circular 19/2000*. London: Home Office.
Humphreys, C., Hester, M., Hague, G., Mullender, A., Abrahams, H. and Lowe, P.

(2000) *From Good Intentions to Good Practice: Mapping Services Working With Families Where There Is Domestic Violence*. Bristol: Policy Press.

James-Hanman, D. (2000) 'Enhancing Multi-Agency Work', in C. Itzen and J. Hanmer (eds) *Home Truths About Domestic Violence*. London and New York: Routledge.

Jeffreys, S. (1985) *The Spinster and her Enemies: Feminism and Sexuality 1880–1930*. London, Boston and Henley: Pandora Press.

Kelly, L. and Humphreys, C. (2000) *Outreach and Advocacy Approaches in Reducing Domestic Violence: What Works?* Home Office, Briefing Notes. www.home office.gov.uk/rds/pdfs05/dpr35.pdf

Lock, J. (1979) *The British Policewoman: Her Story*. London: Hale.

Malos, E. (2000) 'Supping with the Devil? Multi-Agency Initiatives on Domestic Violence', in J. Radford, M. Friedberg and L. Harne (eds) *Women, Violence and Strategies for Action: Feminist Research, Policy and Practice*. Buckingham and Philadelphia: Open University Press.

Mama, A. (1996) *The Hidden Struggle: Statutory and Voluntary Sector Responses to Violence against Black Women in the home. 2nd Edition*. London: Whiting and Birch.

Mullender, A. and Hague, G. (2001) 'Women Survivors' Views', in J. Taylor-Browne (ed.) *What Works in Reducing Domestic Violence: A Comprehensive Guide for professionals*. London: Home Office.

Parliamentary Select Committee on Violence in Marriage (1975) *Report from the Select Committee on Violence in Marriage Together with the Proceedings of the Committee*. Session 1974–75. Vol. 2. Report, Minutes of the Evidence and Appendices. London: HMSO.

Patel, P. (2003) 'Shifting terrains old struggles for new?' in R. Gupta (ed.) *From Homebreakers to Jailbreakers*. London: Southall Black Sisters.

Pence, E. and McDonnell, C. (2000) 'Developing policies and protocols in Duluth, Minnesota', in J. Hanmer and C. Itzen (eds) *Home Truths about Domestic Violence*. London: Routledge.

Plotnikoff, J. and Woolfson, R. (1998) *Policing Domestic Violence: Effective Organisational Structures, Home Office Research Study 191*. London: Home Office.

Radford, J. (1987) 'Women and Policing: Contradictions Old and New', in *Women, Policing and Male Violence: International Perspectives*. London and New York: Routledge.

Radford, J., Harne, L. and Trotter, J. (2005) *Good Intentions – Disabling Realities: Disabled Women Experiencing Domestic Violence, Report for Middlesbrough Domestic Violence Forum*. mdvf.org.uk

Rhodes, D. and McNeill, S. (1985) *Women Against Violence Against Women*. London: Only Women Press.

Robinson, A. (2004) *Domestic Violence MARACs (Multi-Agency Risk Assessment Conferences, for Very High Risk Victims in Cardiff, Wales: A Process and Outcome Evaluation*. Cardiff: Cardiff University.

Robinson, A. and Tregidga, J. (2005) *Domestic Violence MARACs (Multi-Agency Risk Assessment Conferences for Very High Risk Victims: Views from Victims*. Cardiff: Cardiff University.

Southall Black Sisters (1990) *Against the Grain: A celebration of survival and struggle*. London: Southall Black Sisters.

Women's Aid (1998) 'Families without Fear: Women's Aid Agenda for Action on Domestic Violence: Recommendations for a National Strategy'. http://www.womensaid.org.uk/page.asp?section=00010001000900010001

Women's Aid (2006) womensaid.org.uk/home page.

Index

Locators shown in *italics* refer to case studies.

Related books from Open University Press
Purchase from www.openup.co.uk or order through your local bookseller

---

DOMESTIC VIOLENCE
A MULTI-PROFESSIONAL APPROACH FOR HEALTH PROFESSIONALS

June Keeling and Tom Mason (eds)

This book takes a multi-agency approach to domestic violence and looks at a large range of issues that impact on those working in the health and social care field. It begins with identification of situations where abuse may occur, including intimate partner violence, child and adolescent abuse, same-sex violence, and elderly abuse.

The book considers the commonalities for survivors of abuse - such as the right to feel safe and protected from violence - and evaluates how health and social care professionals can work towards a positive outcome for all of the individuals involved.

The book is divided into four parts, Recognition, Reaction, Involvement and Outcome and includes chapters on:

- Sexual Coercion and Domestic Violence
- Abuse and the Elderly
- Treatment and Alcohol
- Multi-Disciplinary Working
- Relationship Conflict and Abuse Outcomes

Domestic Violence is a key reference resource for students and professionals across a wide range of health and social care occupations.

Contributors
Georgia Anetzberger, Michael Kimmel, Jacquelyn C. Campbell, Adrian Sutton, Poco Kernsmith, T Shackelford, Aaron T. Goetz, Marianne R. Yoshioka, Karel Kurst-Swanger, Julie Schumacher, Jay Peters, Dana DeHart, Iona Heath, Albert R. Roberts, Anne Cools, Melanie Shepard, Patricia O'Campo, Ajitha Cyriac, Farah Ahmed, Richard E. Heyman, Iona Heath, Chris Murphy, Beth Mattingly, Laura Dugan, Katherine van Wormer.

Contents
The editors - The contributors - Preface - Acknowledgements - Introduction - Part one: Recognition - Abuse and the elderly - 'Gender symmetry' in domestic violence: A falsely-framed issue - Female victims of violence - A child psychiatry perspective: Children as victims of adult–adult violence - Sexual coercion and domestic violence - Evolutionary psychological perspectives on men's violence against intimate partners - Effective educational strategies - Part two: Reaction - The impact of the cultural context on the experience of domestic violence - The political, societal and personal interface of abuse - Battered women who use violence: Implications for practice - The role of health care professionals in preventing and intervening with intimate partner violence - Multi-disciplinary working - Part three: Involvement - Treatment and alcohol - Domestic violence myths - Offenders' experiences of interventions - Couples' approaches to treating intimate partner violence - Domestic violence: A family health perspective - Part four: Outcome - Partner homicide including murder-suicide: Gender differences - Relationship conflict and abuse outcomes - How female victims' responses affect the risk of future assaults by their male intimate partners - Conclusion - References - Index.

2008   300pp
978–0–335–22281–0 (Paperback)   978–0–335–22282–7 (Hardback)

FAMILIES, VIOLENCE AND SOCIAL CHANGE

Linda McKie

This comprehensive analysis on abuse committed in the home provides insights at both the micro and macro levels... The book combines legal and social science approaches in a way that makes it essential reading for anyone studying or working on violence-related issues.

> *Kevät Nousiainen, University of Helsinki, Johanna Niemi-Kiesiläinen,*
> *University of Umeå and Anu Pylkkänen, University of Helsinki*

This excellent book offers a timely intervention into debates about violence. Whilst most debates still focus on the spectacular rather than mundane forms of violence, Linda McKie uses a synthesis of legal, sociological and feminist research to show how current debates fail to deal with the violence that under-pins our lives.

> *Prof Beverley Skeggs, University of London*

An exciting new addition to the series, this book tackles assumptions surrounding the family as a changing institution and supposed haven from the public sphere of life. It considers families and social change in terms of concepts of power, inequality, gender, generations, sexuality and ethnicity. Some commentators suggest the family is threatened by increasing economic and social uncertainties and an enhanced focus upon the individual. This book provides a resume of these debates, as well as a critical review of the theories of family and social change:

- Charts social and economic changes and their impact on the family
- Considers the prevalence and nature of abuse within families
- Explores the relationship between social theory, families and changing issues in familial relationships
- Develops a theory of social change and families through a critical and pragmatic stance

Key reading for undergraduate students of sociology reading courses such as family, gender, health, criminology and social change.

Contents

Series editor's foreword – Acknowledgements – Introduction – Part one: Families, violence and society – Your family, my family, their family – Identifying and explaining violence in families – Families: Fusion and fission – Part two: Gender, age and violence – Embodiment, gender and violence – The ambiguities of elder abuse: Older women and domestic violence – Part three: Towards a critical theory – Unpalatable truths: Recognizing and challenging myths – A critical social theory of families, violence and social change – References – Index.

2005   192pp
978–0–335–21158–6 (Paperback)   978–0–335–21159–3 (Hardback)

THE VALUE BASE OF SOCIAL WORK AND SOCIAL CARE

Adam Barnard, Nigel Horner and Jim Wild (eds)

Featuring contributions from key commentators including Lena Dominelli, Sarah Banks, Peter Beresford, Michael Flood and George Ritzer, this diverse text explores an array of concepts and themes that are vital to our understanding of the value base in social work.

Each chapter contains a range of exercises and activities that are intended to encourage students to take a creative and active learning approach to defining and understanding values. Among the key themes examined in the book are the tensions between values such as justice, anti-discrimination, compassion, and empathy, and the need for professionalism, accountability, cost codes, and performance measurement.

Also included are chapters on:

- anti-oppressive practice
- service user values
- anti-social care
- violence prevention
- valuing equality

The Value Base of Social Work and Social Care is a key text for students undertaking the qualifying social work degree, and for those studying youth work, youth justice, education welfare, probation, health care, counselling and community work. Due to the range of contributors and the current emphasis placed on interprofessional working, it is also relevant to an international audience of practitioners and professionals within the field of social care.

Contents
The contributors – The editors – Foreword – Introduction – Values, ethics and professionalization: A social work history – The social work value base: Human rights and social justice in talk and action – Globalization defined – An anti-racist strategy for individual and organizational change – Social work and social value: Well-being, choice and public service reform – Service user values for social work and social care – Community intervention and social activism – Anti-oppressive practice as contested practice – Engaging men: Strategies and dilemmas in violence prevention education among men – Social work and management – Anti-social care: Occupational deprivation and older people in residential care – Index.

2008   160pp
978–0–335–22214–8 (Paperback)   978–0–335–22215–5 (Hardback)